D1084523

Agile Software Development

Evaluating the Methods for Your Organization

For a listing of recent titles in the *Artech House Computing Library*, turn to the back of this book.

Agile Software Development

Evaluating the Methods for Your Organization

Alan S. Koch

Artech House
Boston • London
www.artechhouse.com

Library of Congress Cataloging-in-Publication Data
A catalog record for this book is available from the U.S. Library of Congress.

British Library Cataloguing in Publication Data
Koch, Alan S.
  Evaluating Agile software development: Methods for your organization.—(Artech House computing library).
  1. Computer software—Development   2. Computer software—Evaluation
  I. Title
  005.1

  ISBN 1-58053-842-8

Cover design by Yekaterina Ratner

"CMM® " and "Capability Maturity Model" are registered in the U.S. Patent and Trademark Office by Carnegie Mellon University.
SM "PSP," "TSP," "Personal Software Process," and "Team Software Process" are sales marks of Carnegie Mellon University.
"PMBOK Guide"® and "Project Management Body of Knowledge" are registered trademarks of the Project Management Institute.

© 2005 ARTECH HOUSE, INC.
685 Canton Street
Norwood, MA 02062

All rights reserved. Printed and bound in the United States of America. No part of this book may be reproduced or utilized in any form or by any means, electronic or mechanical, including photocopying, recording, or by any information storage and retrieval system, without permission in writing from the publisher.

  All terms mentioned in this book that are known to be trademarks or service marks have been appropriately capitalized. Artech House cannot attest to the accuracy of this information. Use of a term in this book should not be regarded as affecting the validity of any trademark or service mark.

International Standard Book Number: 1-58053-842-8

10 9 8 7 6 5 4 3 2 1

To you, the war-weary software professional who just seeks a rational way to develop software.

And to Laurie, my wife, who always believes in me and supports my work, even when she wishes I was planting a tree!

Contents

10   Face-to-Face Communication   73

11   Sustainable Pace   83

12   The Unstated Principle: Appropriate Processes and Tools   89

21   Simplicity 177

22   Retrospectives 183

Foreword by Kent Beck

I was ready to dislike this book from the first. It begins with the false dichotomy of agility versus discipline. Would you ask a gymnast if they were agile or if they were disciplined? No. Gymnasts are agile to precisely the same degree they are disciplined. So it is with software development. Agility in software requires iron discipline—absolutely fixed time schedules, rigid and high-quality goals, and a devotion to collaboration and communication even when communicating with those who have very different perspectives than your own.

Once I got beyond my initial reaction, though, I found myself enjoying my reading. Here is my work and that of my community seen through a very different set of eyes than mine. The parts of Extreme Programming that have been hard for those in large organizations to apply are presented fairly. However, this book clarifies the difficulties some have with practices such as full-time customer involvement in projects. The book makes the case for such practices' value even while presenting their drawbacks.

The other theme I learned from this book was the comparison and contrast of the various "agile" methods. Different methods are quite different, and readers should be able to choose wisely from the discussion here which path to take towards agility.

In the end, agility is simply a measure of software development. How agile is yours? Not very, taking years to respond to change? Very, responding in hours or days? Your software development lives somewhere on the continuum already. You don't get to pick "agile" or "not agile."

The question is, is your agility enough for your organization and if not, what are you going to do about it? This book presents the alternatives for improvement fairly and impartially.

Kent Beck
Three Rivers Institute
Merlin, Oregon
October 2004

Foreword by Mark Paulk

I have been involved with software process improvement since 1987. I led the team at the Software Engineering Institute that wrote the Capability Maturity Model® for Software, which formalized Watts Humphrey's vision for transforming software organizations. I have had the pleasure of seeing the Software CMM® become a de facto standard for the software community—and I have seen it abused in ways that astonished and saddened me.

There have been many debates over "software process." In the early days, we debated whether software projects could be managed or whether software was a creative, artistic endeavor that could not be constrained by plans and budgets; in recent days, we debated whether software processes could be placed under statistical process control.

I like to think that "my" side has won these debates over the years, but one thing that I have repeatedly observed is that some people stake out extremist positions when discussing controversial issues. One of the more controversial topics to arise in recent years is agile methods. Some of its proponents have taken the extreme position that "we don't need no stinkin' processes around here!" Some of its opponents have taken the extreme position that agile methodologists are just hackers who are unwilling—and perhaps unable—to do the hard work necessary to build high-quality software. Unfortunately, both extremes can find justification in the opposing camp for their extremism.

Perhaps we live in a *time* of polarization, when extremism is the norm. If so, I choose to live in the middle ground. In my work, I have attempted to steal the best ideas from everyone—whether they come from project management, statistical process control, or the agile methods.

One of the virtues of the agile methods is that they have taken good engineering and management practices to an extreme implementation. Further, the agile methodologists have identified a "sweet spot" of small teams, colocated, working on small-to-medium-sized systems, with active customer collaboration, with high requirements volatility, and stated that this is where the agile methods are the methods of choice. With the exception of volatile requirements, this sounds like nirvana to most software professionals! This may be the source of some of the resistance to agile methods—they've taken over the territory most of us would like to work in!

Why would we challenge the principles of the agile methodologies? The values expressed in the agile manifesto should be captured in any modern software project, even if the implementation may differ radically in other environments. Customer satisfaction, communication, working software, simplicity, and self-reflection may be stated in other terms, but without them, nontrivial projects face almost insurmountable odds against success.

The problem, of course, is that enlightened folks like Kent Beck, Bob Martin, and Ken Schwaber are the exception rather than the rule. Bob Martin told a story at XP Universe about running into someone who said his organization was using Extreme Programming. Bob asked how pair programming was viewed... and the reply was, "We don't do that." Bob asked how refactoring was working out... and the reply was, "We don't do that." Bob asked how well the planning game was working... and the reply was, "We don't do that." "Well," Bob asked, "then what are you doing?" "We don't document anything!" was the answer. Success carries the seeds of failure, and the agile methodologists are concerned that some adopting these new ideas do not really understand what an agile methodology is—and it is not ad hoc, chaotic programming.

We have had the same problem in the software process world, and I must admit to some amusement at watching the agile methodologists struggle with the abuses of their methods, just as I have struggled with those who abuse the Software CMM®. The cruel reality in using any model or method is that they have to be applied with common sense and good professional judgment. If the day ever comes when that is no longer true, then humans won't be needed anymore to build software because we can just automate the process!

Much of the controversy with respect to the technical issues centers on what happens as projects scale up. Practices that rely on tacit knowledge and highly competent professionals may break down in larger teams with their rapidly expanding communication channels and coordination challenges, and replacing those practices with ones appropriate for large teams may result in losing the emergent properties of the agile methodology.

My conclusion is that the middle ground is the most profitable place to stand—pick the agile methods most pertinent to your problems; take advantage of their good ideas; adapt them as necessary; and don't try to tailor them beyond something recognizable as "agile." I hope that sounds like good (and obvious) advice. The problem lies in implementing that advice.

That's where Alan's book, *Agile Software Development: Evaluating the Methods for Your Organization* comes in. There are a number of good books on Extreme Programming and Scrum. There are only a handful of books that I would recommend on comparing and evaluating agile methods. Barry Boehm and Richard Turner have written an excellent book, *Balancing Agility and Discipline*, that takes a risk-oriented view of the agile methods. I would also recommend Craig Larman's *Agile and Iterative Development: A Manager's Guide*.

Alan views agile methods as a new process that organizations need to learn how to make work, building on the insights gained from the software process world. The element missing from the agile methodologies, which is crucial for the Software CMM®, is the concept of establishing the culture that "this is the way we do things around here." Although implicit in some agile practices, such as the peer pressure implicit in pair programming, "culture" is crucial to the adoption of the agile methods.

Organizations considering the agile methods should read Alan's section on hierarchical versus cooperative cultures closely. Different cultures have different strengths and weaknesses. Any substantive process improvement involves cultural change—including the adoption of agile methods. Alan compares and contrasts six different agile methods; selecting the agile method (if any) that best fits an organization's needs and business environment is the first step to successful adoption. It is also vital to the disciplined change management that underlies true process maturity.

The cultural changes required by the agile methods extend beyond the team and the organization employing the methods. One of the crucial aspects of dealing with volatile requirements proactively is customer collaboration—and folding the customer into the cultural shift required for implementing agile methods can be daunting. The greatest challenge in taking advantage of the virtues of the agile methods may lie in convincing customers to "step up to the plate" and use them where appropriate. We have to decide where to place the "balance point" in documentation and planning to alleviate the concerns of the stakeholders (and regulatory requirements) while achieving the flexibility and benefits promised in the agile philosophy.

Many of the practices in the agile methodologies are good practices that should be thoughtfully considered for any environment. While the merits of any of these practices can be debated in comparison with other ways of dealing with the same issues, none of them should be arbitrarily rejected. Perhaps the biggest challenge in dealing effectively with both agile and plan-driven methodologies is dealing with extremists in both camps who refuse to keep an open mind. Alan's book can be a useful tool for making informed decisions about the appropriateness of agile methods in your environment and maintaining a strong position in the middle ground.

Mark Paulk
Carnegie Mellon University
Pittsburgh, Pennsylvania
October 2004

Preface

Are you interested in using an Agile method for developing software? Or are others lobbying you to approve the use of one? Or is your interest more casual; perhaps you are merely wondering if an Agile method is worth considering? Whichever is the case, this book is for you.

I come from the "disciplined process" world. After 13 years at the Software Engineering Institute (SEI) and a few years running ASK Process, Inc., I received a query from a prospect who asked about Extreme Programming (XP). To answer that query, I began researching XP, and that turned into research into the Agile methods in general. So began my foray into the Agile world.

The more research I did, the more I became intrigued with the Agile methods. Far from being a license to hack (as I, like many of my "disciplined process" colleagues believed), these methods have some interesting practices that make a whole lot of sense to me. There are ways in which they are not so very different from the disciplined methods I have come to respect so much, like the Capability Maturity Model® (CMM)® and the Team Software Process℠ (TSP)℠. But there are other ways in which they are dramatically different — different in ways that solve problems that are so common in software organizations. I told myself, "There is a *lot* that we can learn from the Agile methods!"

The Agile and the disciplined process communities have not gotten along well. You are likely to hear process-philes disparaging the Agile methods. At the same time, you are likely to hear the Agilists crying about the terrors of disciplined process. The truth, of course, is somewhere between those two extremes. Disciplined processes are good and necessary, as long as they do what processes *should* do: support the work of professionals and make them more effective. And agility — the ability to move quickly and adapt to changing realities while maintaining one's balance — is also critical, as long as it remains focused on meeting the customer's needs in a way that also meets the needs of the development organization.

The Agile methods and the disciplined processes share a common objective: making all software projects as successful as they possibly can be. They differ only in the means they employ and their guiding philosophies. Neither of them is completely correct. Each has good recommendations, and each leaves opportunities for its users to abuse it and cause problems. Each can learn from the other, and indeed, so they must.

This book had its genesis in my research. I came to realize that executives, managers, and software practitioners alike are faced with making decisions about the Agile Methods, but hear only the voices of those two extremes to guide them. Must they trust one and discard the other? Must they embrace one and throw the other out with the trash? What is needed is a middle perspective. A voice that is neither enamored of the Agile methods nor repulsed by them. A voice that points out both the good and bad things about the Agile methods. A voice that is believable and can help people like you make a well-informed decision based on unbiased information.

This book provides that unbiased, balanced view of the Agile methods. It does not blindly advocate for them (though it *does* identify what is good and noteworthy). It also does not automatically malign them (though it does identify potential problems of which one should beware.) It provides information in a form that can be read, digested, and used. And there is a workbook that you can download and use to organize your thoughts and draw conclusions. (See Chapter 7 for more on the workbook.)

It is arranged so you can either read it straight through to get a complete picture of the Agile methods, or you can let the Table of Contents guide you to the chapters that are particularly relevant to your needs. It talks about the considerations you should keep in mind while thinking about the possibility of adopting an Agile method, it is structured around the Agile Manifesto (which enumerates the values on which the Agile methods are based), and it includes a short description of each Agile method in the appendixes.

This book is designed for you. Use it (and the supporting workbook) in any way that makes sense to you, to help you make a sound and well-founded decision about whether your organization should adopt an Agile method.

PART

I

Adoption Considerations

In the first part of this book, we lay the foundation for your evaluation of the Agile methods.

Chapter 1 provides a brief introduction to the Agile methods. Each of the next five chapters discusses a dimension of your organization that you will want to keep in mind as you do your evaluation. They are:

- Chapter 2: Considering Your Organizational Culture;
- Chapter 3: Considering Your Customers;
- Chapter 4: Considering Your Projects;
- Chapter 5: Considering Your Tools and Processes;
- Chapter 6: Considering Your Staff.

Chapter 7 (the final chapter in Part I) contains guidance on how to use the information in this book and the available "Evaluating Agile Methods Workbook" to reach a decision about using Agile methods at your organization.

Contents

Introducing the Agile Methods

This chapter provides a brief and basic introduction to the Agile methods. It is designed to provide a minimal foundation for the contents of this book but also contains pointers to sources of more complete information for those interested in investigating them more deeply.

Historical and background information

Although some of the Agile methods have existed in one form or another for a decade or two (a relative eon in the software business), the term "Agile Method" was coined more recently, in February 2001, by 17[1] of the leading developers and proponents of what were then known as the "light" methodologies. These people met "to see whether there was anything in common among the various light methodologies" [1]. The meeting resulted in four levels of agreement among participants.

1. There is a need for methods designed to respond to change during software projects. Further, they adopted the term "Agile" to identify those methods. They agreed that the term "light" was not appropriate because certain projects (e.g., those with many programmers or those that develop safety-critical software) would not employ a "light" methodology but could still require agility.

2. The second level of agreement was on the four statements of the "Agile Manifesto".[2] These four statements capture the

---

1. The 17 people were Kent Beck, Mike Beedle, Arie van Bennekum, Alistair Cockburn, Ward Cunningham, Martin Fowler, James Grenning, Jim Highsmith, Andrew Hunt, Ron Jeffries, Jon Kern, Brian Marick, Robert C. Martin, Stephen J. Mellor, Ken Schwaber, Jeff Sutherland, and Dave Thomas.

2. The Agile Manifesto is quoted and discussed in Appendix A.

core values on which all of the Agile methods are built, as well as the spirit in which they should be implemented. The Agile Manifesto states:

> We are uncovering better ways of developing software by doing it and helping others to do it. Through this work we have come to value:
>
> - **Individuals and interactions** over processes and tools.
> - **Working software** over comprehensive documentation.
> - **Customer collaboration** over contract negotiation.
> - **Responding to change** over following a plan.
>
> That is, while there is value in the items on the right, we value the items on the left more.

3. The next level of agreement was on a set of 12 Agile Principles.[3] In these statements, the values are fleshed out in more detail and given more concrete meaning.

4. The final level of agreement was that agreement at a more detailed level (e.g., actual activities or tactics for running projects) was beyond their grasp at the time. They were content to leave that fourth level for each of the Agile methods to define in its own way.

Since that meeting, the Agile methods have become a popular topic in software development circles, giving rise to much confusion and contention. The Agile Alliance[4] has grown to become the voice of the Agile methods. Their Web site is an active forum for practitioners to share their experiences and the practical matters related to using the Agile methods. The Web site is probably the best source of up-to-date information about the Agile methods.

This book is designed to cut through the partisan positions of the various factions in the Agile method debate. It presents a balanced view of the Agile methods to give you the information you need to make an adoption decision based on an analysis of facts and consideration of your organization's needs.

The Agile methods, generally

The suspicion that led to that February 2001 meeting where the Agile Manifesto was developed was confirmed. These methods do, in fact, have much in common. The commonalities revolve mainly around the topics of agility, change, planning, communication, and learning.

---

3. The 12 principles are quoted and discussed in Appendix B.

4. Refer to http://www.AgileAlliance.org.

Agility

The name that they adopted, "Agile," pinpoints one of the key attributes that these methods share. What image does the word "agile" bring to your mind? Perhaps it makes you think of a gymnast's performance, or a mountain goat navigating steep rocky crags, or a gazelle running in the wild. Someone who is agile is able to move quickly but decisively, to react to changing situations with speed and grace, to change direction while maintaining his or her balance and poise.

This image contrasts sharply with the more traditional software development methods, which more closely resemble a large military encampment. These methods commit to a war plan and then steadfastly march forward toward the stated goal, all the while controlling and mitigating any outside effects, as opposed to accommodating them.

That the Agile methods are designed to be able to move quickly and react to change is clear. What is less clear is the extent to which they can do these things with speed and grace ... with balance and poise. The concern many people have about these methods is the cost that may be incurred in order to achieve agility. What must be given up to achieve those ends? And is the achievement worth the cost?

Change

The philosophy of agility shows up most pointedly in the methods' approaches to change. The Agile methods treat change as an equal partner in the project. Change is welcomed to the table and encouraged to shed new light and introduce new information continually throughout the project. These methods are designed not just to *accept* change, but also to welcome it and capitalize on it.

The traditional methods treat change as the enemy. They accept that it cannot be avoided, so they spend significant effort to control it and mitigate its effects. Far from welcoming change, most methods shackle it in Change Request systems and try it in the court of Configuration Control Boards (CCB). Each change is interrogated and examined in an effort to determine what should be done about it.

An appropriate position on the subject of change is a point of contention that we will discuss in some detail in Part V. For most projects, neither of the two extremes described is optimal; rather, some middle ground is more likely to be to the project's advantage.

Planning

Although planning is as central to the Agile methods as to any traditional method, the Agile methods treat deviations from plan very differently. When an Agile project does not progress as planned, the methods treat the deviation as new information about the project, and they generally replan in light of that new information. Their goal is to bring the plan into conformance with reality.

The more traditional methods view deviations from the plan as undesirable events. Therefore, they react to deviations by adopting corrective actions. In extreme situations, the "corrective action" may involve replanning, but these methods much prefer to bring reality back into conformance with the plan.

So, should reality be molded to the likeness of the plan? Or should the plan be reworked to match reality? Clearly, neither position is optimal. Rather, each deviation should be evaluated and an appropriate reaction adopted. This subject will also be discussed in Part V.

Communication

All of the Agile methods are designed to optimize communication among the various stakeholders. They strongly favor face-to-face communications and tend to de-emphasize written documents, except where those documents provide real-time support for the more favored face-to-face communication. Although none of these methods actually intends to eliminate all documentation, they do militate against documentation that is primarily archival in purpose. They all pay primary attention to communication among project team members and between the team and the customer (in whatever way the word "customer" is defined).

The traditional methods do not argue *against* communication; rather, they tend to *assume* that appropriate communication will result from the prescribed activities and documents. Unfortunately, this assumption sometimes remains unmet as each party does what is required of them and reads their own biases into documents, only to find that misunderstandings surface later in the project.

While the Agile methods' emphasis on communication is welcome, their tendency to not document the results of those communications can cause problems. People's memories are often faulty, and two people can have very different memories of the same exchange. So, a more appropriate philosophy might state, "If something is worth talking about, then it is also worth recording what was said." These topics will be addressed in Parts II and III.

Learning

Each of the Agile methods treats a project as a learning experience. They acknowledge that, at the beginning of the project, neither the customers nor the developers have a complete understanding of what must be built. Therefore, the following occurs:

- The methods foster copious communication among stakeholders to accelerate the learning that will take place.

- The new learning results in changes to the requirements for the system, the technical constraints on it, and the ways in which it will be used.

> ▸ Those changes become the basis for evolving plans, as the project adapts to the new information.

The traditional methods regiment learning into the project life cycle. It is assumed that all that is needed to plan the project is available during the planning phase, that all of the requirements are understood during the Requirements phase, and so on. When this turns out not to be the case, the resulting deviation is documented, and corrective action is taken.

The reality is that every stakeholder in every project continually learns throughout the life of the project. To expect that this will not be the case is to expect miracles. But at the same time, (as discussed in the "Change" and "Planning" sections) not everything that is learned is necessarily beneficial to the project. Each new piece of information should be evaluated and integrated into the project only if it provides value. These topics will be addressed in Parts IV and V.

The Agile methods, specifically

This book focuses on the following six[5] major Agile methods:

> ▸ *Adaptive Software Development (ASD)*, as discussed in Appendix C, is based on Complex Adaptive Systems theory and treats software development as a collaborative learning exercise. ASD is based on the "Adaptive Life Cycle" (which continually cycles through three phases named "Speculate," "Collaborate," and "Learn) and the "Adaptive Management Model" (also called "Leadership-Collaboration" management).

> ▸ *Dynamic System Development Method (DSDM)*, as discussed in Appendix D, is not properly a "method" because it does not provide guidance about how development projects should be run. Rather, it is mainly a philosophy about system development that consists of nine principles. DSDM focuses on *system* development and does not get into the details of writing software, so it can be used in conjunction with any of the more software-intensive Agile methods, like XP.

> ▸ *Extreme Programming (XP)*, as discussed in Appendix E, is a collection of 12 practices that focus specifically on the mechanics of developing software. These practices include such topics as The Planning Game, Pair Programming, Refactoring, and Testing.

> ▸ *Feature-Driven Development (FDD)*, as discussed in Appendix F, treats software development as a collection of features that are implemented one at a time. Unlike the other Agile methods, FDD includes upfront

5. These six methods were chosen because they are widely recognized as being Agile methods and there was enough published information about them at the time of this writing to support evaluation. Absence of any particular method from this list should not be interpreted as a judgment of that method. It is merely an artifact of the available information at this time.

architectural analysis, such as the development of a Domain Object Model, which becomes the basis for planning the project iterations. It also includes a unique (among the Agile methods) mechanism for objectively reporting progress against plan.

▶ *Lean Software Development (LD)*, as discussed in Appendix G, is not really a software development method. Based on the principles of lean manufacturing, LD provides a set of seven principles for making software development more efficient, and it amplifies those principles with 22 tools.

▶ *Scrum*, as discussed in Appendix H, is primarily a product development method. Its seven practices focus on planning and managing a development project but do not address any specifics about software. Therefore, it can be used in conjunction with any software development method.

Each of these six methods embodies the philosophies of the Agile Manifesto. Each is widely recognized as an Agile method. And each provides a good basis for the discussions in this book.

Reference

[1]   Cockburn, A., *Agile Software Development*, Reading, MA: Addison-Wesley, 2002, p. 215.

Contents

Considering Your Organizational Culture

The culture of your organization is a prime determinant of the degree to which any change you attempt will succeed. Although your culture can be changed, such change is a slow and long-term effort. For this book's purposes, your culture should be considered static. The culture you have today is the one into which any change in your software development methods will be inserted.

Corporate culture has many facets, most of which we will not discuss. Rather, we will focus on the specific parts of your culture that are relevant to the Agile methods. These cultural elements revolve around issues such as division of responsibility and authority, lines of communication, and how change is handled. For this discussion, we will divide the world into two broad dichotomies: hierarchical versus cooperative organizations, and those that control change versus reacting to it.

Although most organizations' formal structure aligns with their culture, this is not always the case. Generally, a mismatch between formal organization and culture is the result of a relatively recent change. For example, when a hierarchical organization rearranges into a more cooperative structure, it will take significant time (likely years) for the culture to realign with the new formal structure. Therefore, as you consider your corporate culture, be sure to focus on how people actually think and behave today, as opposed to any formal structure you have adopted or how you *intend* for them to think and behave.

Hierarchical versus cooperative organizations

This dichotomy deals with the ways in which people are organized and communicate within the organization.

Hierarchical organizations

In hierarchical organizations, there are clear divisions of responsibility and authority, with specific positions being responsible for discrete activities. For example, some companies have a project management organization whose members provide planning and management services to all projects. Figure 2.1 pictures this environment, where work processes (gray arrows) tend to look very much like an assembly line, with each individual receiving items or information or assignments from his or her predecessor, performing the required operations on them, and then passing them forward to the next position on the line.

Communication paths in these organizations (boxed arrows in Figure 2.1) tend to be clearly defined and restrictive. That is, the communication paths required to perform normal activities are predefined and well understood. When communication outside of the normal channels is required, it generally must flow up the hierarchical chain and back down again following the existing communication channels. Communication across the hierarchy, or skipping over levels of the hierarchy, is generally seen as a breach of etiquette and may even be considered insubordination and punished accordingly.

Cooperative organizations

In cooperative organizations, as shown in Figure 2.2, both work patterns and communications (shown by boxed arrows) are fluid. When something needs to be done, a group of relevant people will (sometimes spontaneously) form an ad hoc team. The composition of that team will likely not be constrained by people's job titles or place in the organization; rather, it will be driven by the needs of the job at hand and the skill sets of the available people. This team would then work closely together and draw any needed information directly from its source, within or outside of the organization.

Considerations: Hierarchical versus cooperative

Start-up organizations tend to be more cooperative in the beginning and then grow more hierarchical as they become established and grow in size. In a highly cooperative organization, you may even find the company president wrestling with the compiler or banging test cases against the latest

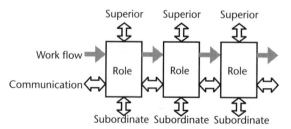

Figure 2.1   Hierarchical organization.

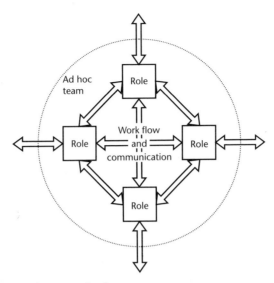

Figure 2.2 Cooperative organization.

version of the software. No such things could happen in a hierarchical environment.

Each of the Agile methods has many elements that are clearly cooperative. They tend to assume that the project team is composed of the appropriate people who are drawn from all parts of the organization to work together on the project. In addition, they all stress the need for copious communication both within and outside of the project team.

But the Agile methods also have some hierarchical elements. For example, they tend to define the constitution of the development team and how it interacts with others in a hierarchical way. Some of the methods even define a hierarchy and responsibilities within the project team.

Therefore, any of the Agile methods could present challenges to your organization, regardless of where it falls on the hierarchical-to-cooperative continuum. Adopting an Agile method could require your organization to stretch in either the hierarchical or the cooperative direction, or possibly in both.

Controlling change versus reacting to it

This dichotomy deals with how an organization addresses change or deviations from plans.

Controlling change

An organization that controls change tends to value continuity and conformance to plans and requirements. When any deviation from those plans or requirements is presented to such an organization, it is captured, cataloged, and scrutinized, and then corrective actions are adopted.

These organizations generally have well-defined procedures and tools in place to capture, track, and manage the changes and deviations that come along, as shown in Figure 2.3. They would be happiest if no changes were encountered, but because changes are inevitable, they carefully manage those changes to mitigate their effect on the project.

Reacting to change

Organizations that react to change tend to value the satisfaction of their customers (or whomever is deemed to be in power and important). When this type of organization encounters a change (either suggested by the customer or deemed by the organization to be instrumental in satisfying the customer), it is adopted as a matter of course, with little regard for the cost. As shown in Figure 2.4, the changes tend to drive this sort of project.

These organizations tend not to keep close track of the changes they adopt. Instead, they are more likely to have well-tuned mechanisms for taking the pulse of the customer and quickly reacting to any problems or opinions that the customer may express. Because they count the costs of change as normal costs of doing business, projects' budgets and schedules can become unpredictable when trying to please a fickle or demanding customer.

Considerations: Controlling versus reacting

A controlling type of organization might face some challenges in adopting an Agile method, because these methods tend toward being reactive to change. The projects' plans and initial requirements are often treated as approximations, with the assumption that as the project moves forward, both the customer and the development team will learn about it. Many of the Agile methods use time-boxing[1] to control schedule and rely on the customer to prioritize functionality that will be delivered. Clearly, a cooperative customer[2] is the key to making this arrangement work.

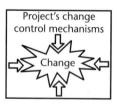

Figure 2.3   Controlling change.

---

1. "Time-boxing" is a method for managing projects that sets hard begin and end dates for the project or project iterations and allows the delivered functionality to change in order to complete work within the specified period. Refer to the description of "Sprint" in Scrum (Appendix H) for an example of how an Agile method might use time-boxing.

2. See Chapter 3 ("Considering Your Customers") for more discussion about your customers.

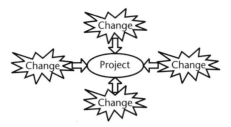

Figure 2.4 Reacting to change.

The role of organizational culture

The culture of your organization has grown up over a long period of time and is based on the challenges your organization faces and the people who have been instrumental in its success. Although culture *does* change over time, that change is a very slow process because it requires members of the organization to learn new behaviors and adopt new ways of interacting with each other. As anyone who has ever tried to lose weight knows, changing ingrained behavior is very difficult to do.

It is virtually guaranteed that some of the practices of any Agile Method you may choose to adopt will clash with your existing organizational culture. The members of the organization will find it difficult to change their behaviors to align with those clashing practices because it will require them to act in a way that is counter to what has made them successful over the years. For example, managers who have been successful in a highly hierarchical organizational structure are likely to have great difficulty operating in a more cooperative environment. Even if an individual manager *wants* to adopt cooperative methods, his or her past experience will make it difficult to actually do it.

Do not underestimate the role of organizational culture in defining how people behave. Beware of the behavior changes that adopting an Agile Method may require of your staff. In cases where those changes are counter to an organizational norm, people will be reticent to change. And even when behaviors *are* changed, the underlying cultural norm will exert pressure to revert to old behaviors for a long time into the future (possibly for years). The only way to succeed in such a change is through a conscious program of continual reinforcement of the desired behaviors until they become a natural and automatic part of daily business.

3

Contents

Considering Your Customers

This chapter provides insight into how the customers you serve will affect your decision to adopt an Agile method.

The Agile Manifesto[1] includes the value statement: "Customer collaboration over contract negotiation." This value provides a snapshot of the Agile methods' approach toward customers. They assume that customers are willing to accept a fluid relationship that is defined less by up-front agreements and more by ongoing collaboration and cooperation. This assumption about the customer is consistent with these methods' philosophy of projects as learning experiences for all involved.

There are three main parts of your relationships with your customers that will be affected by adoption of an Agile method; the nature of the contractual terms, how requirements are established and maintained, and the type and intensity of interactions your customers have with your development teams. Each item will be discussed in this chapter.

Contracts and statements of work

While the Agile methods acknowledge that contracts and other forms of agreement must exist, they do not explicitly identify what those agreements should or should not contain. This omission is unfortunate, but from these methods' treatment of the customer's role in Agile projects, it becomes clear that they do not expect these vehicles to fully and precisely define what is to happen on the project. Rather, the customer and the developers are treated as colearners who work together to figure out the project's results as it progresses.

Traditional project managers, contract administrators, and lawyers generally want agreements to fully specify the roles

---

1. The Agile Manifesto describes the four values behind the Agile Methods. It is described in Appendix A.

and expectations of all parties, as well as the budget and schedule to be adhered to and the functionality and quality to be delivered. They are often uncomfortable with open-ended agreements because they perceive risk in them. As depicted in Figure 3.1, the traditional view often uses contracts to protect the parties from each other.

The Agile methods acknowledge the risks involved in more open-ended agreements, but rather than trying to avoid them through careful specification upfront, they seek to mitigate the risks through close collaboration with the customer. These methods are all based on the assumption that not all project parameters can be known ahead of time. They generally establish some of them, then set goals for others, allowing them to change as the project progresses. For example, the use of time-boxing usually means that budget and schedule are held constant, whereas the delivered functionality is allowed to vary. In this sort of project, the functionality to be delivered cannot be known with certainty before the project is complete.

A contract for an Agile project must of necessity be different from those we normally see, because it acts as a platform for collaboration, as depicted in Figure 3.1. Its mix of "shalls" and "shoulds" must be based on the practices of the specific Agile method being employed, and it must be explicit about those terms that are targets rather than guarantees. In addition, it must clearly establish how the product requirements will be managed over time, as well as the nature and extent of customer involvement required. These last two items are significant considerations and will be discussed in the remainder of this chapter.

Establishing and changing requirements

Traditional project management holds that the requirements for the system being developed should be baselined at some relatively early stage in the project. That is, the customer and development team should agree that the

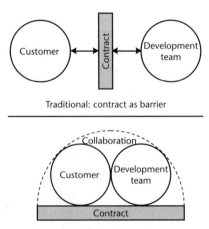

Traditional: contract as barrier

Agile: contract as platform

Figure 3.1 Contracts: barrier versus platform.

requirements as documented at that point in time are an accurate description of what will be delivered. This agreement becomes the basis for the developers' work, as well as the customer's acceptance activities. Once this agreement has been reached, the baselined requirements take on the formality of a contract, requiring explicit negotiation and mutual agreement before they can be changed or added to. The net result of this, as shown in Figure 3.2, is that the early requirements baseline defines the bulk of the work that will be done, and changes to that baseline are controlled so that they represent a (hopefully) small part of the project.

The Agile methods treat the system requirements as one more aspect of the project about which both the developers and the customer will learn over time. So they tend to call for specification of initial requirements only at a very high level, leaving much room for interpretation and adaptation as the project moves forward. They expect that both the customer and the developers will propose changes to the requirements throughout the project. But the authority to approve, disapprove, and prioritize the ever-changing requirements vests solely with the customer (with technical input from the developers). The net result of this, as shown in Figure 3.2, is that the initial requirements form a base upon which the system requirements grow by accretion over the life of the project. Its intent is to ensure that the functionality that is delivered will satisfy the customer's needs.

As an example of the difference in approach between the traditional and the Agile methods, consider a system for managing customer data:

▸ A traditional requirements baseline would likely comprise hundreds of pages that would include such details as a full entity-relation diagram for the database, identification of all fields on each user interface screen, and the content, structure, and layout for all reports the system will produce. Once this baseline is established, there is an expectation that changes to it will be limited in scope and impact.

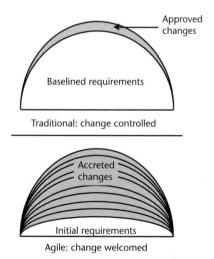

Figure 3.2 Requirements change: controlled versus welcomed.

▸ An Agile project would begin with a much less complete description of the requirements, perhaps a dozen pages, or as little as one page. This description would identify the users of the system and its intended use but leave the majority of the details undefined. Then, as each detail needs to be addressed during the project, the development team would work with the customer to determine what those details should be.

So, Figure 3.2 depicts the two key differences between how the traditional and Agile methods manage requirements: 1) the level of detail with which the requirements are initially specified; and 2) the response to requirements changes. Where the traditional methods seek to establish a baseline and then *control* changes, the Agile methods actually encourage and welcome continuing evolution of the requirements. This manner of managing requirements demands an actively engaged customer (which can be its own problem), which we will discuss next.

Expectations about collaboration

Traditional projects tend to use contracts, gatekeepers, and requirements specifications to mediate between the development team and the customer, as shown in Figure 3.1. In many organizations, developers are not allowed to meet the end users, let alone interact with them regularly. Even when interaction *is* allowed, the contracts and gatekeepers often circumscribe it so that its potential results are limited.

The Agile methods all depend on regular and significant interaction between the development team and the customer. Most of these methods define "customer" to be either an end user or a representative of the end users who has direct and regular contact with them. Because the customer representative has such a central role in the project (for example, see the previous discussion of requirements), some Agile methods prescribe that this person be available to the project team significant amounts of the time. The most extreme example is XP, as described in Appendix E, which prescribes that the customer representative actually *be* a member of the project team and be continuously collocated with the team.

The Agile methods prescribe a significant amount of interaction between the customer and the development team to engender a positive working relationship. The philosophy is that this collaborative relationship should result in a smoother-running project that ultimately produces a product that satisfies the customer's needs.

But these methods also place demands on the customer, demands that will be foreign to most customers' experience. Most organizations contract for software development because they do not have the resources to do the job themselves. The Agile methods demand that the customer commit as much as a full-time person to a project. This demand could be a burden that a customer would not able or willing to assume. If you are not able to secure the required level of involvement from your customer, then the success of your Agile project will be threatened.

Your customers

Adopting an Agile method will have a noticeable impact on your relationships with your customers. It will change the nature of the contractual terms, the way in which requirements are established and managed, and the degree of customer involvement on your projects. Success with any Agile Method will depend on your customer's willingness to embark with you on this new way of doing business.

CHAPTER

4

Contents

Considering Your Projects

This chapter discusses a number of project attributes you need to keep in mind when anticipating adopting an Agile method.

Some Agile methods provide guidance about the types of projects for which they are best suited. For example, XP as described in Appendix E explicitly states it is best suited to experimental projects that require a small colocated development team. Others provide no such guidance. But even in cases where guidance is provided, proponents of the various methods generally say there is no reason why their methods should not work for almost any type of project.

In fact, in recent years the Agile methods have been used in a variety of project environments. The discussion groups associated with the Agile Alliance Web site (http://www. AgileAlliance.org) include anecdotal reports of results on many kinds of projects. At the time of this writing, there does not appear to be any statistically significant data that can guide us in determining the types of projects most likely to succeed with an Agile method. Therefore, you would do well to seek out the most recent information available on the Internet.

With this cacophony of voices as a background, we will discuss some attributes of your projects that are particularly pertinent to the Agile methods.

Size of project teams

All Agile methods seem best suited to small project teams, that is, teams that do not exceed 10–15 individuals. Although some methods do not explicitly place a limit on team size, their preference for face-to-face communication over written documentation places a *practical* limit on size, as shown in Figure 4.1. Only a limited number of people can actively participate in a meeting, and regardless of whether a method calls for regular

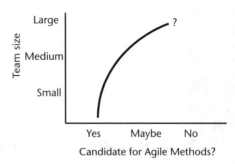

Figure 4.1   Team size.

team meetings or not, each Agile method requires continuous communication among all team members.

When a project's scope mandates a larger team, the Agile methods are not necessarily inappropriate. In any project of 50 people or more, individuals are almost always grouped into smaller subteams (as shown in Figure 4.2) for practical purposes. Each subteam will often operate somewhat independently of the others and integrate its work products at appropriate milestones. In such an environment, one or more (or even all) of the subteams could use an Agile method for its work. (For more on this idea, refer to the "Multiple teams" section later in the chapter.)

Colocation of team members

The Internet and technologies that enable it have resulted in the growth of distributed teams. Many organizations have found that with the appropriate tools in place, there is no longer a hard requirement for team members to be colocated. Sometimes one or two members are remote from the rest of the team, and in other cases team members are widely dispersed.

The Agile methods have a bias against distributed teams. Some (like XP) explicitly specify that the team should be colocated (although recent discussions of experiences with XP seem to contradict this restriction). As with team size (previously discussed), the communication assumptions of *all* Agile methods are easiest to meet when all team members work in the same location.

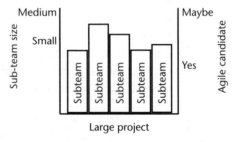

Figure 4.2   Subteams in large projects.

As depicted in Figure 4.3, one of the primary features of a location in which people work is a communication bubble. A location's communication bubble is saturated with a tremendous amount of verbal and nonverbal communication that goes on constantly. This communication includes formal documents and meetings, in addition to the casual hour-to-hour contact that team members have with one another. A telephone call opens a temporary portal between two locations and can transmit a relatively small amount of information between them. And while a teleconference portal has a much greater bandwidth than a telephone call, it is still temporary and quite limited when compared with the regular communication within either location.

Yes, a distributed team *could* use an Agile method, but such a situation would present communications challenges that would have to be addressed in order for the team to operate as the methods intend. Some recent advances in teleconferencing might be able to partially mitigate the communications problems. For example, some teleconferencing systems provide not just audio and video links but also the ability to share computer screens, whiteboards, and other communication devices. When the bandwidth becomes great enough, the teleconferencing experience begins to approximate face-to-face interaction. But even in such cases, this relatively rich communication is still temporary and not a complete substitute for the communication bubble of colocation.

Criticality of projects

How important is your project to the organization? If the project fails, what will be lost? Convenience? Information? Capability? Money? A customer? An industry? The company? As indicated in Figure 4.4, every project falls somewhere along a continuum from "The project does not matter" to "Failure is not an option." The level of criticality for a particular project is an important driver for many decisions about it. Generally, the more critical a project is, the more important it is to mitigate risk by using appropriate techniques, tools, and methods. But how do you determine what is appropriate?

The first consideration is the experience of the organization. Generally, it is ill advised to try out a new method or tool on a critical project. The first use of a tool or method is usually attended by surprises as people learn how to use it, and the organization works to figure out how it meshes with (or does not mesh with) existing organizational mechanisms and norms.

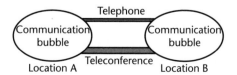

Figure 4.3   Multiple location communication.

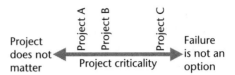

Figure 4.4 Project criticality.

Adaptation to a new tool or method will often require more effort and time than anyone can foresee, and at times, the surprises are severe enough to jeopardize the entire project. Trying an Agile method for the first time would represent a significant risk to a project.

This does not mean you should not use an Agile method on a critical project, or even that a critical project should not be the test case. The risk of trying an Agile method on a project must be balanced against other risks to determine an appropriate course.

For example, suppose that your critical project is exploring new ground (like an application domain in which you have no experience or a technology that is new to the organization). If your existing methods have already proven to be ineffective on that sort of project, then using them would constitute a substantial risk to the project. In such a case, it may be appropriate to use an Agile method to mitigate the risk of that project.

Safety and security requirements

Safety and security requirements are special cases of system requirements. These requirements necessitate a special class of product features — features that are nonnegotiable and which absolutely must work correctly.

As discussed in Chapter 3 in "Establishing and changing requirements," the Agile methods often allow the functionality that is to be delivered to change over time. This tendency means that although an Agile project has general goals, many of its exact deliverables are not known until they have been delivered. But this does not mean that an Agile method cannot be used where some features are nonnegotiable. Each Agile method contains a mechanism for prioritizing functionality, and so these critical features can simply be assigned the highest priorities. By doing this, you can ensure that the nonnegotiable features will be implemented, even while following the Agile method's normal processes.

The need for absolute correctness of these features could be a reason to *prefer* using an Agile method (depending on your normal method's track record in ensuring correctness). All of the Agile methods have a strong focus on developing high-quality software. For example, XP prescribes that the tests for a feature be written first, then the code developed to fully satisfy the tests. It requires that *all* tests for *all* features run 100% correctly before integration of a feature is considered successful. In addition to their focus on developing high-quality software, all of the Agile methods are fully compatible with independent Verification and Validation, which would further boost confidence in the product.

Safety and security requirements, like business criticality, may prompt you to either embrace an Agile method or avoid it. Your decision must be based on an analysis of the relative risks of your available options.

Multiple teams

The Agile methods simply do not address the special requirements of projects in which multiple separate teams collaborate. Rather, they make the assumption that a system is being developed by a single cohesive team of individuals that is answerable to a single customer.

As discussed in "Size of project teams," breaking a larger team into relatively independent subteams can allow one or more (or even all) of those subteams to use an Agile method. But that does not answer some important questions about the project. For example, how would the work of all those subteams be managed and coordinated? And with all of the interaction among the various teams, who would have the role of the single customer to whom each team is responsive?

One example of a paradigm that could work is shown in Figure 4.5. In this example, a project management office that would manage the overall project would play this coordination and customer role. This office would have to include a customer representative, but it might also provide other resources that would be needed at the global-project level. (These resources could include a professional project manager, requirements analyst, configuration manager, and independent acceptance testers.)

The relationship between the subteams and this program office might be modeled after the chosen Agile method's customer-interaction model, but it would likely have to be extended to provide the level of support and coordination required to meld several successful Agile subprojects together into a single successful project.

While this example is only one option, it shows the degree to which an Agile method would have to be adapted and augmented to be used successfully in a multiteam environment. Clearly, the challenges would be significant, and while they are not insurmountable, making them work effectively will require innovation and flexibility.

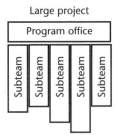

Figure 4.5 Multiteam example.

Subcontractors

The subject of managing subcontractors[1] is not addressed by any of the Agile methods. They all operate under the assumption that the system is being developed entirely in-house. Although any part of a system that is subcontracted must of necessity be discrete and self-contained, it must also integrate cleanly with the rest of the system. The two greatest risks in subcontracted software revolve around; (1) integration of the subcontracted work with the in-house developed software, and (2) ensuring that the subcontractor will deliver software of the required quality by the date needed.

The integration points are significant sources of risk when different parts of a system are development by different teams. So, if an Agile method is used in such a case, the details of the integration points would have to be treated in much the same way as safety and security requirements (as previously discussed). They would have to be defined and prioritized in such a way that their integrity in the software developed in-house could be ensured.

Managing the relationship with the subcontractor would add a dynamic to the project that is not anticipated by any of the Agile methods. Figure 4.6 shows that, where the Agile methods define interactions between two entities (customer and developers), the subcontractor would be a new type of entity, requiring a new set of interactions. Working out the details of the subcontractor interaction in the context of an Agile method would require significant adaptation and innovation.

It may be advisable to avoid using an Agile method on a project that includes subcontracted work unless the project's needs require it and the organization is able and willing to make the requisite adaptations and innovations.

Integration with hardware and other software components

An Agile project might operate in the context of a larger system development effort, developing a software component that must integrate with other software or hardware components. This is feasible because in that type of environment, there is almost always an over-arching program office that coordinates the development of all of the components by the different project teams. (This sort of arrangement was discussed under "Multiple teams and depicted in Figure 4.5.)

---

1. As used in this book, the term "subcontractor" refers to an organization to which a discrete part of the software development work is delegated. Commonly, such subcontractors manage their own work and treat the prime contractor as their customer, receiving requirements from them and delivering a finished product (or product increments) to them.

   We do *not* use the term "subcontractor" to refer to contract (or 1099) employees or temporary help provided by an agency. Generally those individuals will work and be managed in-house by the contracting organization and will function as members of the project team.

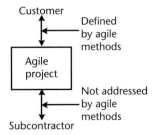

Figure 4.6 Subcontractor interactions.

In this context, the program office is the Agile project's "customer." It will provide the project's requirements and maintain ongoing interaction with the project. The program office will generally include a CCB that will act as a forum for resolving any integration issues that will arise among the components. In short, the program office serves all of the functions of the customer in an Agile project.

CHAPTER

5

Contents

Considering Your Tools and Processes

This chapter discusses some assumptions that the Agile methods make about the tools and processes used in your software development organization. In some cases, these methods assume relatively mature tools and processes, and in others, they require a level of informality that may be a source of challenge. The three classes of tools and processes we will discuss are Requirements Management, Project Management, and Configuration Management (CM).

Requirements Management

Requirements Management systems in software organizations run the gamut from completely informal to rigorously formal. At the first extreme, the product is developed on the basis of little more than a flow of phone calls and e-mails. At the other extreme, the agreed-upon requirements are documented in a tool that traces their implementation to specification sections and product components and modules. In this case, a sophisticated change management system is generally used to record every proposed new requirement or change to one, so that it can be tracked, deliberated over, and formally approved (or disapproved) by a Configuration Control Board. For any change that is approved, a corrective action system is used to track all of the necessary activities to closure.

Some Agile methods specifically address Requirements Management, and those that do not assume a system much like those that are specified. The best example of such a system is described in Scrum, as described in Appendix H, which manages requirements this way:

- Each and every requirement is documented as one item in the "Product Backlog." The Product Backlog includes both user requirements and technical or implementation requirements.
- Any person can add an item to the Product Backlog at any time.
- The customer has sole responsibility for prioritizing the Product Backlog items.
- For each iteration of development (each Sprint), the team chooses items from the Product Backlog to constitute the "Sprint Backlog" (using the items' priorities as one consideration in their choices).
- The Sprint Backlog is not allowed to change during a Sprint.
- At the end of each Sprint, the customer determines which Product Backlog items have been satisfied, and those items are removed from the Product Backlog.

You can see from this description and from Figure 5.1 that the Agile methods tend to need a system for managing requirements that is somewhere in the middle of the range described above.

Agile Requirements Managment includes the following:

- Requirements are written down.
- Tracing from those requirements to components is never suggested.
- The customer actively manages the set of requirements.
- Although new requirements as well as changes to them are usually accepted without deliberation, the changes are documented just as the original requirements were. But because no traceability is maintained, determining the impact of each requirements change is left up to the development team.

If your organization has already adopted a requirements methodology or a tool that enforces certain levels of documentation and activities, you will

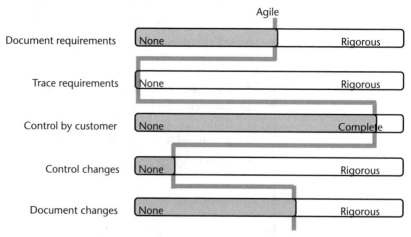

Figure 5.1   Agile Requirements Management.

need to examine the nature of the tool's imposed restrictions to determine if an Agile method will fit within them. You may also want to explore the extent to which an Agile method can be adapted to your existing ways of managing requirements.

If your organization has no set methods or tools for managing requirements, or if your existing tool or methodology is not compatible with the Agile method you intend to adopt, then you will want to identify the extent to which an Agile method will demand changes to the way requirements are managed. Will you need to also adopt a new requirements tool? Will the Agile method require more rigor in managing requirements than your staff is prepared to exercise?

Project Management

Like requirements management, project management systems in software organizations run the gamut from completely informal to rigorously formal. At the first extreme, the team is given an objective and expected to do whatever is necessary to achieve that objective. At the other extreme, detailed estimates and plans are assembled, and then the project's progress against those plans is assessed regularly. When actual performance varies from the plan, corrective actions are taken to bring the plans and the actual performance back in line with each other.

As you can see in Figure 5.2, the Agile methods tend toward the less rigorous end of that continuum.

Agile Project Managment includes the following:

▸ Estimates of product attributes such as size are not generally made.

▸ However, the effort and schedule for the project (and especially for the current iteration) *are* estimated to some intermediate level of detail.

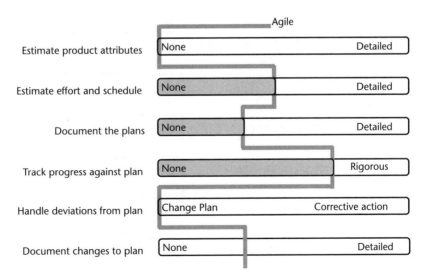

Figure 5.2   Agile Project Management.

- The plans are not generally documented in any great detail.

- While the project's progress is tracked against the plans with relatively great care, corrective action is almost never taken. Instead, deviations from the plan are treated as a fact, and the plans are changed to conform to the newly understood reality.

- Those changed plans are documented to the same degree as the original plans were.

These attributes of Agile project management may or may not fit well with the norms in your organization. For example, if your projects usually produce large Ghant charts that lay out tasks and dependencies in great detail, then an Agile method's plans will seem inadequate to many people. Or, if status is carefully compared with plan, and corrective actions implemented when there is a deviation, then an Agile method's tacit acceptance of plan changes will be a major shock (or perhaps a welcome relief).

Conversely, if your organization's projects tend to run "by the seat of the pants," then an Agile method will represent a new level of detail and rigor that will be foreign to your staff. Even so, the light nature of Agile project management should not present a great challenge to even the most undisciplined project managers.

Configuration Management

CM covers a variety of topics, some of which are addressed by most organizations' processes and tools, and others that tend to be totally overlooked in all but the most rigorously formal organizations. The Agile methods do not explicitly discuss *any* aspect of CM. But from the practices involved in each of them, it is clear that certain levels of CM process and tool support are

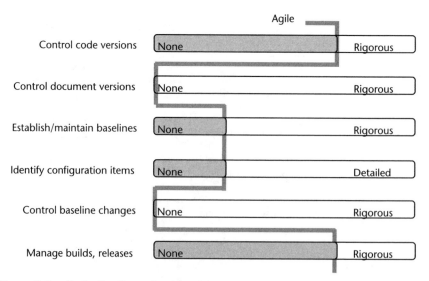

Figure 5.3   Agile Configuration Management.

assumed. This level of support is depicted in Figure 5.3 and discussed in the following sections.

Code control

Most organizations have a code control tool that automatically maintains file versions as they are updated and prevents two people from updating the same code at the same time. The Agile methods clearly require good version control for program code. Many expect continuous and uncoordinated changes to be made to code throughout the project. Some explicitly say that changes should be made freely, because any change can be undone. These practices and this philosophy would not be possible without a good automated version control system.

Document control

Automated control of documents (such as specifications and plans) is much less common than code control. At one extreme, project managers are left to devise their own methods for controlling documents, and many do so in a barely adequate way. At the other extreme, a few organizations purchase specialized systems to provide rigorous control of documentation.

The Agile methods explicitly de-emphasize the role of documents, so implementation of an Agile method would require little in the way of document management practices or tools. By the same token, if you currently use a sophisticated method or tool for managing documents, there is little reason that your Agile projects could not easily use those methods and tools.

Baseline maintenance

Although the term "baseline" is never used in any of the Agile methods, the concept is central to their practices. All of the Agile methods rely on incremental development processes, with each increment resulting in a working product or other substantial deliverable that becomes the basis for future increments. Because the Agile methods' increments are quite short (a couple of weeks to a couple of months), this product baseline is established early and updated on a regular basis.

The Agile methods dictate no formality in the baselining process, so the required level of baseline control can be satisfied by relatively simple build and release management tools and processes (as later described in "Build and release management"). If your organization currently uses specific processes and tools to establish and maintain your baselines, then there appears to be no reason why those processes and tools could not be used on your Agile projects, provided they are agile enough to meet the speed demands of those projects.

Configuration Item identification

As with baselining, Configuration Item (CI) identification is not explicitly addressed by any Agile method, yet its principles are assumed to be in place. Some Agile methods call for collective ownership of all code and other artifacts produced by the project. This practice would not be feasible without mechanisms for each project member to be able to identify what each source code file is for, what it is named, where it is stored, and which version is the current one.

Any reasonably robust code management system includes features that support CI identification, and it appears that the Agile methods assume the use of those facilities. If your projects do *not* use such a robust system, or if they fail to use the CI identification features of the system, then adopting an Agile method will require some changes.

Change control

Classical CM practices treat changes as if they are an enemy to be cataloged, held for interrogation, and finally dispatched. Even projects that do not employ formal classical CM tend to treat changes as unwelcome intruders on their projects, tolerating them if they must, but ignoring them when they can. The Agile methods, on the other hand, treat change as an ally to be welcomed or as an honored guest. (Refer to Chapter 18, "Welcome Changing requirements," for further discussion of this dichotomy.) It is likely that regardless of how formal or informal your change control processes may be, adopting an Agile method will require a significant shift in philosophy as well as action.

Build and release management

Each Agile method has specific practices for managing builds and releases of products, specifying when they are done, how they are accomplished, and what is done with them. The build and release cycles in Agile projects are generally much more rapid than most organizations are used to. (Some Agile methods call for daily or even "continuous" builds. And because Agile iterations are generally short, releases are expected every month or two.) Although this pace will likely be foreign to your organization, builds and releases are such a natural part of the Agile methods that they are not likely to cause adoption problems.

However, there may be reason for concern over whether your configuration management tools and processes can adequately track and control such fast build and release cycles. As with CI identification, any robust code control tool will have the necessary facilities. But many people may need training to ensure that they can manage Agile builds and releases easily.

Your tools and processes

Regardless of how rigorously you use processes and tools, adopting an Agile method will most certainly impact how you use them. In some cases it may lead you to abandon a process or tool, and in others you may need to acquire a new tool or learn to better use the capabilities of a tool you already have. In all cases, it is well worth your time to carefully consider how an Agile method will affect and be affected by your processes and tools.

CHAPTER

6

Contents

Considering Your Staff

In this chapter, we will discuss attributes of your programming staff that will affect adoption of an Agile method. Specifically, we will look at the variety of expertise they possess and how they are likely to react to the changes in their work environment that adoption of an Agile method would necessitate.

Superstars

All of us try to hire only the best and brightest people, and we will often tell them so to stroke their egos and inspire them to extraordinary effort. But, in truth, most organizations have a relatively average mix of software professionals who have a relatively average mix of talent and motivation, with a few superstars, and a few disappointments. For most of us, our average programmer is only average, and about half of our staff members are below average.[1] Your current method of choosing members for teams and assigning tasks to people is based on the mix of talents and skills in your organization.

A change to an Agile method has the potential to upset your organizational balance. Most Agile methods make the assumption (some explicitly) that the Agile project is staffed by technically expert and highly motivated individuals. They tend to place the project team members in empowered positions, expect them to identify the correct path to follow, and then take the necessary steps on their own.

Proponents of the Agile methods point out that these methods do not just empower the programmers but also build their professional capabilities at the same time. For example, Feature-Driven Development's, as described in Appendix F, "Chief Programmer," XP's, as described in Appendix E,

---

1. Yes, I know that mean and median are not necessarily the same! But for the sake of rhetorical effect, I am assuming a normal distribution.

"Coach," and Scrum's, as described in Appendix H, "Scrum Master" are all technical experts and mentors to other project team members. So, over time, it is expected that your staff of merely average professionals will grow to become extraordinary, if not superstars.

But, of course, as with any learning, if this improvement in your staff's capabilities does in fact take place, it will not happen immediately. There will be some period of time when your Agile projects will be staffed with mere mortals. Unless your software shop is *truly* populated with exceptional individuals, you will want to carefully consider the assumptions that any Agile method makes about the staff's ability to innovate and self-motivate. Be sure that you are not setting your staff up for failure by placing responsibilities on them that they are not yet ready or willing to accept.

Changing work patterns

How comfortable is your programming staff with their existing work patterns? Do they have a history of doing things in a certain way from which they would be loath to deviate? Or are they chafing under the stress of work patterns that they despise? Even if the impetus for exploring the adoption of an Agile method is coming from the ranks of your programming staff, you still must consider whether the clamor is coming from a vocal few or if there is a general sense of dissatisfaction with the status quo.

Adoption of any of the Agile methods will mean significant changes to how your software projects work. Everyone's job will change (including yours), and for some people that change will be significant. For example, self-managing teams require less management oversight and depend on the team members themselves to make decisions that were once the purview of managers alone. Will those changes be exciting to those people? Or will they add stress and anxiety?

Significant changes in the work environment can cause surprising reactions among your employees. They can experience a sense of loss as the old ways of working slip into the past. Even individuals who are glad to see the old ways go may display the symptoms of grief and loss. Figure 6.1 shows the stages that people tend to go through while dealing with changes in the work environment.

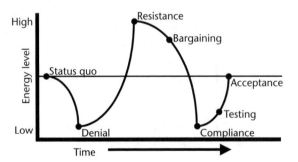

Figure 6.1 Responses to change.

These stages include:

- *Status Quo*—This is the steady state that exists before the change, and to which you will want to return after the change has been fully implemented.

- *Denial* — Initial reactions to change are often a hope or expectation that the change is not permanent, and things will return to "normal" if the change is simply ignored.

- *Resistance*—This is an active lashing out against the change, often in the form of either overt or covert attempts to stop or even sabotage the change.

- *Bargaining*—When it becomes clear that the change cannot be avoided, attempts may be made to evade its direct impact, for example, by seeking exemption from it.

- *Compliance* — When resistance and bargaining fail to stop the change, a sullen compliance can set in. People may comply with the change, but they do it grudgingly, and productivity often suffers.

- *Testing*—After some time of bare compliance, people may begin to actually test out the meaning and extent of the change to discover how it can benefit them.

- *Acceptance*—Finally, the change is accepted as the new status quo when people decide that it is not as bad as they had feared, and that it provides some benefit to them.

While not every person will go through these exact responses, they form a pattern that you are likely to observe within your organization any time significant change is introduced.

Making changes stick

Most organizations have a history of failed change efforts. People's "denial" reaction (as discussed above) is often well founded, because they have seen that strategy work in the past. They have found that if they ignore changes, those changes often *will* go away! Making a change successful over the long term is a complex topic about which much has been written.[2] In this section, we will discuss a few dimensions of this topic that are particularly pertinent to adopting an Agile method.

Making the right change

The first point is probably the most obvious. The most important part of assuring that a change will be successful is to make a good decision about

---

2. If you search the Internet or your local library for "managing organizational change," you will find a wide range of books and other resources on this subject.

the change in the first place. Too often, changes are adopted based on very little information and analysis. This results in a bad decision and, ultimately, in a failed change effort.

The fact that you are reading this book indicates that you are intent on avoiding this pitfall. You are collecting the information you need to be sure that adopting an Agile method is indeed the right thing to do in your organization. In this book, Part I, Chapter 7 "Using This Book to Make Your Adoption Decisions," and Part VII: "The Adoption Decision" will guide you in getting the greatest value from this book and making the right decision.

As you will see in Chapter 23, making this decision should not be a solo activity. Your staff members will have unique perspectives on the subject on which you will want to capitalize. If you are being lobbied to adopt an Agile method by some of your staff, it would be prudent to find out if others disagree with that position. When you have collected enough information (e.g., after completing most of this book), it would be healthy to engage all parties in a debate of the question. Their viewpoints will provide valuable information that you can use to make this decision, which is ultimately *your* responsibility.

If you decide that adopting an Agile method is the right thing for your organization, then you will surely continue your research by gaining an intimate knowledge of the method you decide to adopt through further reading and by hiring a consultant or employees with the requisite expertise. Understanding the details of that method will be critical to successfully making it part of your organization's way of doing business.

Building buy-in

Because a successful change effort requires effort and cooperation by many people throughout the organization, you have to take steps to ensure that those people "buy into" the decision. That is, that they understand the decision and will do their part to make it successful, even if they do not fully agree with it.

Even if you are the most senior executive, you still need to "sell" the adoption decision to others within your organization. Although you can *command* compliance, remember (from the "Responses to change" section) that bare compliance is not your goal. Your goal is to reach a new state of status quo. And this can only be achieved when your staff *embraces* the change as the new norm for the organization.

Engaging people during the adoption decision (as discussed in "Making the right change") is an important first step. But it must be followed with continuing communication to the entire staff about the change, including:

  ‣ Regular reinforcement of the reasons for the change;

  ‣ Discussion of the plans for implementing the change;

  ‣ Regular reporting on the progress of the implementation effort;

- Descriptions of problems that have come up (as they surely will), and how they have been dealt with;
- Celebrations of successes.

This topic is discussed in much more detail in Chapter 24.

Changing the reward system

Your organization has a reward system. It may not be formal, and it may not be administered centrally, but it exists. Every employee has a clear understanding of which behaviors are rewarded and which behaviors are not, and the vast majority of employees will practice those behaviors that are rewarded. The reward system in your organization has grown over time to encourage behavior that seems to enhance the organization's success.

The adoption of an Agile method will significantly alter the behaviors required of many of your employees. Some behaviors that used to be desirable will no longer be appropriate, and other new behaviors will need to take their place. If the reward system is not changed, then your staff's behavior will resist change as they continue to act in ways that are rewarded.

For this reason, you must look carefully at the behaviors that are encouraged and discouraged by your reward system and take decisive action to change that system. This topic is also discussed in more detail in Chapter 24.

Your staff

Considerations about your staff are nearly the most important ones you should make. After your organizational culture, your staff and their abilities and attitudes about adopting an Agile method will be critically important to the success of any adoption effort you undertake.

CHAPTER

7

Contents

Using This Book to Make Your Adoption Decisions

In this final chapter of Part I, we change our focus from the Agile methods and how they may affect your organization to the nuts and bolts of how to get the greatest value out of this book. This chapter first discusses the structure and order of the book's parts and chapters. It then provides instructions for downloading and using the supporting workbook that is designed to provide an easy mechanism for you to record your thoughts as you read, then analyze and draw reasonable conclusions from them.

Structure of this book

Figure 7.1 illustrates that this book is structured to facilitate your rapid understanding of the Agile values, principles, and practices so you can assess how adopting an Agile method might affect your organization. This book consists of seven parts and eight appendixes.

Part I: Adoption Considerations sets the stage for the remainder of the book with a brief introduction to the Agile methods, discussions of considerations you should keep in mind as you read the remainder of the book, and pointers to maximize the value you derive from the time you are investing.

- Chapter 1: Introducing the Agile Methods.
- Chapter 2: Considering Your Organizational Culture.
- Chapter 3: Considering Your Customers.
- Chapter 4: Considering Your Projects.
- Chapter 5: Considering Your Tools and Processes.
- Chapter 6: Considering Your Staff.

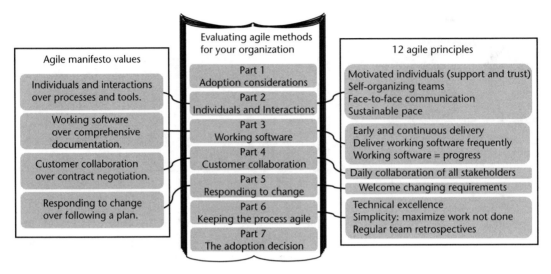

Figure 7.1 Structure of this book.

> Chapter 7: Using This Book to Make Your Adoption Decisions.

Parts II–VI are the meat of this book. They are structured around the value statements of the Agile Manifesto, the principles that amplify them, and the practices by which each Agile method implements them.

Part II: Value: "Individuals and Interactions Over Processes and Tools" discusses the Agile Principles and Practices that support the first value from the Agile Manifesto.

> Chapter 8: About People, Processes, and Tools.

> Chapter 9: Motivated Individuals and Self-Organizing Teams.

> Chapter 10: Face-to-Face Communication.

> Chapter 11: Sustainable Pace.

> Chapter 12: Supporting Processes and Tools.

Part III: Value: "Working Software Over Comprehensive Documentation" discusses the Agile Principles and Practices that support the second value from the Agile Manifesto.

> Chapter 13: The Role of Documentation in a Software Project.

> Chapter 14: Incremental Delivery of Working Software.

Part IV: Value: "Customer Collaboration Over Contract Negotiation" discusses the Agile Principles and Practices that support the third value from the Agile Manifesto.

> Chapter 15: Defining the Customer Relationship.

> Chapter 16: Daily Collaboration of All Stakeholders.

Part V: Value: "Responding to Changeover Following a Plan" discusses the Agile Principles and Practices that support the last value from the Agile Manifesto.

- Chapter 17: Understanding Change in Software Projects.
- Chapter 18: Welcome Changing Requirements.

Part VI: The Unstated Value: Keeping the Process "Agile" discusses the Agile Principles and Practices that, although they are not related to one of the four values from the Agile Manifesto, are nonetheless critical to the Agile methods.

- Chapter 19: Maintaining the Process.
- Chapter 20: Technical Excellence.
- Chapter 21: Simplicity: Maximize Work Not Done.
- Chapter 22: Regular Team Retrospectives.

Part VII: The Adoption Decision wraps up the book with a discussion of how to use the information and impressions you have gained to make your adoption decision.

- Chapter 23: Making the Adoption Decision.
- Chapter 24: Adopting the New Practices.
- Chapter 25: Evaluating the Effects of Your Agile Method.

Finally, the appendixes provide more detailed information on the Agile Manifesto, the 12 Agile principles and the Agile methods, including references for further information.

The "Evaluating Agile Methods" Workbook

To assist you in deriving the greatest value from this book, we have provided a workbook for your use. As Figure 7.2 shows, this workbook matches the book's structure. It provides mechanisms for you to record your observations as you read this book and then roll them up for a summarized view afterwards.

You can download this workbook from the author's Web site, as shown in Figure 7.3.

- Go to http://www.ASKProcess.com/eval-agile.
- Scroll down to the "Supporting Workbook" section.
- Click "Download the workbook" and follow the instructions.

Refer to the "Instructions" page of the workbook for detailed instructions on its use.

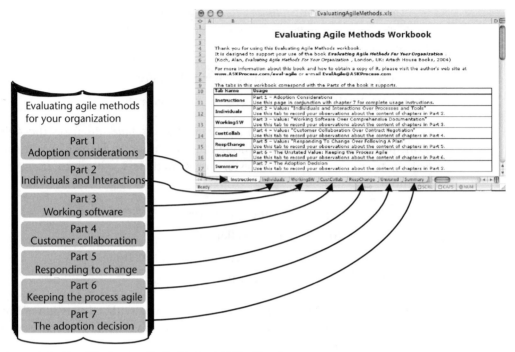

Figure 7.2   The "Evaluating Agile Methods" Workbook.

Supporting Workbook	Readers are encouraged to download the workbook that augments this book. This workbook provides a framework for the reader to record his or her evaluations of the Agile practices and compile a set of preliminary conclusions. The final chapters of the book will guide the reader in transforming the results from the workbook into an adoption decision, and (if the decision is to adopt some form of Agile method), into an action plan.

Figure 7.3   Download the workbook.

Evaluating the practices

As you read each part of this book, you should use a different page of the workbook to record your observations. For example, as shown in Figure 7.4, while reading Part II: Value: "Individuals and Interactions Over Processes and Tools," you should use the "Individuals" tab of the workbook to record your notes.

The chapters of Parts II–VI (after the initial chapter of each part) correspond with the Agile principles listed on the appropriate page of the workbook. Figure 7.4 shows that Chapter 9 corresponds with the first two Principles on the "Individuals" worksheet. (Scroll down on this worksheet to see the sections for Chapters 10–12.) Associated with each Agile Principle are places for you to record your ratings and notes about each of the Agile Practices discussed in the book's relevant chapter.

For each Agile Practice, the workbook provides places for you to record your thoughts and impressions about the following topics:

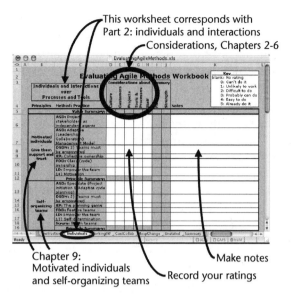

Figure 7.4   Using the workbook.

- *Considerations about culture*—This refers to the considerations about how well the Agile practices will fit with your organization's current culture. Since organizational culture is slow to change, adopting an Agile method will result in some friction within your organization. These were discussed in Chapter 2.

- *Considerations about customers*—This refers to the considerations about how the Agile practices will affect your relationship with your customers. The Agile methods prescribe much more customer involvement in software development projects than most people are used to. These were discussed in Chapter 3.

- *Considerations about projects*—This refers to the considerations about how well the Agile practices will work on the types of projects your organization undertakes. Different types of projects have different needs, and the Agile Methods were designed with certain types of projects in mind. These were discussed in Chapter 4.

- *Considerations about tools and processes*—This refers to the considerations about how the Agile practices will affect (or be affected by) the processes and tools your organization uses. Since processes and tools must support the methods being used, adopting an Agile method may necessitate changes to processes and tools (eliminating some, adding others, or changing how they are used). These were discussed in Chapter 5.

- *Considerations about staff*—This refers to the considerations about how well your staff may adapt to the Agile practices. Any change will require people to operate differently from the way they have in the past, and some may be more willing to make those changes than others. These were discussed in Chapter 6.

As you evaluate each Agile practice, you are encouraged to assign each consideration a numeric value between zero and five to indicate increasing suitability of that practice to your organization. If you believe that the consideration is not important to your decision (be careful about believing this), or that you are unable to make a valid judgment, then leave that consideration blank, and the workbook will ignore it. (Zero and blank entries are treated differently.)

The valid ratings are as follows. If you make any entry other than the six listed below, it could affect the workbook's summary computations. However, you are free to use the workbook in any way that you see fit.

- 0—The Practice *absolutely could not work* with this consideration in our organization.

- 1—The Practice is *unlikely to work* with this consideration in our organization.

- 2—The Practice would be *difficult to do* with this consideration in our organization.

- 3—The Practice *probably can be done* with this consideration in our organization.

- 4—The Practice would be *easy to do* with this consideration in our organization.

- 5—The Practice is *already in place* with this consideration in our organization.

Finally, there is a place for you to make notes about each Agile Practice. It would be good to record the reasoning behind the ratings you assign, especially any ratings of zero or one. You can enter as much or as little information in these areas as you like. The notes areas are for you to use in any way you like.

Compiling the results

As you enter your ratings of each Agile Practice/Consideration, the workbook will keep running summaries of these entries, as shown in Figure 7.5, including:

- *Practice Summary*—A summary of your ratings for all Considerations for a single Practice.

- *Principle Summary*—A summary of your ratings for all the Agile Practices for each Consideration, and a summary of those Consideration Summaries for a single principle.

- *Value Summary*—A summary of the Principle Summaries for a single value (worksheet).

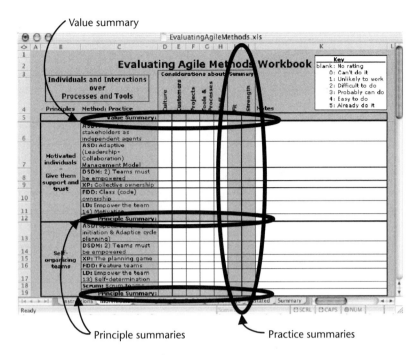

Figure 7.5 Workbook summaries.

You should watch these summary values as you enter your ratings. If they do not appear to reflect your opinion about a particular Consideration, Practice, Principle, or Value, then you should check your individual entries to be sure they are accurate. A data entry mistake could lead you to inaccurate conclusions.

However, you may also find that your initial assumptions are not supported by the analysis this book is leading you through. The intent of the workbook is to provide a place for you to record your detailed impressions. If you have recorded well-thought-out ratings, then you should let your own data guide you in making rational decisions and revising your initial assumptions, if needed.

Final steps

The Summary page of the workbook copies all the Principle and Value Summaries together onto a single page. This provides you with a summary view of all the ratings you made. After you have completed Parts II–VI and recorded all your impressions about the Agile Practices, you can use the Summary page to help draw conclusions about the Agile Methods.

Part VII leads you through the decision-making process using this data. Refer to Chapter 23 for a complete discussion of using the workbook's Summary page.

PART

II

Value: "Individuals and Interactions over Processes and Tools"

In this part of the book, we will explore the implications of the first Agile value, which states, "We have come to value individuals and interactions over processes and tools." We will begin this exploration with a general discussion in Chapter 8, "About People, Processes, and Tools," regarding the relative roles of people, processes, and tools and how they are interrelated. We will then look at several Agile Principles that embody this value.

> ▸ Chapter 9: "Motivated Individuals and Self-Organizing Teams" discusses the two people-related Agile Principles;
>
> ▸ Chapter 10: "Face-to-Face Communication" discusses communication in Agile projects;
>
> ▸ Chapter 11: "Sustainable Pace" discusses avoiding the overuse of overtime.

Finally, Chapter 12, Supporting Processes and Tools, discusses how the Agile methods affect and are affected by the processes and tools you use. We refer to this as the "Unstated Principle" because several practices of the Agile Methods relate to this topic and it is important to all of the Agile methods, even though none of the 12 Agile Principles addresses it.

CHAPTER

8

Contents

About People, Processes, and Tools

This first chapter of Part II lays the foundation for our exploration of the Agile Principles that embody the Agile value, "Individuals and interactions over processes and tools." The following chapters in Part II will each delve into one or more of those principles.

People versus processes versus tools

The very first value in the Agile Manifesto draws a line in the sand. In it, the Agilists clearly state their belief that people are of greater importance in determining software project success than are processes or tools. Naturally, this is an overstatement of their case. As we will see in Chapter 12, all of the Agile methods depend on good processes and tools to enable the project's people.

> **Agile Manifesto:**
> We have come to value...
> **Individuals and interactions**
> over processes and tools

The Agilists are not alone in their emphasis on people; it has been with us in the software industry for decades. Many people believe that if you compose your team of the right people, and you attend to their needs, then those people will be able to succeed no matter what. Some go so far as to say that disciplined processes and structured tools can get in the way of project success.

While toolmakers would not be likely to argue *against* the importance of people, they naturally place their main emphasis on tools. They focus on the tasks that their tools are designed to do, and work hard to make their tools complete and robust. Unfortunately, there are many cases where toolmakers do not consider the needs and abilities of the people who will use their tools. For example, although "usability" is a critical feature of any tool, many tools are difficult for the novice user to learn. And in addition to the requisite training, tools often assume specific knowledge that is not always present in an organization. For example, some design tools demand the use of predicate logic; something all programmers *should* know but with which many are not proficient.

The other trouble with tools is that they often dictate the processes that must be adopted in order to use them. For example, Requirements tools generally embody a requirements definition process, so that adopting the tool requires that the organization also adopt the tool's process. If the organization already uses a compatible process, this may not be a problem. But in the more common case, the tool may dictate that the organization adopt a new process that differs from the way they normally manage requirements, and in the worst case that new process may not be appropriate to the organization's needs.

The software process community generally acknowledges the importance of people, but the processes they build do not always reflect such a belief. Like the toolmakers, the writers of processes often focus so closely on the completeness and robustness of the processes themselves that the ability of people to follow them is compromised. For example, a person may find that the role he or she is assigned by the process may require activities beyond his or her skills, abilities, or time constraints. Compounding this problem, when people cannot see the value of the work products or activities that a process prescribes, they will consciously or unconsciously undermine or circumvent that process.

Process writers also tend to pay little attention to tools. While they acknowledge that the right tools can make any process more efficient, they do not routinely consider the available tools when designing processes. In light of this discussion about the effects of tools on process, such a lack of attention can have serious negative effects as the organization attempts to integrate a new process with an incompatible tool set.

So we see that of people, process, and tools, *all* are important to our projects' success. As Figure 8.1 shows, they are the three legs on which projects stand. To make one leg longer or shorter than the other two would make the project unstable, and eliminating any of the three would cause the project to fail. The success of our projects depends on all three. In this chapter, we explore the importance of each of these three success factors and identify how they interact with each other to bring about the success of our software development projects.

The role of people

Our people are our most precious resource. In the business of creating intellectual property, people have a preeminent role, as seen in Figure 8.2.

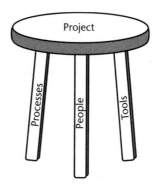

Figure 8.1   People, processes, and tools.

Figure 8.2   People as a project success factor.

Processes cannot create. Tools cannot exercise intellect. Turning ideas into working software requires people. People imagine, people interpret, people envision what they expect to build, and then people turn that vision into reality. Without people, software cannot be written.

But as we can also see in Figure 8.2, people have shortcomings. People make mistakes that result in defective software. People forget things so that their solutions are incomplete. People envision the future imprecisely so that their plans and estimates may be poor. People can keep only a limited amount of information in their minds at one time, so they may miss the consequences of their decisions. People misinterpret what others say so that information is lost in communication. People remember imprecisely so that facts are subject to dispute. People are expensive and may work slowly so that projects run over budget and schedule. People are bored by repetition so that some tasks are ignored or performed poorly.

Because of all these things and more, people by themselves are insufficient to ensure a successful software project. A team of even the best people in the software industry will have an uncertain likelihood of success. All people need the support that is provided by processes and tools to mitigate for their shortcomings so they can do their best work.

The role of processes

Every software development project follows processes, even if they are not recognized as such, and even when the project "team" consists of only one person. It is *not* a matter of having or not having processes; rather, it is a question of how consistently those processes are followed, and how well those processes meet the needs of the people who use them.

Processes identify the roles of the people on the project, the actions those people will take, and the work products those people will produce. In fact, the Agile Manifesto's contention that interaction among individuals is more important than "process" belies a misunderstanding of the nature of process. After all, it is the process that is being followed that determines who will interact with whom, under what conditions the interaction will take place, what will be the subject of that interaction, and what will be its result. Indeed, "interaction" cannot be more important than "process," because interaction is, itself, part of the process!

The importance of process lies precisely in the shortcomings of people, as we already discussed and can see in Figure 8.3. People make mistakes, so their processes include checks and balances. People forget things, so their processes remind them of what needs to be done. People are imprecise, so their processes identify where precision is needed. And people are limited, so they rely on their processes to keep the important facts before them. Processes that do these things provide the support people need to mitigate for their shortcomings.

The most critical attribute of a good process is that it meets the needs of those who use it. A key complaint of many people is that processes inflict undue burden on projects, making people inefficient and endangering the project schedule or other objectives. This complaint reflects problems with the specific processes those people have experienced rather than a problem with processes in general. As we have observed, the appropriate role of process is to make people more effectual in their work. Like any other supporting function, properly designed and executed processes are nearly invisible, doing their intended jobs without calling attention to themselves or their requirements. But processes that are ineffective become painfully obvious to those who must endure them. Thus, our focus must not be to minimize or eliminate process. Rather, it should be to identify those processes that are burdensome and correct or replace them with processes that are actually helpful.

The other critical issue is how consistently the processes are followed. A process that is inconsistently followed will produce inconsistent results. But one that is followed faithfully will produce predictable results. This consistency is not necessarily related to the process's formality, or even to it being documented in writing. Most of us follow a consistent morning routine

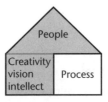

Figure 8.3   Processes as a project success factor.

(process), even though we may never have thought through its steps and procedures and have almost certainly never written them down. Because we are consistent in following this invisible process, it produces predictable results. On those few days when our routine is upset, the results can be embarrassing!

People often do not write their processes down on paper or illustrate them with flow charts, because that level of formality is not of value to most individuals. But when many people must work together, process documentation becomes more important. As organizations evolve, they follow a predictable pattern. In the beginning, the founders often base their work on a mutual understanding with one another, finding little necessity for documenting their processes and procedures. But then, as they grow and begin to hire people, they find that certain things simply must be written down. As the company grows, so does the need to document the processes that members are to follow to ensure that things run smoothly. The growing need for formality in process documentation arises from the simple fact that consistency in following a process becomes progressively more difficult to achieve as more and more people are involved.

Processes are essentially nothing more than tools that mitigate for people's shortcomings. Good processes make people able to harness their intellectual abilities and effectively apply them to solving problems. When consistently applied, good processes produce predictable results. And documenting those processes allows multiple people to share them and work together toward common goals.

The role of tools

All software projects use tools. At the very least, they use an interpreter or compiler and linker. Most also use a code control system and something to track bugs.

The main purpose of tools is to make processes more efficient and people more productive. Many labor-intensive tasks can be done more efficiently by either replacing human effort with a tool (such as when we run automated tests) or by supplementing human effort (as is the case when the compiler converts source code we have written into object code). Repetitive tasks that produce boredom in people (and the resultant errors) can often be relegated to tools. The key to ensuring that a tool is effective lies in making sure that it supports the people who do the work as well as the processes those people use, as shown in Figure 8.4.

A tool supports the process when it makes that process less labor-intensive and easier to follow. Implementing a tool will generally require process changes to incorporate any tool-specific steps into the process. For example, a code control tool will require the addition of special steps to the coding task (steps like check out and check in). But these steps are fairly nonobtrusive, and they certainly do not change the nature of the coding process that programmers follow. An example of a tool *not* supporting a

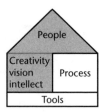

Figure 8.4 Tools as a project success factor.

process might be the case where implementing a requirements tool forced an organization to discard an effective requirements development process because it did not work with the tool. In that case, the tool would be dictating the process, rather than supporting it.

A tool supports the people when those who are affected by it can use it without undue effort or consternation. Implementing a tool almost always requires that people be trained in its use, after which they should become proficient with it in a reasonable amount of time. For example, in order to use a bug tracking system, the programmers will need to learn to enter bugs, change their state, and close them out. An example of a tool *not* supporting the people would be a design tool that requires mastery of predicate logic in an organization where the designs are developed by average coders who are not proficient with predicate logic.

In order to be worth implementing, a tool must make life on the project team better. After reasonable implementation and training time, the tool must earn its keep by supporting the team's processes and making the team members more efficient at their intellectual tasks.

Balancing people, process, and tools

People, processes, and tools: No one of these is more important than the others. Each has an important role to play in ensuring the success of our projects. None can be eliminated or de-emphasized without having an adverse effect on the project.

Our people are the source of the creativity, intellect, and vision that is required to build software. These key strengths make people indispensable to the task of creating software. But people's shortcomings can jeopardize our projects' success. Errors, oversights, miscommunication, and the like are common human frailties. People have come to depend on processes to mitigate for these shortcomings and make success more achievable. Individuals rarely document their processes and often do not recognize that they follow them. But in organizations, attention to and documentation of process is the key to ensuring that the processes are followed consistently and modified when necessary so they remain beneficial to the organization. Finally, tools make both the people and their processes more efficient by leveraging people's effort and taking over some of the more mundane (though critical) activities in our processes.

To be sure, there is a clear hierarchy: People require the support of processes, and tools must support both people and processes. But to claim that any one of them is more important than the others is to add unnecessary risk to our projects.

Motivated Individuals and Self-Organizing Teams

In this chapter, we will discuss the first two Agile Principles that support the value about "individuals and interactions" and the practices of the various Agile methods that embody them.

> **Agile Manifesto:**
> We have come to value...
> **Individuals and interactions**
> over processes and tools

Agile Principles

The two Agile Principles[1] that relate most directly to the first Agile value about "individuals and interactions" are the ones that deal with motivated individuals and self-organizing teams.

Motivated individuals

> *Build projects around motivated individuals. Give them the environment and support they need, and trust them to get the job done.*

This principle highlights the Agile methods' reliance on the motivation of each team member to achieve project success. Most of the practices of these methods make the assumption that team members are going far beyond simply following orders and doing what was assigned. They expect that each person is exercising his or her professional judgment to take the path that he or she believes is best at each juncture of the

---

1. All 12 Agile Principles are quoted and discussed in Appendix B.

project, or at least to raise questions and concerns to be discussed with the team, management, and the customer.

But the Agile methods do not just expect motivated individuals to appear. The second sentence of this principle highlights a few conditions that the Agile Manifesto authors believe are important to *building* a motivated team: an appropriate environment, support for them as professionals, and trust that they will indeed exercise good professional judgment.

These things highlight the Agile methods' differences from the more conventional command-and-control mode for managing projects. The traditional methods assume that intrinsic motivation is rare, and so they enforce specific behaviors. The Agile methods build an environment where each individual is challenged to build his or her capabilities and where motivation is an expected outcome of the environment.

Perhaps a better way to state this principle would be, "Build project environments that generate motivated individuals." This statement aligns more readily with the way the Agile methods are engineered.

Self-organizing teams

The best architectures, requirements, and designs emerge from self-organizing teams.

The Agile methods embrace the recent movement toward self-managed, self-directed, or (as this principle says) self-organizing teams. This philosophy is a movement away from traditional command-and-control management and toward one that counts the team as an entity that has its own knowledge, perspective, motivation, and expertise. In this environment, the team is treated as a partner with management and the customer, capable of providing insight, affecting decisions, and negotiating commitments.

The Agile Manifesto sees this structure not only as a way to achieve a more motivated team but also (as this Principle states) as a way to achieve technical excellence. The Agile methods each count on the team itself to keep the technical issues under control and "on the radar scope" when project decisions are being made.

Agile practices

The two Agile Principles already discussed describe a certain type of project environment in which the development team is challenged to learn from one another, develop their capabilities, maintain their own motivation, direct their own activities, and act as an equal partner in the project with management and the customer.

All of the Agile methods have specific practices that directly support these two Principles and the Agile value about "individuals and interactions." We will briefly discuss each of those practices, one method at a time.

Adaptive Software Development (ASD)

Three of ASD's philosophies bear directly on the Agile Principles about individuals and teams: project stakeholders as independent agents, speculation about project mission and adaptive plans, and the Leadership-Collaboration Management Model. ASD is described in Appendix C.

The Adaptive Conceptual Model: Project stakeholders as independent agents

ASD, discussed in Appendix C, makes the most explicit statements among the Agile methods about the role of the software development team as an agent that is in the position of directing itself and negotiating with management and the customer. It states that as a "complex adaptive system," a software project "is an ensemble of independent agents" and the development group is one of those independent agents.

This radical-sounding philosophy levels the playing field by removing any idea of precedence or hierarchy among the "agents" and making the technical team an equal partner with management and the customer in the quest for achieving the project mission. With no superior power over the team to organize and direct it, the team is expected to capitalize on the freedom to self-organize and self-motivate.

The Adaptive Development Model: Speculate: Project initiation and adaptive planning

As an outgrowth of its philosophy about software projects being "complex adaptive systems," ASD replaces the idea that the project's results can be predetermined with the concept of "emergent results." That is, the agents' expectations about what the project will produce are expected to grow and change over the life of the project. This view of a project results in the activity we would normally call "plan" being renamed "speculate."

The project mission is established as the various independent agents of the project speculate together about the overarching parameters that will guide their work. They establish a vision and set of values for the project and speculate about the product that will emerge.

Adaptive planning is done at the beginning of the project, as the independent agents speculate together about what development cycles will be required to achieve the Project Mission. It is then revisited at the beginning of each development cycle, as they refine that speculation based on project history to date.

This all means that the project mission and plan are not dictated to the technical team. As equal partners with management and the customer, they work together to negotiate the project's critical parameters. In this way, the ASD team has a strong hand in organizing and managing the project environment in which they will work, which is expected to motivate them to meet the commitments to which they have agreed.

The Adaptive (Leadership-Collaboration) Management Model

A natural result of adopting the concepts of independent agents and speculation is the rejection of traditional command-and-control management in favor of "leadership-collaboration" management.

In this philosophy, the role of the manager is to lead (as opposed to direct), and to foster an environment in which the various independent agents can collaborate to produce the project's emergent results and ultimately achieve the Project Mission. Again, this is expected to result in a self-organizing team that is highly motivated.

Dynamic System Development Method (DSDM)

DSDM's second principle (empowered teams), directly relates to the Agile Principles about individuals and teams. DSDM is described in Appendix D.

Principle 2: DSDM teams must be empowered to make decisions

DSDM takes a more traditional view than does ASD of the relationships among the technical team, management, and the customer. But it stresses that the team must be given wide latitude to make technical decisions that are congruent with the direction already agreed to by all parties to the project (including the team itself).

DSDM envisions that the customer, management, and team collaborate in establishing overall goals and directions for the project (including functionality, budget, and schedule). Then the technical team is empowered to do what team members believe is necessary to satisfy those goals, appealing to management and the customer only when they discover that some aspect of the agreed-upon goals must be renegotiated.

With this empowering of the team to negotiate with management and the customer and of individual team members to exercise their professional judgment, DSDM establishes an environment in which the team can self-manage and self-motivate.

Extreme Programming (XP)

Two of XP's practices address the Agile Principles about individuals and teams: The Planning Game and collective ownership. XP is described in Appendix E.

The Planning Game

XP's Planning Game is an ongoing collaborative activity that includes all stakeholders in the project, including the technical team and the "business people" (which includes management and the customer). In this game, each party is expected to bring its own unique perspective to bear on the job of planning the work to be done. The customer knows what he or she wants, management knows the project's constraints, and the technical team knows the technical limitations and how quickly they can work.

As with other Agile methods, the Planning Game results in the technical team being treated as a collaborator with management and the customer, rather than being subservient to them. This is a key part of self-management and a key motivational aspect of XP.

Collective ownership

Within an XP project, each pair of programmers is empowered to take any actions that they agree is necessary to reach the desired result. To make this happen, XP declares that there is no ownership of code. Every pair is encouraged to make any changes that are needed to any code at any time, with the only requirement being that they do not cause the existing automated test suites to fail. This empowerment to make significant decisions is expected to be a motivating factor for XP team members.

Feature-Driven Development (FDD)

Two of FDD's practices (class ownership and feature teams) illustrate the Agile Principles about individuals and teams. FDD is described in Appendix F.

Class (code) ownership

FDD takes code ownership to the opposite extreme from XP; it establishes a single owner for every class and mandates that the owner be the *only* one to ever change that class. This philosophy is designed to motivate each individual to assume full responsibility for the correct operation of his or her classes.

By itself, class ownership does not differ much from normal practice in the software industry. But it is important when taken in combination with the next practice, feature teams.

Feature teams

An FDD project revolves around implementing the identified features. Each feature is implemented by a team that consists of the owners of all the classes affected by implementing that feature. Therefore, the FDD project team is continuously, dynamically reorganizing itself into feature teams.

As work progresses, various feature teams are established, do their work, and then disband. Every project member will be a member of one or more feature team at any point in time. Each feature team has full authority to do what is necessary to implement their feature. This includes augmenting the team with owners of classes not originally identified as being affected by the feature.

This FDD practice is the essence of self-organization. No one tells FDD team members who should work with whom. Each feature team forms as team members see the need, and within the feature team, each individual is expected to take responsibility for his or her classes.

Lean Software Development (LD)

Two of the tools under LD's Empower the Team principle (self-determination and motivation) address the Agile Principles about individuals and teams. LD is described in Appendix G.

Empower the Team: Tool 13, Self-determination

LD states that the people who do the work are in the best position to determine *how* that work should be done. This philosophy means that a software project team should be free to identify its methods, determine the processes it will use, and determine for itself if those methods and processes are meeting its needs. This LD practice is essentially the same as the Agile Principle about self-organizing teams.

Empower the Team: Tool 14, Motivation

LD defines "motivation" by focusing on the supportiveness of the environment in which individuals work. It asks questions about team members such as: "Do they share a goal they believe in?" "Do they feel that they belong?" "Do they feel safe from punishment?" "Do they feel able to accomplish their work?" "Can each person sense regular progress?" This LD practice is essentially the same as the Agile Principle about motivated individuals.

Scrum

Scrum's practice, "Scrum teams," deals with the Agile Principles about individuals and teams. Scrum is described in Appendix H.

Scrum teams

The members of the Scrum development team are key participants in Sprint (development cycle) planning in a Scrum project. They participate fully along with other stakeholders in planning each Sprint, and their commitment to achieving the Sprint goals is a key criterion for an acceptable Sprint plan.

During each sprint, the Scrum team has full authority to do whatever they believe is necessary to achieve the Sprint goals. They even have the authority to abort the Sprint if they discover that the agreed-upon goals cannot be met. Thus, the Scrum team self-manages and (it is expected) also self-motivates.

Adoption implications

As we can see from descriptions of the various Agile practices, all Agile methods address the Agile Principles of motivated individuals and self-organizing teams in essentially similar ways. There are some differences in degrees (e.g., ASD's conception of the team as an independent agent versus DSDM's treatment of the team as part of a hierarchy), and even some differences in approach (e.g., XP's collective ownership versus FDD's class ownership by individuals), but the basic philosophies of these methods are remarkably similar.

Trusting the technical team

For most organizations, adopting any of the Agile methods will mean significant changes to the way project teams are managed. ASD's "Leadership-Collaboration" Management Model describes the sort of management under which any Agile method would thrive: abandonment of command-and-control style management; replacing it with clear respect for the team:

- Include the team in all deliberations about the project.
- Give them unfettered access to the customer.
- Seek their input on all technical issues.
- Believe their concerns about schedule goals.
- Expect them to learn (along with everyone else) as the project progresses.
- Gain their willing commitment to all plans.
- Negotiate with them to reach acceptable plans.
- Empower them with broad authority.
- Provide the tools and support they need.
- Trust them to exercise their best professional judgment in all circumstances.

This essentially means entrusting the development team with the authority to self-organize and self-manage. How big a change would this be in your organization? How collaborative is your current environment? How strongly entrenched is the command-and-control management style? To what degree are your technical staff believed, respected, and trusted to exercise professional judgment? Take a moment to consider these things and jot down some notes.[2]

Staffing with "motivated individuals"

You may be asking yourself, "Where am I going to find all of these motivated people?" "And what will I do with the unmotivated lumps I am stuck with now?"

It is true; most of your staff members are *not* superstars. In fact, most of them are pretty average. The point behind the Agile methods is *not* that you must find a whole bevy of highly motivated and technically expert people. Rather, it is that by adopting an Agile Method and what ASD calls the "leadership-collaboration" management style, you can motivate most of your current staff to behave more like superstars.

Behavioral psychology has long told us that people tend to live up to (or down to) the expectations placed on them. This is as true with your technical staff as with any other population. The average person, in an environment where his or her expertise and knowledge is valued, will not only bring those attributes to bear on the topic at hand but will also seek to improve them, to make himself or herself more capable of rising to such challenges in the future.

This is not to say that *every* person will pleasantly surprise you. Just as you have a small minority of superstars, you also have a small minority of career nonperformers. But in the context of a self-organizing team of motivated individuals, these people will stand out in ways that they will *not* appreciate. So, they will be likely to either find ways to operate as a productive member of the team, or they will find a position somewhere where they will not stand out so much. Either way, the effectiveness of your teams will be enhanced.

Are you willing to put the Agile management theories to the test? Would you be able to place such trust in your heretofore average staff? Do you fear that developing their abilities and confidence would make them more likely to be spirited away by your competitors? Or would they be so pleased with the environment that they would be less likely to leave it? Take a moment to consider these things and jot down some notes.

Team structure and roles

The various Agile methods present a variety of new roles as well as new definitions for some existing roles. In this section, we will explore some of the role changes that may affect your adoption decision.

---

2. You are encouraged to use the "Evaluating Agile Methods Workbook" that is available to support this book. Refer to Chapter 7 for information on downloading and using this workbook.

Pair Programming

XP's practice of "Pair Programming" is unique and foreign to almost all organizations. It states that pairs of individuals working together perform *all* technical work. These pairs are expected to form and trade partners from time to time. All designing, test case development, coding, and testing is done in pairs. While one member of a pair is "driving" the computer, the other is watching, assessing the partner's work, and asking questions. The pair switches roles on a regular basis.

Although this practice sounds wasteful of your most precious resource (your engineers' time), XP's proponents claim just the opposite. They claim that a pair working together can be as much as 50% more productive than the two individuals would be if they worked separately. This is expected for a variety of reasons:

- The real-time review being done by the observing partner results in many defects being discovered and corrected within minutes of being created, instead of showing up later in tests when the diagnosis and correction could be more time-consuming.

- The person in the observer role tends to think about the big picture, making him or her more likely to identify architecture, design, or testing issues early, so they can be corrected before much rework would be required.

- The constant interaction between the individuals allows them to learn from each other, sharpening both of their skills and making each of them more capable.

- Because two individuals become intimately familiar with every part of the system, the loss of any one person cannot cripple the project.

- It provides a way for any new project member (even a recruit fresh out of school) to become a contributing member of the project very quickly.

Pair Programming should be quite motivational for programmers who benefit from its use. While we know of no wide-based studies of the productivity improvement claims, many organizations that have tried Pair Programming swear by it. Do you believe it would be worth experimenting with? Take a moment to consider this and jot down some notes.

Chief Programmer

FDD includes a Chief Programmer role. This role is generally reserved for highly respected team members who have superior technical knowledge. By placing such individuals into this role, FDD seeks to capitalize on their expertise and reputation to strengthen the skills of the rest of the team.

In addition to their normal technical tasks, Chief Programmers act as coaches and mentors on technical matters, being a resource to team members who have questions about the work they are contemplating. Is this a good design? Is there a cleaner way to code this? What have I overlooked? Why does this seem too hard? … or too easy?

But can you really afford to tax one of your best people with this role? Would it not be better for him or her to be designing and coding all the time? In most projects, we tend to overload our best people, because we trust them to do better work than most of their peers. But if we structure our projects so these experts can share the wealth of their knowledge with their teammates, then it is no longer so critical that these people actually do the hard jobs themselves.

No matter who is working on a hard problem, a Chief Programmer will likely have a hand in it and able to bring his or her expertise to bear on it. Not only will the hard job be done well, but also the person who benefited from the Chief Programmer's input will have learned how to approach a problem that may have been beyond his or her capabilities before. In this way, Chief Programmers contribute directly to continuously improving the team's capability to self-manage, self-motivate, and produce excellent work.

Who among your staff would be good Chief Programmers? What would be the effect of having these people available to mentor the rest of the staff? Can you see how the work you now pile on this person will get done? Take a moment to consider this and jot down some notes.

Method Coach

Some Agile methods (e.g., XP and Scrum) recommend that the project have a person whose job is to coach the team in using the method. This is a good recommendation in any environment where the team is being asked to change how they do their work. Changing old habits can be difficult, and a coach may be indispensable in helping people recognize old habits and exchange them for new ones.

But even after the "new" method becomes your team's normal way of doing their work, a coach can still add great value. Your technical folks will always be immersed in the technical job at hand. The method they use and how well they enact it will usually be secondary to them (if they think of it at all).

A coach can keep things running efficiently by being the person who is *always* concerned about the method and how well it is serving the project's needs. And, of course, when team members *do* become aware of the method (because it is impeding their work), the coach will be prepared to help them work through the problem and come up with ways of working that serve the team better. The Coach ensures that the Method you have adopted is indeed creating a project environment in which the team can self-motivate and self-manage.

How useful would a coach be to your team if you adopt a new development method? What about after the team reaches a new steady state? Take a moment to consider this and jot down some notes.

Project Manager

If you adopt an Agile method, the role of the project manager is likely to change dramatically. Instead of planning the project, the manager would now collaborate with the team to establish the plan. Instead of assigning work to people, the manager would collaborate with them to identify what should be done, when, and by whom. Instead of telling each person what they will have done when, the manager will negotiate that with them.

Many project managers will feel like all of their power is being stripped away and given to the technical team. In a way, this is the case, because what most managers do by themselves, an Agile team will do collaboratively. But the Leadership-Collaboration Model has another side—the "leadership" side. And that is where the project manager's new influence will lie.

As the leader, the manager will always focus on the project mission, articulate a vision that will motivate the team's best effort, build a culture of collaboration, and provide the support the team needs. Rather than commanding that tasks be done, a leader points out the direction and encourages the team to tackle the tasks by his or her own example. This change in behavior is a key step in building an environment in which Agile project teams can thrive and realize the benefits of motivation and self-management.

Changing the nature of the manager's role from commanding to leading is difficult. It requires that the manager learn a whole new set of behaviors and interact with the project team in whole new ways. For many, it is not an easy transition, and for some it is impossible. How will your project managers adapt to the Leadership-Collaboration Management Model? How will *you* adapt to it? What will it take to make the transition? What will you have to do to support it? Take a moment to consider this and jot down some notes.

Motivated individuals and self-organizing teams

Motivated individuals and self-organizing teams are critical principles behind all of the Agile methods. These things do not happen automatically. If you are going to adopt an Agile method, then beginning to follow these two principles will require dedicated work, both on your part and on the parts of all your managers and staff.

Deciding if your organization is up to this challenge is an important consideration.

Face-to-Face Communication

In this chapter, we will discuss the third Agile Principle that supports the value about "individuals and interactions" and the practices of the various Agile methods that embody it.

> **Agile Manifesto:**
> We have come to value...
> **Individuals and interactions**
> over processes and tools

Agile Principle

The third Agile Principle[1] that relates directly to the first Agile value about "individuals and interactions" is the one about face-to-face communication.

Face-to-face communication

The most efficient and effective method of conveying information to and within a development team is face-to-face conversation.

The Agile methods all prefer personal face-to-face conversation over any other form of communication, especially written documents. This preference does *not* mean that any of these methods completely dispenses with documents. Every one of them acknowledges that written communication has its place in a software project. They just stress the importance of personal communication, for reasons we will now discuss.

   The Agile methods take this position to counteract their perception that many organizations place too much stock in written documents and not enough in face-to-face conversation. Have

---

1. All 12 Agile Principles are quoted and discussed in Appendix B.

they carried this reaction too far in overemphasizing conversation and de-emphasizing documents? That is a matter of interpretation, so you will have to decide for yourself.

Agile practices

All of the Agile methods make heavy use of face-to-face communication and minimize written documents to varying degrees. However, only two have practices that address this principle, Scrum's Daily Meeting and XP, with several of its practices.

Extreme Programming

The Agile Principle about face-to-face communication shows up in four ways in XP as discussed in Appendix E: in its "Facilities Strategy," (which is not one of its 12 practices), and in its practices of Pair Programming, The Planning Game, and On-Site Customer.

Facilities Strategy

Although XP does not call it out as one of its 12 practices, its Facilities Strategy is the clearest embodiment of face-to-face communication in any of the Agile Methods. An ideal XP work environment for an eight-person team, as articulated by Kent Beck (XP's author), is depicted in Figure 10.1. Each piece of this facility is designed to enhance the team's face-to-face communication.

▸ The Pair Programming workstations table at the center of the room is the locus of activity. Most of the time, each pair of programmers is busy collaborating at a workstation.

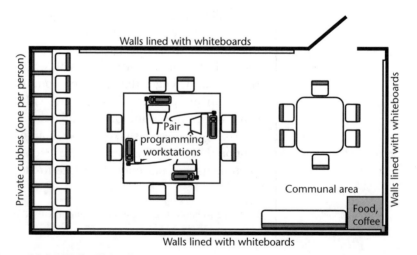

Figure 10.1 XP Facilities Strategy.

- The communal area is a meeting place used for relaxation and discussion. It has a table, chairs, and a couch and is stocked with coffee, food, and toys.

- All available wall space is covered with whiteboards. They are one of the best facilitators of face-to-face conversation and can also be used as information radiators. (See "Availability" near the end of this chapter for more on "information radiators.")

- Finally, there is a small cubby for each programmer, where he or she can keep personal stuff and can go for privacy (e.g., to make a phone call). But work is usually *not* done in the cubby.

- There are no private offices or even cubical walls; the only door is the door to the room.

This strategy is designed to maximize face-to-face conversation within the team. It also facilitates "accidental communication," as people overhear what other pairs are discussing. Some people could interpret this "accidental communication" as annoying or distracting noise. But, even though programmers (like any other workers) prize private office space as prestigious, XP proponents report that programmers actually like this sort of working environment because of the richness of the communication that it fosters.

How different is XP's Facilities Strategy to the working environment in your organization? What would it take to try this sort of arrangement? What would be your technical staff's reaction to such an arrangement? Take a moment to consider these things and jot down some notes.[2]

Pair Programming

XP's Pair Programming is face-to-face conversation taken to the extreme. It states that pairs of people working together do *all* technical work. This includes designing, creating test cases, coding, testing, and building and integrating the system.

Of course, a computer has only one keyboard and mouse, so members of each pair take turns "driving" the computer. The individual who is not driving is reviewing the work his or her peer is doing, considering the wider ramifications of the direction the work is taking, and asking questions of the driver to be sure they both understand and agree about the reasons for each action. This practice results in a continual dialog between the pair and is said to result in higher productivity, fewer defects, and better technical work as the two pool their expertise and knowledge to attack the problem at hand.

Do these arguments make sense to you? What opportunities might you have to try Pair Programming? How might your technical staff members react to it? Take a moment to consider these things and jot down some notes.

---

2. You may want to use the "Evaluating Agile Methods Workbook" that is available to support this book. Refer to Chapter 7 for information on obtaining and using this workbook.

On-Site Customer

XP is the extreme among the Agile methods when it comes to the customer's role in the project. XP requires that a customer representative be located on-site with the development team at all times. The point behind this is to use face-to-face communication as a means of ensuring that the project team's work is steadily progressing toward a conclusion that will satisfy the customer.

With the customer so easily accessible, the technical team is not likely to make assumptions about what is needed. Questions will be posed to this person as they arise, and they will be answered with a timeliness that will ensure that progress on the project is not impeded. And there is less possibility of misunderstanding because the communication is face-to-face, and the customer can observe what the developers are doing as a result of what he or she said.

In addition, just as "accidental communication" helps programmers stay informed about what their peers are doing, it also keeps this resident customer informed. This will result in the customer remaining better informed about the project status, and it allows the customer to raise questions if some part of the project appears to be moving in the wrong direction. The on-site customer uses face-to-face communication to keep the project on track.

The Planning Game

XP's Planning Game is yet another exercise in face-to-face communication. This "game" is "played" in a workshop setting that brings all of the project stakeholders together to plan the next project iteration. They work face-to-face to adjust overall project expectations based on progress so far, make changes to the Project Metaphor and Stories as needed, and determine what will be delivered to the customer at the end of the planned iteration.

Because all stakeholders do this in a workshop environment, the Planning Game is the prime opportunity for those who are not part of the project's day-to-day activity to work with the project team face-to-face. It is here that questions should be raised and disagreements settled, while all of the key people are together in one room.

By doing the project planning face-to-face, XP works to keep communication flowing among all project stakeholders.

Scrum

Scrum's practice, "Daily Scrum Meetings," supports the Agile Principle about face-to-face communication. Scrum is described in Appendix H.

Daily Scrum Meetings

Scrum's practice of daily stand-up meetings takes the standard team meeting concept to a whole new level. Although daily stand-ups are not unique to Scrum (or even to Agile methods), they are not widely practiced in the software industry.

The Daily Scrum Meeting is a time when each team member briefly shares status and concerns with the team. The meeting is supposed to be quite short, with a target of 15 minutes or less. Because the meeting happens every business day, each person can generally provide a complete-enough status in a minute or two, allowing the team to finish within the time limit on most days. Usually, these meetings are done while standing to encourage brevity (hence the common moniker, "daily stand-up").

Although problems and roadblocks may be mentioned during the Daily Scrum Meeting, there is a strict policy of *not* solving them, or even discussing them during the meeting itself. The team leader generally takes action items to correct any roadblocks outside of the meeting. And a few interested team members usually will address issues that need to be discussed after the meeting so the remainder of the team can get back to work.

The Daily Scrum Meeting is designed to maximize information exchange while minimizing disruption to the technical work. It also serves to highlight problems so they can be addressed later, and to stimulate discussions of issues, again, outside of the meeting. How does this practice compare with your teams' methods of sharing status? Could a daily stand-up improve your teams' effectiveness? Take a moment to consider these things and jot down some notes.

Adoption implications

The Agile methods are right to highlight communication as a key issue in software projects (actually, in *any* projects). Any project will thrive with the right communication in the right amounts and will slowly die when communication is withheld or done in ineffective ways. Face-to-face communication has a number of beneficial attributes (which is why the Agile methods focus on it), but it also has some drawbacks.

In this section, we will discuss some critical issues surrounding communication so you can consider the effectiveness of your current communication modes, along with those proposed by the Agile methods.

Richness

"Richness" refers to the amount of information that a particular communication method can transmit. The Agile methods prefer face-to-face conversation precisely because it is about as rich a mode of communication as there is. This richness derives from the variety of clues that are available to help the listener understand the speaker's intent.

> ‣ *Words*—When we think of communication, we generally think of words. Most of the modes we use in business make use of words in either spoken or written form. Although the words tend to be the

heart of what we hope to communicate, they are too often misunderstood. That is why the other clues that follow are so important. They help the listener understand the speaker's intent more readily.

E-mail wars are common mainly because it is so easy to misconstrue written words when they are absent from other communication clues.

▸ *Voice inflections*—The ways we inflect our voices add a tremendous amount of information to our message, often more than we would suspect. Try saying the same sentence several times, but putting the emphasis on a different word each time. For example:

  ▸ "*You* were wrong," can imply that others were *right*.

  ▸ "You *were* wrong," can imply that you may not be wrong *now*.

  ▸ "You were *wrong*," can imply that one of us thought you were *right*.

The importance of these sorts of clues is what makes a speech more valuable than a document. From the lectern, the speaker uses his or her voice to make the message clearer.

▸ *Clarifications*—Two-way communication adds richness by allowing listeners to communicate the need for more explanation, or to test their understanding. Asking questions about the speaker's intent or feeding back your understanding to the speaker are important ways to ensure that the message you received was what the speaker intended to send. Even something as simple as a quizzical or confused look can be important to accurate communication.

This is why a Q&A session after a speech can be so important, or why a phone call is richer than a voice-mail message.

▸ *Body language*—How we move our body also adds to the message we communicate. Often this level of communication is unconscious, and at times it can contradict the spoken words (giving us insight into the speaker's real thoughts). Take, for example, the sentence, "Tell me what you think."

  ▸ If it is said across a large desk by a person with his arms folded and a mocking look on his face, you might get the impression that the request is not sincere.

  ▸ But if the speaker comes alongside you as he says it, gestures with an open hand, and has a friendly but concerned expression on his face, you will be more likely to take it as a sincere request.

  ▸ The added richness of body language is why a face-to-face conversation provides more information than a phone call.

▸ *Illustrations*—When words are augmented with pictures, comprehension goes up significantly. The images act as thought-holders and become handy references as the conversation goes on. They can also show relationships among ideas by their relative positioning and by lines that connect or separate them.

> ‣ XP highly recommends that copious amounts of whiteboard space be available to the team, because the whiteboard is such a powerful addition to face-to-face conversation.

Memory

We humans can have difficulty accurately recalling things from the past. (Some of us have more difficulty than others!) What we remember and how accurately we remember it is affected by a variety of influences, including our perceptions about the importance of the information, its relevance to our tasks at hand, and our beliefs about how it can be applied. For this reason, it is not uncommon for two people to have significantly different memories of an interaction in which they both participated.

Although a face-to-face conversation in front of a whiteboard may be very rich, it is also fleeting. The spoken words slip into our memories, and the markings on the whiteboard are soon distorted or erased. For casual interactions, this may not be important. But in a software project, we interact in order to share knowledge, bring multiple people's expertise to bear, examine alternatives, and make decisions. These are all very important things, and our ability to accurately recall their results is important to the smooth functioning of the project.

Persistence

Because human memory is of uncertain reliability, we also need modes of communication that are persistent; that is, they are available to be reviewed after the fact. Contrast a verbal interchange with a written document, which can be stored away and referred to in the future when the need arises. The document's content will remain unchanged over time, and it will serve to remind you of things you may have forgotten in the mean time.

Because of the importance of our project-related communications, many interactions on our projects deserve some form of persistence. Practitioners of the Agile methods use the software work products themselves as the persistent records of their face-to-face communications. For example:

‣ Test cases "document" the expected functionality of the product.

‣ The program code itself "documents" implementation decisions.

‣ Comments that are embedded in the program code provide additional information to clarify the code itself.

While these are important records of decisions made along the way, the amount of information they convey can be highly variable. Where one person's program may be quite readable, and the comments may provide key information, another's program may not. And even in the best of cases, the information contained in these vehicles is compressed and encoded so that it records *not* what was said but how the implementer interpreted what was said. And, as we previously observed, those two can be quite different.

Contrast those things with meeting minutes, which are designed to capture what was said and agreed upon during face-to-face communication. Minutes, when done well, can be documented quickly and scanned by meeting participants to ensure a common understanding by all participants before any of them acts on a faulty understanding, wasting time and effort.

Availability

Most communication modes suffer from limitations to their availability. Face-to-face communication is rich for an instant, and then it is gone (except for our memories). Whiteboards get erased. Books are loaned and not returned, and documents are filed away (often never to be seen again). Information that cannot be accessed easily is of little use to your project. Although some vendors sell tools that they claim will correct many of these problems, a few of the Agile methods advocate a simple low-tech method called "information radiators."

Information radiators are displays of useful information that are posted around the team's work area. They are more persistent than conversation, more up-to-date than your memory, and easier to locate than any document. Your staff can ignore them when they do not need them, and they can instantly find them when they do. And you can find out how the project is progressing at a glance, without interrupting someone's train of thought to ask them about it.

An example of an information radiator is shown in Figure 10.2. This simple wall chart shows the current status of the project by allowing each team member to record what he or she is doing. The team, the manager, or anyone else can understand the exact status of the current iteration simply by looking at this information radiator.

	Story	Pair	Start	Finish	Comments
1.	Dhfkdhflrhkj	John/Sue	1/12	1/15	
2.	Oirejijgoihrgr	Joe/Bill	1/17		
3.	Srjghghwohrgtwg	Joe/Barb	1/12	1/17	Beware of class "Clown"
4.	Hfhferkj				
5.	Rwiogfjoirjgoirioj	John/Sue	1/15		
6.	Whrghker				
7.	;w'erjgjrepjr				
8.	Woivmslvjd;	Bill/Sean	1/12	1/13	
9.	Leifjeijerkil				
10.	Owepjgk[work				
11.	Opwpeopjrgjp	Bill/Sean	1/13	1/17	
12.	Oritrjgpowjero				
13.	Dskjfh9erihoe				
14.	Lkfjrioeihgrhgel	Barb/Sean	1/18		

Figure 10.2 Information radiator.

Communication

Communication is the lifeblood of your projects. There are many ways that we may choose to communicate on our projects, and each has its strengths and weaknesses. There is no single communication mode that is best in every situation. In spite of the Agile methods' focus on face-to-fact communication, it too has limitations and must be augmented with other forms to be effective.

Consider the communication modes currently used on your projects. Are there persistence problems? Miscommunication? Availability problems? What can you learn from the Agile methods to make your projects' communication more effective? Take a moment to consider these things and jot down some notes.

CHAPTER

Contents

Sustainable Pace

In this chapter, we will discuss the fourth Agile Principle that supports the value about "individuals and interactions" and the practices of the various Agile methods that embody them.

> **Agile Manifesto:**
> We have come to value...
> **Individuals and interactions**
> over processes and tools

Agile Principle

The fourth Agile Principle[1] that relates directly to the Agile value about "individuals and interactions" is the one about maintaining a sustainable pace on software projects.

Sustainable pace

Agile processes promote sustainable development. The sponsors, developers, and users should be able to maintain a constant pace indefinitely.

The Agile methods are all designed around an incremental development approach. They each suggest (or require) that each increment of the project be relatively short (2 weeks to 2 months), and that it result in the delivery of some recognizable value. Such an approach means that these methods establish a consistent rhythm of work that makes regular progress apparent, and avoids alternating downtimes and frantic headlong rushes toward deadlines.

---

1. All 12 Agile Principles are quoted and discussed in Appendix B.

That is why this principle states that a sustainable pace is not just a laudable goal; rather, it is a natural result of adopting an Agile method.

Agile practices

Although all of the Agile methods will result in a sustainable level of effort because of their use of incremental development, only XP has a practice that directly addresses this Principle.

Extreme Programming (XP)

XP's practice about the 40-hour workweek addresses the Agile Principle about maintaining a sustainable pace. XP is described in Appendix E.

40-hour week

XP's 40-hour week practice states that overtime should be rare on a software project. It goes on to state that when overtime *is* worked, it is allowed only one week at a time. In other words, if a person worked overtime last week, it is not allowable for that person to do it again this week.

Although putting "40-hour" in the name of this practice makes it sound restrictive, XP clarifies what is meant by saying that people should work their *normal* number of hours, however many that may be. For most people, that will be some number in the vicinity of 40 hours, but there are unusual individuals for whom 40 hours a week would seem like an unreasonable limit.

In one shop I was a member of, when the director told us, "I want to eliminate overtime. Each of you should work only 40 hours every week," a hand immediately shot up. "Sir," ventured the twenty-something with the long ponytail and sandals, "Do you mean that I'm not *allowed* to be here any more than that?" The rest of us smiled, as we imagined him clawing at the walls of his apartment while he waited for "working hours" to return.

Just as our director clarified, XP has no trouble with someone working as much as he or she *wants* to work, even if it is 60, 80, or more hours a week. What XP is precluding is most *forced* overtime.

Adoption implications

The elimination of most overtime work represents quite a change from business as usual in many shops. For too many programmers, their bosses expect that overtime is a normal part of the job, especially when a deadline is approaching. There is often a stigma attached to *not* working overtime, as if a person who avoids overtime work somehow lacks commitment to the company or project.

Overtime versus the Agile methods

Overtime work is common in many businesses because of the peaks and valleys in the workflow. No company wants to pay people to sit on the bench when there is little work for them to do. But that is precisely what would happen if they kept the number of people on staff that they need during peak times. So instead of staffing for the peak, they staff for the norm and require their staff to work overtime during busy times.

As Figure 11.1 shows, many traditional projects require significant amounts of overtime during the final testing and release phases, pushing their effort requirements above what is sustainable for the long haul. The Agile methods work actively to ramp up quickly, then smooth out the peaks and valleys in a software development project by changing the workflow dynamics. In the following sections, we look at various project phases to see how the Agile methods achieve this effect.

Initial analysis

Figure 11.2 illustrates that many of our projects begin with an extended period of analysis and planning. During this phase of the project, only a few of our most experienced people are involved in establishing the project's parameters and plans.

The Agile methods, as Figure 11.2 also indicates, eliminate much of this upfront analysis. They assume that it is unreasonable to expect that you can establish a detailed understanding of the system at the beginning of the project. So, this initial analysis is replaced with an incremental development approach that allows the project team (as well as the customer) to learn and discover as the project progresses. This includes discovering both the details of the system as it is being built, and what must happen on the project as it unfolds.

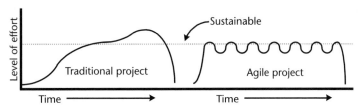

Figure 11.1   Level of effort.

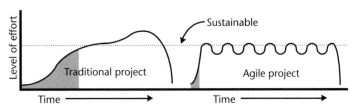

Figure 11.2   Initial analysis.

Any analysis that *is* undertaken is done by the entire project team, usually in collaboration with the customer. The Agile methods teach that each team member has a valuable perspective to contribute to any deliberations about the project. Also, because of their strong focus on learning, these methods view such full-team work as a critical method for strengthening the team by building each team member's experience base and knowledge about the project.

Incremental development

Although it is unusual for software projects *not* to be iterative in some way, most do not practice incremental development, as Figure 11.3 depicts. And those that *do* incremental development do not take it to the same extremes as the Agile methods. Where we might be comfortable with delivering increments every 3 months to a year or more, the Agile methods explicitly minimize the length of each increment. Many of us find it difficult to believe that the Agile methods' guidelines of 2 weeks to a maximum of 2 months for each increment can be effective.

▸ By keeping the time frame for each increment very short, the Agile methods help the team maintain a reasonable level of pressure almost continually. Since the end of the current increment is always close, the end-of-the-project pressure is always present. But because the goals for each increment are relatively modest, the pressure is not excessive, and the work that needs to be finished in that time frame is rarely overwhelming.

▸ The short time frames also result in measurable achievements on a regular basis, even as often as several times each month. This not only helps maintain the enthusiasm of the project team, but it also gives management and the customer a good level of comfort about the project's progress.

▸ Testing is generally the project phase that can stretch beyond expectations, resulting in forced overtime. The Agile methods' small increments mean that only a limited amount of new functionality is being tested at any one time. With a limited scope, testing can be more easily managed, and fixing defects is less likely to become a bottleneck.

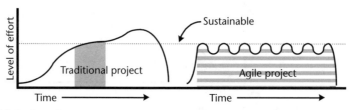

Figure 11.3 Development.

Testing

Figure 11.4 shows that in the Agile methods, "testing" is not a phase at the end of the project. Instead, it is an activity that the entire development team is engaged in throughout the life of the project.

Each Agile method has a unique view of testing and other quality activities. They all place the responsibility for quality squarely in the hands of the developers. None of the Agile methods even addresses the concept of independent verification and validation (V&V) beyond the customer's acceptance test (although there is no reason why independent V&V cannot be done on an Agile project).

▸ Testing by the developers is integrated into the development activities in most Agile methods. This establishes a whole new definition for "coding complete." Instead of feeling that they are done when the code compiles and a cursory unit test of some kind succeeds, the Agile methods expect developers to perform a complete set of tests on their code. XP's "test first" practice calls for developers to write their test cases first, then develop code to pass the tests. But even after completing a full battery of tests, the developers' work is still not done.

▸ Peer reviews are a common element of the Agile methods. Although each method addresses this subject differently, the result is that (in the methods that include peer reviews), the developer's code must clear this additional hurdle in order to be "done."

▸ Finally, integration testing is also the responsibility of each developer, as we will discuss next.

Integration

Integration is also changed by most Agile methods. Figure 11.5 shows that, rather than being done after all of the code for an increment has been written, the system is integrated continuously. Some Agile methods refer to "daily" or even "continuous" builds. But regardless of the details, they all boil down to this: Integration testing is not a separate phase at the end of each increment. Rather, it is an ongoing activity that is done continuously.

Most Agile methods call for developers to integrate their own code into the growing system immediately, as soon as the code is ready. If anything they have written causes problems when integrated into the system, then

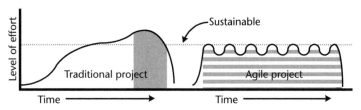

Figure 11.4   Testing.

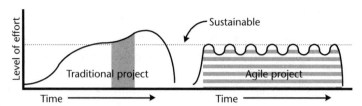

Figure 11.5   Integration.

their work is not yet complete. Only after their code has been fully tested (both at the unit level and during integration) is the developer's work on that code considered complete.

A sustainable pace

A sustainable pace is not just a goal to seek. The Agile methods build a project environment that is likely to result in the project maintaining a sustainable pace. What effect would such a change have in your organization? Is overtime a basis for rewards? Is it a badge of honor? Or is it an evil of which most people would like to rid themselves? What would it take to make the Agile Methods' philosophy (of overtime being rare) an accepted part of your organization? Take a moment to consider these things and jot down some notes.[2]

---

2. You may want to use the "Evaluating Agile Methods Workbook" that is available to support this book. Refer to Chapter 7 for information on obtaining and using this workbook.

The Unstated Principle: Appropriate Processes and Tools

In this chapter, we will discuss the unstated Agile Principle that supports the value about "individuals and interactions" and the practices of the various Agile methods that embody it.

> **Agile Manifesto:**
> We have come to value...
> **Individuals and interactions**
> over processes and tools

To say that "appropriate processes and tools" supports this value may seem contradictory, since the value explicitly downplays "processes and tools." But when you look at the specifics of the practices of the Agile methods (as we will in this chapter), the picture becomes much clearer. Far from saying that processes and tools are bad, the authors of the Agile methods recognize that processes and tools are absolutely necessary to the success of the Agile methods.

Actually, this principle is not *entirely* unstated. It is buried within the first Agile Principle that we discussed in Chapter 9. That Principle says:

> *Build projects around motivated individuals. Give them the environment and support they need, and trust them to get the job done.*

For purposes of the discussion in this chapter, the key phrase is the one in the middle, "give them the environment and support they need." Indeed, one of the most critical aspects of the project environment is the processes and tools that are available to support the team.

Agile practices

Almost all of the Agile methods specify a development process that is to be followed. We will not spend time discussing each of those processes, as they are all touched on throughout this book and explained in some detail in the appendixes. Instead, we will discuss the practices of the Agile methods that bear directly on processes and tools. Then, in the "Adoption implications" section of this chapter, we will look at some process and tool assumptions that are apparent in all of the Agile methods.

FDD and LD have specific practices that directly support the unspoken Principle about processes and tools. We will briefly discuss each of those practices, one method at a time.

Feature-Driven Development (FDD)

FDD's Configuration Management practice illustrates the unspoken Agile Principle about processes and tools. FDD is described in Appendix F.

Configuration Management

FDD is alone in stating what is unmentioned but assumed by all of the other Agile methods; that good, reliable CM is important to the health of an Agile project. FDD raises the subject of CM but does not specify the depth or breadth of the CM practice that should be exercised. It merely points out that in addition to source code, documents (e.g., requirements and design specifications, test cases, and results) are worth controlling.

We will discuss CM in considerable depth later in this chapter.

Lean Software Development (LD)

LD has the strongest focus on processes and tools among the Agile methods. Fully five of LD's tools deal with these subjects. These tools fall under the three LD principles: Amplify Learning, Deliver as Fast as Possible, and See the Whole. LD is described in Appendix G.

Amplify Learning: Tool 5, Synchronization

Whenever more than one person is involved in developing software, synchronization issues are likely. What those issues might be, and how they might manifest themselves, will differ depending on the nature of the development methodology being used and the size and dispersion of the project team. For example, a four-person XP team (adhering to XP's collective ownership) working in a single room will have different synchronization challenges than a geographically dispersed multiteam project. XP is discussed in Appendix E.

This LD tool discusses synchronization in general terms and suggests a number of processes and tools that could be used, depending on the needs of the project.

Code ownership policies affect synchronization issues. FDD recommends that each class be owned by a single individual, so it uses "feature teams" to synchronize the work. XP, on the other hand, calls for collective ownership of the code, in which each pair of programmers should change whatever code they deem necessary to implement their story, so it uses the build process to work out synchronization issues.

The build process can be done in a variety of ways depending on the size and complexity of both the system being developed and the project composition. Continuous or daily builds are a great synchronization mechanism and are prominent in most Agile methods.

Smoke tests can be the quickest way to uncover synchronization issues. Simple tests are run to ensure that the software will work at some basic level. It is good practice to make smoke tests a regular part of your build process, so that if a smoke test fails, then the build is considered unsuccessful. (The term "smoke test" comes from the hardware practice of leaving a device turned on for some period of time to see if it starts smoking.)

Stubs and harnesses are tools that can speed up the build and smoke test processes for very large systems that take multiple hours to build or test. "Stubs" are stand-ins for parts of a system. They have a functioning interface, but do not actually do anything, and are usually used to allow system testing before the stubbed-out part has been developed. "Harnesses" are stand-ins for an entire system. They have functioning interfaces for one or more components, but do not actually do anything, and are usually used to allow component testing before the rest of the system has been developed. LD suggests that stubs and harnesses can also be used to reduce the system's size (to make builds run faster) or to increase the system's speed by removing slow operations (to make tests run faster).

Automated test tools are an important way to speed up the testing process. Manual testing is not only intellectually taxing, but it is also slow. Automating successful tests allows the project team to rerun them often to ensure that previously working code has not been "broken" by the continuing work. Using automated testing tools to perform the smoke test as a part of the build process is commonly recommended by the Agile methods.

Automated build tools go one step further in speeding up the build process. Not only do such tools allow the build and smoke test to be done with a simple click of a button, but they also ensure that the builds are done correctly each time so that time is not wasted by build errors.

The Matrix development approach is especially useful with geographically dispersed multiteams. In this approach, the system is partitioned among the various teams, and the interfaces among the parts of the system are developed and tested first, ensuring that any synchronization problems are worked out early.

Deliver as Fast as Possible: Tool 10, Pull Systems

In "Pull Systems," what is done and when it is done is determined by demand. The most recognizable example of this is "just-in-time" manufacturing or delivery, which reduces most requirements to carry inventory by making the manufacturing and delivery processes more sensitive to product demand.

In applying this concept to software development, LD focuses on ensuring that each project team member maintains a clear understanding of exactly what needs to be done at any point in time. Several suggestions are made for accomplishing this, and they all revolve around communication.[1]

- The short increments recommended by all Agile methods can result in greater focus for team members. The increment goals tend to be clearly articulated, and the activities required to complete the increment are usually obvious. For example, in XP, a set of Story cards is selected for implementation during a particular increment. So each pair knows that when they finish work on a Story, they should just choose another one and get right back to work.

- All of the Agile methods advocate regular face-to-face communication. The most obvious of this is Scrum's daily stand-up meetings. This sort of regular communication helps keep everyone on the project working productively. Scrum is described in Appendix H.

- Information radiators serve to keep key information in front of everyone at all times. If anyone is unsure of what comes next, they can just glance at the chart on the wall to refresh their minds about current priorities.

Deliver as Fast as Possible: Tool 11, Queuing Theory

LD recommends using queuing theory to analyze and remedy bottlenecks in the software development process. For example, if the group that does independent testing is a bottleneck, you can use queuing theory to analyze the arrival rate and processing rate of work. This analysis can result in suggestions for changes to the development life cycle or division of responsibilities that could reduce overall cycle time.

Deliver as Fast as Possible: Tool 12, Cost of Delay

This tool revolves around using financial analysis to make trade-off decisions. Specifically, it says that a financial analyst can normalize any project-related information by restating it in terms of money. That way, project personnel can make decisions by comparing the financial value of each option. For example, to answer the question, "Should we buy this tool?" you can

---

1. Each of the communication topics touched on in this chapter is discussed in more detail in Chapter 10.

restate the benefit of the tool in terms of dollars saved over time, allowing you to compare the purchase and support costs with the financial benefits.

As the authors of LD say, "How can a developer decide if it is better to save a week, save $10,000, or add new features? If all of these decisions are expressed in dollars—or Euros, or yen—the decision will be more straight-forward" [1].

See the Whole: Tool 21, Measurements

LD's Measurements tool is focused not so much on encouraging measure-ment of the development process as it is on warning of the dangers inherent in doing so. This is not to say that LD encourages dispensing with measure-ment. On the contrary, it encourages a variety of measures, so long as they are carefully engineered to avoid significant dangers.

LD states the maxim that "You get what you measure." Since software development is an inherently complex activity, it should be clear that we can measure only a small subset of this activity's important attributes. So there is a real danger that the measurements we make are likely to cause suboptimization. For example, if programmers are rated according to the number of lines of code they produce per hour worked, then you are likely to get bloated systems of uncertain quality.

LD's conclusion is that the least dangerous measurements are those aggregated at a relatively high level. For example, rather than measuring people's productivity at their individual jobs, measure the amount of time it takes for the team to make the trek from a customer's need to an acceptable solution. This is more likely to provide useful information, and less likely to result in suboptimization.

Because all of the Agile methods recommend development in relatively short increments of 2–8 weeks, there is little need for measuring individual attributes in an Agile project. Instead, every month or so, you have an incre-ment of completed code that can be measured against the requirements for a good understanding of project progress. Other measures tend to provide details behind this one primary measure: working programs.

Adoption implications

The Agile methods are mainly silent on the topic of processes and tools, and the Agile Manifesto discounts their value. This, however, belies their impor-tance to the successful implementation of any of the Agile methods. Let's take some time to think about their roles.

Processes

Though it may be obvious, it goes unsaid that each Agile method (with the exception of LD) prescribes its unique software development process. A process structure and flow is defined, the various roles are identified, and the steps that should be followed in running the project are enumerated. Many include specific planning steps and status reporting methods. And they all spend significant effort defining the process for managing the customer requirements. Finally most warn that their process must be followed strictly (at least at first) to gain the advertised benefits.

The Agile methods do indeed focus on processes. What distinguishes them from more rigorous methods is the level of detail in the process descriptions, and the weight of documentation required by the process. While rigorous methods tend to be heavy in those things, Agile methods are, by design, much lighter. (Before the term "Agile" was adopted, they were referred to as the "Light" software development methods.)

So, adopting an Agile method will *not* mean that your organization will avoid processes. Rather it will mean focusing on a new process and learning how to make it work. A few Agile methods recommend having a coach for the project team to help them follow the processes effectively.

What effect would such a process change have in your organization? How difficult would it be for your staff to adopt new processes for doing their work? Take a moment to consider these things and jot down some notes.[2]

Configuration Management

As previously discussed, CM is a discipline that is of great importance to the Agile methods, in spite of being practically ignored by them. Each Agile method prescribes incremental development and expects continuous changes to the requirements and code throughout the project. Many also describe unique code management modes (like XP's collective ownership). All of these things require solid CM processes and a good CM tool.

CM is a lot more than just version control of code; it includes several topics, each of which is important to the success of any Agile method. We will discuss each of them.

Code control

The most primary CM topic is simple version control of code and other files. This is so basic that most organizations have at least a simple tool for doing code control, and those few that do not have one institute code management processes and naming conventions to keep everything under control.

Although code control is critical on any software project, the Agile methods make it even more important. This is because changes to the code are likely to be happening more dynamically, and (as with XP's collective ownership) the likelihood of collisions from different people changing the same code at the same time is increased. Without a version control tool to maintain the code's integrity, an Agile project would become very chaotic.

---

2. You may want to use the "Evaluating Agile Methods Workbook" that is available to support this book. Refer to Chapter 7 for information on obtaining and using this workbook.

Establishing baselines

Although they do not use the word "baseline,"[3] the Agile methods' incremental development makes heavy use of them. A baseline is nothing more than a "line in the sand." It is a stable basis from which the development work proceeds. The essential characteristics of baselines are:

» They are established after some level of verification proves the system is ready.

» They are available to appropriate groups to use in the project.

» They are often the basis for releases to the customer (e.g., for acceptance testing).

» They are periodically updated to reflect changes and enhancements that have taken place.

» Such updates are done in a controlled manner with the approval of the governing body.

This describes how any of the Agile methods uses incremental development; building an increment, verifying it, establishing it as the basis for ongoing work, and then updating it to form the next increment.

In such an environment, the best way to manage the baselines is with a tool that is a bit more capable than the simple tool required for version control of code. A good tool for baselining would also provide the facilities for identifying which version of each code module is included in each baseline, easily building an older baseline after new versions have been checked in, and store information about each baseline so that it can be uniquely identified and fallen back to, if necessary.

Change requests

The Agile methods do a better job of managing changes (bug reports as well as enhancement requests) than they seem to at first glance. People's initial reaction is that changes are wholly unmanaged in the Agile methods. But, in fact, handling change is what the agility of these methods all about.

What the Agile methods do *not* do is *control* changes. They accept and embrace changes throughout the project's life. And in order to do this, they must also track and manage those changes.

Each Agile method defines a process for documenting changes, and in most cases, the customer is given the authority to prioritize the changes and determine when they will be implemented. Since these methods do not envision change requests being screened and rejected, they do not discuss change requests and CCBs. They simply document each change as a new requirement that is added to and prioritized with all other system requirements.

---

3. DSDM does use the term "baseline" but only in reference to establishing the initial high-level requirements for the project.

Therefore, each Agile method describes a change request process that needs, as its only tool, the mechanism used to document requirements. And in some of the methods (like XP), that mechanism is as simple as 3×5 cards.

Configuration integrity

The last CM topic is the one that ensures the integrity of the system being built. CM is really just insurance. That is, if nothing ever went wrong there would be no reason to bother with it. But things do go wrong; people make mistakes, computers crash, and disasters happen. And when they do, the integrity of your CM system is the key to recovery.

CM practice ensures integrity is two ways, baseline auditing and status reporting.

When a baseline is established, it usually consists of a number of different components put together in a particular way. The baseline audit verifies that the baseline is correct; that it:

- Is composed of all of the correct pieces;
- Contains the right version of each piece;
- Has no unwanted pieces;
- Was built and assembled correctly;
- Was described accurately.

Status reporting is a less obvious method of ensuring the integrity of baselines, yet it is equally important with auditing. By reporting the information about each baseline to all affected parties, two things are ensured. First, each person becomes aware of the exact status of the system and the fact that the new baseline is now available for use. Second, each person represents one more opportunity to check that the baseline was in fact correctly established and documented.

Baseline audits and status reporting are easy steps to skip, but when (not "if", but "when") the project must recover from a mishap, the integrity of your baselines will be the main factor in the length of your recovery time.

The Agile methods do not explicitly address these integrity issues. Automated regression testing of every build can detect many (but not all) build mistakes that could happen. But this is only a secondary effect of the build process, so you would do well to add appropriate steps to any Agile method to actively ensure the integrity of your baselines.

Will your organization's Configuration Management tools and processes provide adequate support for Agile projects? What will need to be done to provide the CM support that Agile projects will need? Take a moment to consider these things and jot down some notes.

Build automation

Because most Agile methods call for builds to be done often (daily, or even continuously), it is a good idea to automate the build process. There are various tools available to do this, and although the initial setup can be time-consuming, the benefits of build automation are well worth the investment.

The obvious benefit of automating the build process is to speed up the build process. If your developers are doing builds all the time, making the build a one-click procedure makes a lot of sense. But the other benefit is consistency. Since it is likely that a different person will be doing the build each time, automation ensures that it is done the same way each time. This will make the whole development process smoother by avoiding most mistakes in the build process.

Is your build process automated? If not, what will it take to automate it? Take a moment to consider this and jot down some notes.

Test automation

The Agile methods place a unique focus on testing. Developers are made responsible for the quality of their code (more so than with more traditional methods), and they are expected to do significant testing, as well as retesting. When things change (as they are expected to do often in an Agile project), regression testing is the only way to be sure that the changes have not invalidated parts of the system that worked previously. And automation is the only reasonable way to do any significant amount of regression testing.

XP mandates automated testing. It states that a pair is not done implementing their Story until all of the tests run 100% clean — this includes the tests for the new Story as well as the tests for all of the other stories that have already been integrated into the system. As the project progresses, this rule can be feasible only when all of these tests have been automated.

Do you have the capability to automate testing? Have your developers been trained to use the testing tools you have? What would it take for your developers to create and use automated tests routinely? Take a moment to consider these things and jot down some notes.

Processes and tools

Processes and tools are important support mechanisms for the Agile methods. Although these methods value "individuals and interactions" over processes and tools, they are, nonetheless, dependent on good processes and tools for efficient projects. Adopting an Agile method may necessitate enhancing your organization's process and tool sets.

Reference

[1]   Poppendieck, M., and T. Poppendieck, *Lean Software Development: An Agile Toolkit*, Reading, MA: Addison-Wesley, 2003, p. 91.

Value: "Working Software Over Comprehensive Documentation"

In this part of the book, we will explore the implications of the second Agile value, which states, "We have come to value working software over comprehensive documentation." We will begin this exploration with a general discussion in Chapter 13, "The Role of Documentation in a Software Project," about documentation and how it should be used on projects. We will then look at three Agile Principles that embody this value in Chapter 14, "Incremental Delivery of Working Software."

The Role of Documentation in a Software Project

This first chapter of Part III lays the foundation for our exploration of the Agile Principles that embody the Agile value, "Working Software over Comprehensive Documentation." Chapter 14 will delve into those three principles.

Purpose of a document

Why do we produce documents? The short answer is, "To communicate information." I am writing this book because I have important information for you. And you are reading it because you want to use that information for some purpose.

Documents are not the only way of communicating information. In Chapter 10, we discussed the Agile methods' preference for face-to-face communication and saw that each of the different modes of communication has its own benefits and drawbacks.

We concluded that documents as a form of communication are limited by the amount of information they can convey, because they consist merely of words and have no other cues to help the reader understand them. There is no body language, no inflection of the voice, no eye contact, and usually no opportunity to ask clarifying questions. Using documents as a primary communication mode on projects is problematic because of readers' penchant for misinterpreting the writer's intent.

The value of a document lies in its persistence. Where any form of person-to-person communication is fleeting, a document can be reread at any time by any person, and the words will be exactly the same each time. This is not to say that the readers will *interpret* the words the same each time (they will not), but the words on the page persist unchanged from one reading to the next. There are two project-related purposes for which written documents excel:

▸ The first purpose is to provide information in preparation for person-to-person interaction. Whether the information is historical, technical, or proposals of discussion topics, a written document can help participants achieve a more productive interchange than might have occurred if they had not had the opportunity to prepare. When used for this purpose, documents' shortcomings are mitigated, because participants can correct any misinterpretations when the interaction takes place.

▸ The other purpose is to record the results of person-to-person interactions. When used for this purpose, the document's strengths act to mitigate the shortcomings of person-to-person interaction. Specifically, it allows participants to reflect after the fact on what was said to be sure that everyone's understanding and memory of it is accurate. It also serves as a corporate memory, so that the results of the interaction will be less likely to come into dispute in the future, when people's memories have faded.

Audience for a document

So, if a document's purpose is to communicate information, then an important question becomes, "To whom is the document addressed?" No document can be all things to all people. The writer must make assumptions about the reader's knowledge and experience, the amount of time the reader will be able to invest in reading the document, and how the reader will use the information the document contains. These assumptions will affect not only the document's content but also the way in which the information is grouped, packaged, and presented.

For example, many technical reports begin with an executive overview. Such an overview serves both of the likely audiences of the document, though in different ways.

▸ Most busy executives will count on the executive overview to contain all of the document's salient points in a concise and compact form. In many cases, they will not continue reading the rest of the document because their information needs will have been satisfied.

▸ For technical people, the executive overview serves to frame the document's content and provide a preview of the conclusions toward which it is driving. As they read the body of the document, their memory of the overview helps them understand the overall message and how the details fit together.

Only by identifying a document's audience and their information needs can a writer ensure that a document will satisfy its purpose.

Value of a document versus its cost

Agile Manifesto:
We have come to value…
Working software
over comprehensive documentation

The Agile value that is the subject of this part of the book uses the adjective "comprehensive" in its discounting of documentation. This word is key to our understanding of this value. None of the Agile methods dispenses with documentation completely. Rather, they each seek to avoid wasting time and effort in producing documentation.

When does producing documentation become a waste of time and effort? When the documentation:

▸ Does not have a clear purpose;

▸ Does not have a clear audience;

▸ Is overengineered (or underengineered) for its purpose and audience;

▸ Is maintained beyond its useful life.

It may seem strange to think of comprehensiveness as being wasteful, but too many organizations waste significant resources on documentation in the name of being "comprehensive." Any time a document's purpose, audience, and useful life are not kept in mind, waste is a distinct possibility.

For example, what is the purpose, and who is the audience for the Requirements Specification that your projects produce? There are actually several possible answers to this question.

▸ One is that the Requirements Specification is to nail the customer down concerning exactly what the project will produce. In this case, the customer is the audience, so the document should *not* be written to satisfy your designers' or coders' needs. You will likely want to use a professional editor to ensure that the document projects a professional image to your customer. Also, it should record the results of deliberations between the producer and customer, rather than substituting for them.

▸ A second possibility is that the Requirements Specification fleshes out the details of the customer's requirements statements so that the designers and coders can implement what is intended. In this case, the audience would include the designers, coders, and testers, so the document should be focused on their needs. Professional editing would not be worth the cost, as long as the content is clear to these technical readers. Again, it should record the results of deliberations between the producer and customer, rather than substituting for them.

▸ Yet another possibility is that the Requirements Specification will provide important historical information for the people who will ultimately support and enhance the system after it has been produced. The audience and their needs will be similar (but not identical) to those in the second possibility. And in this case, the useful life for the document *begins* at the end of the development project, instead of ending there.

Avoiding waste in documentation

The costs of writing and maintaining documents is significant, so you will want to apply this simple test before spending any effort writing or updating a document.

> • What is the purpose of the document? If there is not a clear purpose or use for the document, then producing it is likely to be wasteful.

> • Who is the audience for the document? If the audience consists of multiple roles, then consider whether a single document can meet the needs of all of them. If there is not a clear audience, or if the audience is too diverse for the document to be practical, then producing it is likely to be wasteful.

> • Does this document record the results of interpersonal communication (or prepare for it)? If not, then it is likely to be wasteful, because words absent from the benefits for face-to-face communication (as discussed in Chapter 10) are a poor communication mode.

> • Is the document still needed? Maintaining a document beyond the time when its audience can use it for its purpose is wasteful.

> • What is the minimum amount of effort necessary to ensure that the document can fulfill its purpose for its audience during the time when it is needed? Overengineering is clearly wasteful. But underengineering is also wasteful, since it results in a document of questionable utility.

Because the costs of writing and maintaining documents are significant, the Agile methods are right to try to avoid wasting them. Whether they go too far in avoiding documentation is a matter of interpretation and opinion. But the intent is entirely appropriate, and it is something we should take to heart whether we implement an Agile method or not.

CHAPTER

14

Contents

Incremental Delivery of Working Software

In this chapter, we will discuss the Agile Principles that support the second Agile value statement.

Agile Manifesto:
We have come to value…
Working software
over comprehensive documentation

Agile Principles

There are three Agile principles[1] that support the second Agile value about working software. Because these three principles are so closely related, we will discuss all of them in this chapter.

Early and continuous delivery

> *Our highest priority is to satisfy the customer through early and continuous delivery of valuable software.*

The Agile methods all have a strong customer orientation. As this Principle points out, satisfying the customer is the highest priority. As we will see in Part IV, this is not just marketing blather, as some companies practice; the Agile methods truly hold this as the highest priority.

This principle identifies three specific ways that the Agile methods work to satisfy the customer, by delivering early, delivering often, and delivering value.

*"…satisfy the customer through **early**…delivery of … software."* The Agile methods are highly suspect of people's ability to do

1. All 12 Agile Principles are quoted and discussed in Appendix B.

significant abstract analysis at the beginning of a project. Therefore they will generally lay a minimal foundation for the project, then begin to produce working software as early as possible.

While the early increments may be only minimally functional, they will, nonetheless, provide both the development team and the customer with a concrete example of the beginnings of the system being built. With this basis in place, deliberations about the details of what is to be built can be more productive. In most cases, the Agile methods prefer producing a working example or prototype to doing abstract analysis.

"...satisfy the customer through...**continuous** delivery of ... software." The Agile methods not only deliver early, they also deliver often. Regular delivery of software provides a continually growing basis for the team and customer as they work out the details of the system being built. An Agile project is a learning experience for both the customer and team, and each software increment that is delivered provides new insights to all parties and accelerates the learning.

"...satisfy the customer through...delivery of **valuable** software." In most Agile methods, the customer has a strong hand in identifying the functionality that is to be delivered. For example, in XP, as described in Appendix E, the customer makes the decisions (with input on feasibility from the technical team). And in Scrum, as described in Appendix H, the customer prioritizes the Product Backlog, and those priorities are a major consideration for the team as they choose which items to include in each increment.

By attempting to deliver value (in the customer's eyes) with each increment, the Agile methods hope to maximize the likelihood that the project will result in a highly satisfied customer.

Deliver working software frequently

> Deliver working software frequently, from a couple of weeks to a couple of months, with a preference to the shorter time scale.

This principle builds on the prior one by defining what "continuous" delivery means. It specifies a range of 2–8 weeks for each increment, and then takes the concept to the extreme by expressing a preference for shorter time frames. Even at 8 weeks, these increments come much frequently more than most of us have experienced. Can 2-week increments really be worthwhile?

The Agile methods prefer to break the project into many, many baby-sized steps. As previously discussed, the point behind incremental delivery is to ensure that the project is progressing toward customer satisfaction. The smaller the steps and the more often the customer can see what is being built, the less likely it will be that the project will go off course.

Working software: Primary measure of progress

Working software is the primary measure of progress.

The prior two principles referred to "valuable software" and "working software," and this one drives that point home. We can and do measure many different things on software projects to try to gauge progress. Of course, working software is our primary objective, but in most traditional projects, the time between increments is too long for this to be an effective way to track progress.

Because most Agile projects deliver software *at least* once within the status-reporting window that most of us use (monthly), they are uniquely positioned to use this primary measure (working software) for regular status checking. The best examples of status reporting among the Agile methods are described in Scrum and FDD.

Scrum, as described in Appendix H, uses changes in the number of items in the Product Backlog to gauge progress. Items are added to the Product Backlog as the team or customer learns about the project and better understands what needs to be built. Then, items are removed from it as they are completed. So the rate of growth or shrinkage of the Product Backlog becomes Scrum's primary method for determining project status.

FDD, as described in Appendix F, uses its feature list in a way that is similar to Scrum's use of the Product Backlog. But FDD goes further by identifying milestones for each feature, like Design complete, Code Inspection complete and Promote to Build. Each milestone is assigned a weight based on the project team's performance so far on the project, so the team can compute the status of partially completed features, as well as the fully complete ones.

Agile practices

Each Agile Method has practices that directly support these principles. We will look at 16 different practices, one method at a time.

Adaptive Software Development (ASD)

Two of ASD's practices support these principles—The "Adaptive Life Cycle," which defines how an ASD project progresses, and "Customer Focus Group Reviews," which explicitly collect customer feedback on each increment of the evolving product. ASD is described in Appendix C.

The Adaptive Life Cycle

ASD prescribes an iterative life cycle, as shown in Figure 14.1. The heart of ASD's "Adaptive Life Cycle" is referred to as the "Learning Loop." Notice

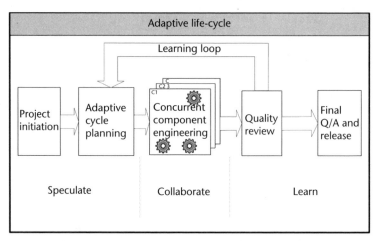

Figure 14.1 Adaptive Life Cycle. (*From:* [1]. © 2000 Dorset House Publishing Co. Inc. Reprinted with permission.)

that this loop continuously cycles through the Speculate, Collaborate, and Learn phases of the Adaptive Development Model. That is, each iteration consists of a planning step, an engineering step, and a review step.

As the name indicates, the point behind each iteration of the "Learning Loop" is to learn about the system that is being built. This learning is achieved by speculating about what will go on during the cycle (most of us call this "planning"), building some things, then reviewing what was built and feeding what was learned into the speculation step for the next iteration.

The key to learning is the Quality Review step, which includes three different kinds of reviews: Customer Focus Group Reviews, software inspections, and the postmortem.

- By "software inspection," ASD does not necessarily mean a formal Fagan[2] inspection. It *is*, however, a relatively rigorous peer review activity that is undertaken to detect and correct defects in the software. In addition to removing defects, this review ensures that the entire software team is familiar with what each person has built during the iteration.

- The postmortem is a review of the development activities that went on during the cycle. Its purpose is to identify what worked well for the team and what could be improved in later cycles. This review allows the team to continually improve its development practices.

- The Customer Focus Group Reviews are discussed next.

---

2. Michael Fagan developed a rigorous formal software inspection method while he was at IBM in the 1970s. This method has come to be known by his name, and it has been written about extensively. Although this inspection method is more expensive than any other peer review method, many studies have concluded that the return on this extra investment is substantial because of the high proportion of defects it can remove before testing begins.

Learn: Quality Review: Customer Focus Group Reviews

The key part of the Quality Review is the Customer Focus Group Reviews. These reviews allow the customer to see what has been built to date and try the evolving system out to see how it works. The word "reviews" is plural because there may be any number of different customer focus groups involved, depending on the nature of the functionality that was added during the cycle (e.g., data entry clerks, financial analysts, and the chief financial officer).

This practice is key because its purpose is to ensure that the system as it is evolving will actually meet customers' needs and expectations. If the development team has not understood a requirement as the customer does, the differences will become clear relatively early in the project, as the system begins to take shape. When this happens, the "learning" phase has done its job by fostering an environment where misunderstandings can be uncovered and corrected before the correction becomes too costly.

Dynamic Systems Development Method (DSDM)

Although DSDM gives projects great latitude in how its principles are implemented, we can see the importance it places on incremental development. Three of its nine Principles deal directly with incremental development. The third, fourth, and fifth principles are Frequent Delivery, Fitness for Business Purpose, and Iterative and Incremental Development. DSDM is described in Appendix D.

3) Frequent delivery

Principle 3: The focus is on frequent delivery of products.

As with the other Agile methods, delivering software to the customer frequently is a hallmark of DSDM. Frequent delivery allows the project's progress to be visible, not only to the customer but also to the team members and management.

4) Fitness for business purpose

Principle 4: Fitness for business purpose is the essential criterion for acceptance of deliverables.

Notice that this DSDM Principle does not say "Satisfaction of Requirements." DSDM, like the other Agile methods, distrusts the stated requirements as an indicator of what needs to be built. Although the requirements serve as a guide for the project team, the ultimate test is whether the customer believes the system will serve the need.

If what was built satisfies the requirements, but does not satisfy the customer's need, then it is not a success, and rework is needed. On the other hand, if the system satisfies the customer's business purpose, then any deviation from the requirements is not considered a problem.

5) Iterative and incremental development

Principle 5: Iterative and incremental development is necessary to converge on an accurate business solution.

At the beginning of a project, each of the parties involved is likely to have a different idea about the project's final outcome. That is, not only will the customer see things differently from the development team, but different members of the customer organization may see things differently from each other. (And the same is likely within the development team.)

DSDM uses incremental development to foster convergence of those varying ideas toward the ultimate "accurate" solution. Figure 14.2 illustrates that as each increment is delivered, everyone's ideas about the system are adjusted and true differences of opinion are highlighted so they can be worked out. The result is that each increment of the project brings participants one step closer to full convergence with each other, and, ultimately, they converge on an accurate business solution.

Extreme Programming (XP)

Two of XP's 12 practices support incremental delivery—small releases and continuous integration. XP is described in Appendix E.

Small releases

XP forces increments to be as short as possible by limiting the content of each release. Each release is supposed to demonstrate one small thing that has value for the customer. Because of this rule, the customer has many opportunities to see the project's progress and to guide the team in building the right product.

Continuous integration

In spite of XP's small releases, its build cycle is even shorter. By "continuous" integration, this principle means that code for each Story is integrated into the evolving system as soon as it is ready. When a pair of programmers

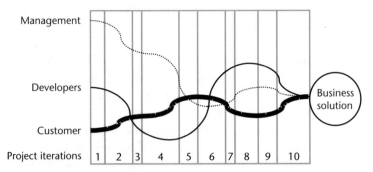

Figure 14.2 Convergence on the business solution.

finishes writing a story, they immediately integrate it into the product. With several pairs of programmers concurrently working on stories, this results in integration going on almost all the time.

The value in this practice is that it provides the fastest possible feedback to the pair on the story they just implemented. If it does not integrate cleanly with the existing system, then they simply continue working on it. Since the system worked before they integrated their Story, there is no doubt about where the problem lies; that pair has more work to do.

This is preferable to the common practice of holding all of the code for one large integration step at the end of the iteration. When the integration test yields unexpected results, it can be difficult to identify the cause of the problem. Then, when the cause has been identified, someone must go back to code that was written weeks or months ago, remember how it was designed, and figure out what needs to be changed.

Continuous integration makes diagnosing integration problems much more straightforward and facilitates learning by the programmers.

Feature-Driven Development (FDD)

Three of the practices support incremental development: developing by feature, regular build schedule, and reporting/visibility of results. FDD is described in Appendix F.

Developing by feature

In FDD, the product is developed one feature at a time. As with XP, this results in very small iterations and short feedback cycles, giving the team and customer insight into the evolving product on a regular basis.

Regular build schedule

FDD does not prescribe any particular frequency for builds, only that they are done regularly. "Regular" could mean weekly, daily, or continuously depending on what the project team thinks would be most advantageous for the project. The intent of this practice is that each new feature is integrated into the product as soon as is practical after it is written.

This avoids problems with more traditional build schedules previously discussed under XP's "continuous integration." But it also acknowledges that some circumstances may necessitate integration less often than "continuously" or even "daily." For example, if the system takes many hours to build, then it may be best to schedule builds for specific times or days.

Reporting/Visibility of results

FDD makes use of the "developing by feature" practice previously described to create a unique method for reporting project status. The project identifies milestones for each feature, and a weight is assigned to each milestone based on the relative effort it requires. A fully completed feature counts as "1," and a partially completed one counts some fraction, based on the milestones it has passed. The project status is computed as the sum of the values earned divided by the total current feature count for the project.

This reporting mechanism avoids the 90% syndrome (90% of the project being 90% complete 90% of the time) by accumulating value only when milestones have been passed. Because the features are small and milestones happen so often, it provides a real-time measure of progress.

Lean Software Development (LD)

LD's "Amplify Learning" principle focuses on the Agile principles discussed in this chapter. This LD Principle makes explicit the pattern we have already observed in the other Agile methods—that learning is a central theme on Agile projects. Two of the four Lean Tools under this LD Principle address these things directly: feedback and iterations. LD is described in Appendix G.

Amplify Learning: Tool 3, Feedback

LD's feedback tool focuses on providing information to every project stakeholder as often as possible to facilitate learning. This includes the customer and management, as well as the developers.

There are a variety of ways to provide frequent feedback to developers. Examples already discussed in this chapter with the other Agile methods include frequent builds, continuous testing, peer reviews, and customer evaluations. This tool urges the Lean Development team to be creative in finding ways to provide feedback to the development team as often as possible, and in as many ways as possible.

The most obvious way to provide regular feedback to the customer (and management) is to complete development increments as often as possible. This allows these stakeholders to see the results of their directions to the development team and to make adjustments when the results are not what they expected. Again, the more often this can happen, the more likely it will be that the project will regularly progress toward a satisfactory end.

Amplify Learning: Tool 4, Iterations

Directly related to Tool 3 is this tool about iterative development. LD recommends iterative time-boxing to manage the project. That is, each increment should have a specific start and end date. Although targets may be set for the functionality to be implemented during the iteration, the time-box is inviolable. That means that during the time specified for the iteration, the work that can be completed is done, and anything that cannot be completed is deferred to a later increment.

Time-boxing is a good mechanism for managing the ramifications of development difficulties. Rather than allowing the iteration to drag on, this mechanism forces the end of the iteration on schedule. Then any problematic features can be discussed and replanned in light of the new information that has been learned. Even if the problem is nothing more than an estimation error, this mechanism provides the opportunity to replan based on the new knowledge about the project.

Scrum

Scrum implements incremental development using practices it refers to as the Sprint and the Sprint Review. Scrum is described in Appendix H.

Sprint

Each increment of a Scrum project is developed in a "Sprint." A Sprint is a time-boxed development increment that is generally set at 30 days in length. The Sprint is characterized by its goal and a set of functionality that it is expected to deliver.

After the Sprint has been planned, the development team has complete autonomy. They are empowered to do whatever it takes to reach the Sprint goal within the time-box. Although this idea is focused on giving the team the liberty to pursue whatever strategies they believe are best, it also allows them to make any change they believe they should make to achieve the Sprint goal. They may even change the details of the functionality to be delivered as long as they believe they will still achieve the Sprint goal.

If they become convinced that the Sprint goal is beyond reach, they are empowered to abort the Sprint, which would immediately result in a new Sprint Planning session. By doing so, they will force the other project stakeholders to reassess the new information they have learned so they can all work together to set a new, achievable Sprint goal to get the project back on track.

As with the other Agile methods, Scrum's time-boxed increments provide a mechanism for all project stakeholders to learn about the system being built on a regular basis. In the case of Scrum, this happens every 30 days.

Sprint Review

Each 30-day Sprint ends with a Sprint Review meeting in which all stakeholders come together to review what was developed during the Sprint. This review includes the entire development team, the customer, and management, and it allows each person to learn from what was developed during the Sprint and to prepare for the planning session for the next one.

Adoption implications

Incremental development is often a very good idea. Consider how rarely we *really* use the waterfall life cycle. In real life, we almost always build in phases. Whether we call it "spiral," "incremental," "cyclical," or "waterfall with feedback loops," we still do it more often than not. The Agile methods have recognized this fact and built incremental development into their basic assumptions.

Time-boxed development

Time-boxing is an interesting concept that turns our development priorities around. Usually, we set a functionality goal and then keep hammering away at the job until we achieve it. If we are late, we work overtime and get it done as close as possible to the scheduled end date. Essentially, when things do not go as planned, the schedule is what gives, although, as Figure 14.3 shows, both the schedule and the functionality are liable to change.

With time-boxing, as Figure 14.3 shows, the schedule is immovable. If things do not go as planned, then the functionality is what changes. We may simplify a function, or drop one, or redefine the extent to which it must work in this increment. There are many options for "slipping" a function, but the schedule does not slip.

Although this is not a common mode of operation, there are many cases where time-boxing makes sense. By completing an increment on time (but with a function missing), we are able to provide all of the other functions to the users as planned. If the functionality is prioritized appropriately, this should cause little in the way of problems for the customer, and may please them more than a slipped schedule. And if the deliveries take place frequently (as the Agile methods all recommend), then the delayed functionality will not be delayed for long.

In what circumstances would time-boxing be appropriate for your projects? Would your customers prefer full functionality delivered late? Or partial functionality delivered on time? Take a moment to consider these things and jot down some notes.[3]

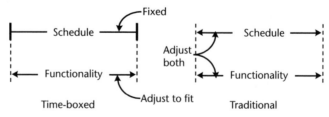

Figure 14.3   Time-boxing.

---

3. You may want to use the "Evaluating Agile Methods Workbook" that is available to support this book. Refer to Chapter 7 for information on obtaining and using this workbook.

Continuous integration

Why not implement continuous integration in your projects? Are there technical reasons why this would not be feasible? How long does it take to build the systems you are developing? If it is under 15 minutes, then there is no technical reason to preclude continuous integration. If it takes more like an hour or two, then daily may be as often as you can integrate. Even for the biggest systems, is there really any technical reason not to integrate at least once each week?

Think about the problems with "big bang" integration. Thousands of lines of new code are thrown together for the first time, and when (not "if," but "when") it does not work, it takes your best engineers days to sort through the mess and figure out what to do. And you hold your breath hoping that there are no serious issues that will take weeks to fix!

When integration goes on regularly throughout the project, the scope of each integration test is small, and the realm of possible problems is very constrained. Also, the impact of any individual problem that is uncovered is going to be much smaller because of the constrained scope of the software being integrated.

The only complication introduced by continuous integration is the demand it places on your CM system. Both the CM tools you use and the processes you employ must work flawlessly. Your people must be trained in how to keep everything straight, and they must do it diligently.

Consider the technical, tool, or personnel issues you may run into with continuous integration. Are they serious? What will it take to correct them? Take a moment to consider these things and jot down some notes.

Incremental delivery

Will your customers *accept* the idea of incremental delivery, as shown in Figure 14.4? Or are their basic assumptions still wrapped up in the waterfall life cycle? Do they want to see a Requirements sign-off, followed in a few months by the Critical Design Review, followed in several more months by Integration Readiness Review, followed many more months later by Acceptance Readiness Review? Or could they be comfortable with receiving increments of software in place of all those reviews? Would they be able to begin using the system before all the functions are available? Would they welcome the opportunity to begin migrating to the new system earlier, rather than later?

Even if they will not be able to actually put a partial system into operation, most customers welcome the opportunity to try out a system as it is

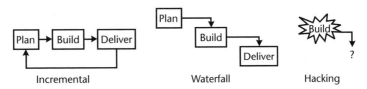

Figure 14.4 Incremental delivery versus waterfall versus hacking.

being built. It allows them to allay their fears about the development project going wrong. They can assure themselves that the system you are building really will satisfy their needs. And, of course, if there *are* surprises, they can raise the issues while work is still ongoing, instead of after the fact.

Are there any reasons why incremental delivery (either for real use or for trial use) would not work with your customers? Take a moment to consider these things and jot down some notes.

Incremental development versus hacking

Do your developers want to do *real* incremental development? Or are they expecting to just hack away at coding while merely *calling* what they do "Agile" and "incremental." True incremental development is planned and managed, as Figure 14.4 shows. The project is laid out as a series of increments, and although we expect to learn as we go through the project, we intend to build those certain increments with some semblance of the functionality we initially intended.

Each Agile method is a well-thought-out process with specific practices and requirements. They are *not* a license to hack. Is that what your people expect? Take a moment to consider these things and jot down some notes.

Deliver working software to whom?

All of the Agile methods advocate incremental delivery of software, but they do not generally indicate to whom those increments should be delivered for evaluation. From the methods' points of view this is appropriate, because the target for delivery will differ from one project to another. But because this subject remains unaddressed, it would be easy to overlook its importance.

If the population of end users for the system being developed is small and homogenous, then it will be relatively easy to determine to whom to deliver each increment. An individual who can represent the entire population will likely be easy to identify and, in some cases, delivering it to every interested end user could be feasible.

But often, determining whom to involve in the project as the "customer" is not straightforward. The larger the population of users, the less likely it will be that a single individual can adequately represent all of them. Also, large populations tend to be more diverse, exacerbating the problem. And, of course, as the population grows, involving *all* of them becomes entirely infeasible.

If you are developing a system under contract for another company, then access to true end users may be a particular challenge. It is not uncommon that the gatekeepers in such situations are unfamiliar with the details of how end users will actually use the product. So your access to end users may be blocked by individuals who do not have the appropriate knowledge or experience to stand in for them.

The most extreme case is when the system will be sold as a commercial off-the-shelf product. In that case, the target population is large and likely to be quite diverse, and no true end users may be available while the system is under development. In this case, a surrogate for the users (e.g., a marketing manager or customer support representative) may be the only option available.

Regardless of your specific situation, careful thought must be given to the question of who is the "customer" for the system that will be developed. That question must take into consideration the size and diversity of the population of end users, access to them, and the feasibility of involving multiple "customers" in the project. The logistics for your projects will be affected by the answers to these questions.

Who is the customer for the systems you produce? Who are the true end users? How large and diverse is the end-user community? How accessible are they? Is there any single individual who can adequately represent all the end users on an Agile project? What complications does this issue raise for your organization? Take a moment to consider these things and jot down some notes.

Minimizing documentation

Before we leave this chapter, and this part of the book, we need to discuss documentation. The Agile value we are focusing on says, "We have come to value… working software over comprehensive documentation." None of the Agile principles says anything about documentation, and none of the Agile methods has a practice about it either. But if we delve into the details of the Agile methods, we will find that this value statement does indeed play out in significant ways.

Each Agile method specifies how requirements are to be documented. And some also discuss other things, like designs. In every case, the level of documentation and detail that the Agile methods call for is far less than what many of us would generally expect.

For example, XP documents requirements in the form of a Metaphor and a set of Stories. The Metaphor—the overarching concept that guides the project—is a simple one-sentence statement, or no more than a paragraph. Each Story—feature—is written on a 3×5 card. So, the sum total of the requirements documentation in an XP project is likely to be no more words than many of us write in the *introduction* to our requirements documents!

XP also stresses that the best way to communicate is face to face with a whiteboard to scribble on. The closest XP comes to any lasting record of these interactions is taking a photograph of the whiteboard before it is erased. Meeting minutes are not even considered worth discussing.

While the intent of making projects more efficient by eliminating unnecessary documentation is laudable, many of us have serious concerns about the degree to which documentation is minimized in all of the Agile methods. The industry has settled on the documentation we normally produce because it has been found to be useful in various circumstances. While it is true that there are cases where some documents carry no value, care must be taken when eliminating documentation. Lacking information that is needed can be much more wasteful than producing documents that are *not* needed.

Consider the documentation that your organization produces. Can you identify a clear purpose and audience for each one? Are some of your documents overengineered? Could they be smaller and more concise? Can you identify documents that have never provided value to the organization? If you implement an Agile method, carefully consider the documents that it may suggest that you dispense with or significantly reduce. Do such changes make sense for you projects? Take a moment to consider these things and jot down some notes.

Incremental development

Incremental development is the hallmark of all of the Agile methods. We have seen in this chapter that it is prominently featured in every Agile method. The purpose for incremental development is clearly tied to the learning that goes on in the project. The Agile methods fully expect that everyone associated with a development project is continually learning, including the customer, the developer, and management. By developing in increments, these methods provide an environment where learning can continually go on. And as the stakeholders learn, the project can adjust to the new knowledge that is generated.

The Agile methods also minimize the role of documentation on development projects. While there are certainly cases when unnecessary documentation wastes project resources, care must be taken to ensure that documentation that is eliminated truly is of no value, either to the project or to the long-term support of the system being built.

Reference

[1]   Highsmith, J. A., III, *Adaptive Software Development, A Collaborative Approach to Managing Complex Systems*, New York: Dorset House, 2000, p. 84.

PART

IV

Value: "Customer Collaboration over Contract Negotiation"

In this part of the book, we will explore the implications of the third Agile value, which states, "We have come to value customer collaboration over contract negotiation." We will begin this exploration with a general discussion in Chapter 15, "Defining the Customer Relationship," about the different types of relationships that you might have with your customers. We will then look at the Agile Principle that embodies this value in Chapter 16, "Daily Collaboration of All Stakeholders."

Contents

Defining the Customer Relationship

This first chapter in Part IV lays the foundation for our exploration of the Agile Principle that embodies the Agile value, "Customer collaboration over contract negotiation." Chapter 16 will delve into that principle.

> **Agile Manifesto:**
> We have come to value…
> **Customer collaboration**
> over Contract Negotiation

Types of customers

As is common in business, the Agile methods (as well as this book) use a broad definition for the word "customer." A customer need not be an individual or a company that is distinct from the organization producing the software. Your customer may be another division or department in your company, or another person within your department. You may even be your own customer (although in that degenerate case, both contracts and collaboration become a moot point)!

We will talk about two broad classes of customers in this book: external customers and internal customers (and we will ignore the case where you are writing software for yourself).

- An external customer is one that is part of a legal entity that is distinct from your organization. This includes any governmental unit (assuming you are not a part of that unit), any part of a totally separate company, and any part of a company that owns or is owned by your company. Relationships with external customers are almost always defined by a contract (and the ones that are not, *should* be)! When separate legal entities are involved in a business transaction, a contract is necessary to define exactly what each party should expect of the other party.

▸ An internal customer is one that is part of the same legal entity as your organization. This includes other divisions of your company, other departments within your division, and even other people within your department. When the business relationship is within a legal entity, a contract is often not written. This is a mistake, because even in the simplest of cases, it is still necessary to define exactly what each party should expect of the other party. And, as we will describe in the next section, that is the primary function of a contract.

The details of your contracts with internal customers will differ from those with external customers (e.g., no need to address intellectual property rights or noncompetition). But the key point of the contract, to define exactly what each party should expect of the other party, is every bit as important with internal customers as with externals ones.

Role of contracts

As with any other document[1] a contract has a purpose and an audience. Actually, contracts have two purposes and three distinct audiences.

The primary purpose of a contract is to define exactly what each party should expect of the other party. And so, the primary audience consists of both the supplier organization and the customer. As such, the contract must address the things that each organization values. For example, the customer is likely to care about the ultimate cost of the work and the functionality to be delivered. On the other hand, the supplier will probably be concerned about controlling changes in the scope of the work and being paid in a timely manner. If the customer is external to the supplier, both will probably be concerned about the system's intellectual property rights and disclosure of privileged information.

Beyond these things, there is a secondary purpose for any contract—to provide a framework for resolving disputes between the parties. The audience for this secondary purpose consists of the other people who will become involved when a dispute takes place. For internal customers, this may be some higher level of management that is common to the two organizations. For external customers, it will include lawyers, arbiters, judges, and, in the worst cases, juries.

So, we see that contracts have a number of important roles. The question, then, is not whether we *need* a contract, but how extensive it needs to be and what it should contain. As with *any* document, the contract's purpose and audience drive the answers to these questions.

---

1. See Chapter 13 for a discussion of the role of documentation in a software project.

Role of ongoing collaboration

Software projects run the gamut from continuous collaboration to almost none at all. The Agile methods tend to be at the high end of the collaboration scale, with XP as discussed in Appendix E carrying the extreme position, requiring that a customer representative be on-site and actively working with the development team every day. At the other end of the spectrum are customers who prefer very little collaboration. Aside from receiving periodic status reports, they prefer not to be involved in the development effort at all.

The most common situation falls in the middle of the continuum. In most projects, the customer and contractor collaborate at a few carefully selected milestones throughout the project. For example, they may schedule a Requirements sign-off, Critical Design Review, and a few other points in the project when the customer receives a full briefing about decisions made to date, perhaps a demonstration of a prototype or of the actual system, and the expected directions the project will take as it moves forward. During these few interaction points, the customer dedicates significant resources to the collaboration exercise and then leaves the contractor to move forward with the project as agreed upon.

Why do most projects engage in some level of collaboration? It all comes back to the key point of Part III: learning. As the development team begins to work through the details of the project, they learn about it, and their original assumptions are replaced with knowledge. Often, this new knowledge is different from the initial assumptions and may result in adjustments to their assumptions about details they have not yet addressed. When customers hear what developers have learned, and see what has been developed to date, their assumptions are likewise replaced with knowledge that is likely to change their future assumptions.

Often, the result of this learning is totally new ideas about what the system can (or should) do. This learning process is the genesis of project scope-creep as the customer, developer, and often both generate new ideas about what the ultimate system should include. So is collaboration good or bad? Scope-creep is almost universally listed as a top problem on software projects. Should we be encouraging it through collaboration? Or should we limit it by limiting collaboration?

The Agile methods mitigate the problem of scope-creep in two ways. First, because the collaboration between developer and customer is so much closer, both parties maintain a clearer understanding of both the evolving system and the customer's needs than would be the case on a traditional project. This results in features and functions being removed and replaced nearly as often as they are added. So, although the requirements may be fluid, they tend not to expand as much as one would expect.

When the scope of an Agile project *does* expand, the Agile methods have a second mitigating strategy: they place the responsibility for addressing the expanding scope on the customer's shoulders. The collaboration on Agile projects is not limited to technical direction and functionality. Most Agile methods involve the customer in planning and prioritizing activities as well. This means that when someone comes up with an idea for a new feature or an extension to a planned feature, the customer is called on to make the hard choices. Does the schedule slip? Does the budget get inflated? Do some other features get cut? The choice is the customer's to make (with input from the technical team on feasibility and costs of the various options).

The Agile methods use close collaboration to ensure the greatest level of customer satisfaction possible. When customers have a strong voice in the project, they are more able to ensure that it results in the system they need at a price they can afford.

If collaboration has this much beneficial effect, then why would my customer *not* want to be so involved in our projects? In a word: cost. Your customers pay you a lot of money to develop the system, and their own people have other jobs to do. The more collaboration you require of them, the higher the cost of the project is to them. For example, using XP's on-site customer practice will require that, in addition to what they pay you, your customers must carry the cost of the additional employee who is nearly dedicated to the project.

Of course, this additional investment in the project is likely to pay dividends in the form of a project that produces a better result more quickly than it otherwise might have. But depending on the customer's constraints and the degree to which that customer believes in the efficacy of using an Agile method, he or she may be unwilling to take the gamble on it.

In reality, the level of collaboration your project team will have with your customers must be negotiated. Since the collaboration is an expense for them more than for you, and it is likely to result in a more satisfactory system, your goal is likely to be to obtain as much collaboration as you can get from them. This negotiation will hinge on the extent to which they believe the value of the "better" system exceeds the cost of the additional collaboration.

Balancing contracts and collaboration

So, your contract says one thing, but through collaboration, you decide on something else. Now what? We need to modify the contract *yet again*, get our contract administrator involved, the lawyers, and higher-level management, too. This could open a whole new set of issues that we thought were already settled!

The key to balancing contracts with collaboration is to *contract* for the level of collaboration that you and your customer agree to. Not only must your customer agree to provide the personnel to participate in the project, but you both must also agree to the extent to which the project costs, schedule, and functionality can be altered without requiring a contract modification.

The contract for an Agile project should acknowledge that learning will take place over the life of the project, and that learning may result in changes to the key issues of cost, schedule, and functionality. Agreeing to this and identifying any applicable limits at the outset can free you and your customer to engage in open and frequent collaboration and take action based on the learning that results.

Daily Collaboration of All Stakeholders

In this chapter, we will discuss the Agile Principles that support the third Agile value statement.

> **Agile Manifesto:**
> We have come to value…
> **Customer Collaboration**
> over Contract Negotiation

Agile Principle

This third Agile value about collaboration versus contracts is supported by the Agile principle[1] about stakeholder collaboration.

All Stakeholders Must Work Together Daily

Business people and developers must work together daily throughout the project.

The wording of this principle is based on a partitioning of the project stakeholders common to all Agile methods but not explicitly described. That partitioning puts the project stakeholders into two broad groups, as shown in Figure 16.1: developers and business people.

▸ "Developers" are the members of the technical team that is developing the software. In addition to the programmers and technical experts like system architects, this group includes the technical lead and supporting roles like testers or

---

1. All 12 Agile Principles are quoted and discussed in Appendix B.

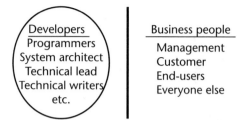

Figure 16.1 Partitioning of Agile project stakeholders.

technical writers. Essentially, "developers" are the people to whom
the Agile methods apply directly.

▸ "Business people" are everyone else. This includes:

  ▸ The entire management structure, including senior and middle
    management and possibly the project manager (if he or she is not a
    technical contributor);

  ▸ Supporting services like human resources, finance, contracts, and
    information technology;

  ▸ The customer, including their management, technical liaisons, and
    contracts people;

  ▸ The end user (who may or may not be part of the customer's organi-
    zation).

The term "business people" refers to everyone with whom the Agile
project interacts.

With this understanding of the Agile methods' partitioning of stakeholders, we can restate this principle as "All of the project stakeholders must
work together with the development team daily throughout the project." In
other words, this principle is all about broad-scale collaboration.

Agile practices

Five of the six Agile Methods have practices that directly support this principle. (FDD is the one Agile method that does not have such a practice. FDD is
described in Appendix F.) We will look at eight different practices, one
method at a time.

Adaptive Software Development (ASD)

Two of ASD's practices support this principle—"Independent Agents,"
which defines how ASD views the roles of the various stakeholders, and the
"Adaptive Management Model," which discusses the ASD management philosophy. ASD is described in Appendix C.

Project stakeholders as independent agents

There are no hierarchies in the ASD view of software projects. Management is not "over" the development team. The customer is not all-powerful. The development team is neither a more important nor a less important player. As shown in Figure 16.2, ASD sets up all the stakeholders in the project as peers.

Each of these peers, or "independent agents," brings value to the project. Each has a unique perspective, each has special knowledge, and different things motivate each. As the project progresses, ASD expects that these agents will self-organize as each situation requires, with each agent being sometimes the learner, sometimes the teacher, sometimes the leader, and sometimes the follower.

The essence of Adaptive Software Development is that the eventual product (of which none of the stakeholders has a complete understanding to begin with) will naturally emerge from an environment (an "ecosystem") in which these independent agents freely interact with each other.

Adaptive (Leadership-Collaboration) Management Model

As you might guess from the discussion of independent agents, the Adaptive Management Model bears no resemblance to the traditional command and control management model. While, like any other manager, the ASD project manager is responsible for keeping the project on track, his or her peer relationship with those being managed necessitates a different approach.

In this environment, leadership is critical because it is the only way the manager can influence the team's behavior. He or she establishes an environment for collaboration, then leads the way in that collaboration. The manager's modeling of behavior gives the team and all of the other stakeholders direction and momentum. And, assuming the manager leads in the right direction and the others follow that lead, the project will progress toward a successful conclusion.

Dynamic Systems Development Method (DSDM)

Two of DSDM's Principles deal directly with collaboration. The first one addresses the role of the end user in a DSDM project, and the ninth speaks in general on the topic of collaboration. DSDM is described in Appendix D.

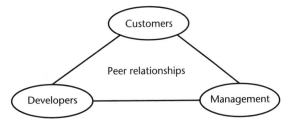

Figure 16.2 ASD—independent agents.

Active user involvement

Principle 1: Active user involvement is imperative.

Its position as the first principle in DSDM, along with the use of the word "imperative," makes it clear that, as with XP, as described in Appendix E the end user is a critical participant in a DSDM project. This is true because of DSDM's primary focus on the fitness of the system being developed for the purpose to which it will be put.

Ultimately, only the user of the system can judge fitness for purpose. So DSDM stresses that the users must be actively involved in the system's development each step of the way. The users give the project team direction, and they validate the results of each project increment. The users direct the progression of the project, and the other stakeholders work to satisfy the users' needs.

Collaborative and cooperative approach

Principle 9: A collaborative and cooperative approach between all stakeholders is essential.

Like the other Agile methods, DSDM is essentially a model for collaboration. It establishes a flat (two-level) hierarchy by placing the end user in the prime position and making all of the other stakeholders collaborators (with the end user and with each other) in pursuit of the product that is fit for its intended business purpose.

Extreme Programming (XP)

XP's on-site customer practice speaks directly to customer collaboration.

On-site customer

By "customer," XP is actually referring to the end user of the system, or at least someone who can speak authoritatively for that person. The point of this practice is to ensure that any questions about functionality, priority of various features, or the appropriateness of what is being built will be answered by this "customer."

This XP practice wants such a person to be physically located with the development team during the entire life of the project. It is assumed that this person's full-time attention to the project will not be required, so he or she should expect to be able to devote some time to "normal" work. But his or her physical presence is required because of XP's preference for face-to-face communication.

By being in the same room with the developers, this customer will engage in informal conversation with them, overhear their deliberations, participate in both scheduled and ad-hoc meetings, validate each Story as it is implemented, and be available at a moment's notice to clarify the intent of a Story or make critical decisions about the product. In short, this "on-site" customer provides prime direction for the project team.

Lean Software Development (LD)

In LD's "Build Integrity In" principle, the tools on perceived and conceptual integrity discuss the customer's role in assuring integrity. Also, its contracts tool, under the "See The Whole" principle, is the only example among the Agile methods of a discussion of contracts. LD is described in Appendix G.

Build Integrity In: Tools 17 and 18, Perceived and Conceptual Integrity

These two LD tools focus on the two kinds of integrity that a system can have. Conceptual integrity refers to the system being built well, including that it is architected well and is easy to use. Perceived integrity is the degree to which the system as it was built is the correct system. The word "perceived" is used because the only judge of this type of integrity is the user. If the user perceives that the system is right, then it is.

So, these two LD tools (especially Tool 17, Perceived Integrity) highlight LD's customer focus. Only the ultimate user of the system can determine if integrity has indeed been built in.

See The Whole: Tool 22, Contracts

The last LD tool (number 22) is the only mention of contracts among the Agile methods. This tool does not suggest certain types of contractual terms or customer relationships. Rather, it explores several common contractual arrangements and comments on the effects each might have on an Agile project.

Scrum

The Scrum practice that highlights customer collaboration is the Product Backlog. Scrum is described in Appendix H.

Product Backlog

The Product Backlog is the main mechanism by which a Scrum project is managed. The Backlog is the list of all the work that remains to be done in the Scrum project. Although any stakeholder in the project can add items to the backlog, the Product Owner has the sole responsibility for prioritizing Backlog items.

This Product Owner is the primary customer representative to the Scrum project. By setting priorities on Backlog items, this person defines the project's direction and strongly influences the order in which the team delivers functionality. This person is also the primary judge of whether the functionality that is delivered actually satisfies the intent of a Backlog item.

Thus, the Product Backlog is the main point of customer collaboration on a Scrum project.

Adoption implications

Emphasizing customer collaboration over contract negotiation will affect your software projects in a variety of ways that revolve around requirements management, customer acceptance, and, of course, the contractual relationship itself.

Establishing requirements

Most of us are used to establishing the requirements for the system being developed before too much work takes place. This is arguably one of the major ways in which Agile methods differ from more traditional ones.

All Agile methods operate under the assumption that a full and complete specification of requirements cannot be made at the beginning of the project. They expect that every stakeholder in the project, including the customer or end user, will be learning and gaining insight into the system's requirements throughout the project. Thus, the requirements specification activities at the beginning of Agile projects are designed to be high-level and incomplete. These initial system requirements are designed to provide a broad understanding of the system to be built and a general direction for the project, but not to constrain or exhaustively identify what will be built.

Although experience tells us it is true that all stakeholders learn about the product throughout the project, actually operating based on this truism can be traumatic, both for the developers and their customers. A "complete" requirements specification provides a feeling of security to all parties. The customer feels that he or she "knows" what will be delivered, and the developers feel that they "know" what the project will entail. Although an honest appraisal will confirm that these perceptions of security are ill founded, abandoning that perception of security will leave us feeling vulnerable.

Making the transition to an Agile method will require a strong dose of realism on the part of both you and your customer, to openly admit that the project will be a learning experience. It will also require a new level of trust that the other party will operate ethically in this environment of uncertainty. (We will explore this in more detail under the section "Contract as a Weapon.") How will your customers react to this new way of working? How will your developers adapt to it? Take a moment to consider these things and jot down some notes.[2]

---

2. You may want to use the "Evaluating Agile Methods Workbook" that is available to support this book. Refer to Chapter 7 for information on obtaining and using this workbook.

Managing requirements changes

Because upfront specification of requirements is virtually discarded by the Agile methods, it follows that the way in which changes to requirements are managed will be affected as well. With the assumption that the initial requirements are only an approximation of what the system will finally look like, the role of requirements changes becomes quite different.

In traditional projects, requirements changes are a destabilizing factor. Where the requirements specification had given us an initial feeling of security, any suggestion that they must change upsets that security. That is why requirements changes must be controlled. We must determine how each change will affect our initial assumptions and try to determine if we want to embrace or reject it. By thus controlling changes, we maintain our illusion of security.

Because Agile projects do not expect that the initial requirements are complete or correct, they treat changes to the requirements as new information that will likely contribute to stability. Since we admit that our initial conception of the requirements was incomplete, this new information is obviously filling a need and moving us toward the final product.

The main concern with requirements changes is that they can lead to scope-creep and result in cost and schedule overruns. The Agile methods mitigate this very real risk by placing the responsibility for scope control squarely on the customer's shoulders. With each change to the requirements (with the developers' input on what they believe it will take to implement), the customer is the one who prioritizes its relationship to other features and determines if it will be done at the expense of schedule, cost, or other functionality.

This new approach to requirements management can be nearly as difficult to embrace as the new approach to requirements specification that necessitates it. What effects will it have on your customer and your developers? Take a moment to consider these things and jot down some notes.

Ensuring product quality

The traditional approach to ensuring product quality is to anoint the requirements specification as the ultimate arbiter of correctness. As soon as the specification is signed off, the testers begin to develop their test plans and test cases based on its content. They work in parallel with the developers so that when the testing phase comes around, a complete test plan will be ready.

This traditional approach tends to segregate responsibilities in a way that can be detrimental to the ultimate goal of achieving a high-quality product. That is, the developers are seen as being responsible for producing code, and the quality assurance (QA) people are viewed as being responsible for the quality of that code. This has resulted in a generation of programmers who do a poor job of testing (if they test at all) and generally poor relationships between the programmers and testers in many organizations.

The Agile methods change the ground rules on which the traditional approach to QA is based by making the requirements specification a moving target. This moving target necessitates the new definition of product quality that is explicitly discussed by some Agile methods and implicitly embraced by others: fitness for business purpose as judged by the customer or end user. The authority now vests with people rather than a document.

Each Agile method makes this new definition work by stressing the importance of direct customer (or end-user) involvement in the project, and by placing explicit responsibility on the programmers for the quality of their code. The customer is responsible for validation (ensuring that the right product is built), and the programmers are responsible for verification (ensuring that the product is build right).

None of the Agile methods discusses the role of independent verification and validation (IV&V), but as the community is working out the details of how to use these methods, the role of testers is being addressed. Indeed they can have an important role to play, albeit a measurably different role than in traditional projects. In general, internal testers become an important ally of the programmers to help them fulfill their responsibility to produce good code. And independent testers become an ally to the customer to help them fulfill their responsibility to validate that what is produced meets their needs. The testing and Agile communities are currently still wrestling with the role of testers on Agile projects and whether their independence is critical or detrimental to project success.

The Agile methods radically alter the quality assurance landscape by moving responsibility for quality to the developers and customer and by defining a new supporting role for the QA professional. Much work remains to be done in fleshing out how this new landscape will work. How will it play out in your organization? Will it be difficult to determine the appropriate role for the testers in your shop? Take a moment to consider these things and jot down some notes.

Acceptance

In traditional projects, "acceptance" is a phase that takes place at the end of the project. After all of the development work is complete, the candidate product is delivered to the customer for acceptance testing. This phase generally results in scores of defect reports and many re-releases of fixed code. It also often gives rise to serious disputes about the meaning of the requirements specification statements that had served as a security blanket throughout the project.

On Agile projects, acceptance is done many times throughout the project. In XP, for example, each 2-week increment culminates with delivery of a product to the customer for evaluation, and possibly for use. In this way, the customer (who is the ultimate judge of acceptability) provides a steady stream of feedback to the project, which is likely to guide the project toward an acceptable final result.

This is a fundamental shift in the role of acceptance in software projects. Rather than being a protracted wrestling match at the end of the project, it becomes part of the project's natural learning cycle. We plan a little, code a little, then accept a little. And when what was written turns out to be unacceptable in some way, it is not a big problem. The necessary corrections are simply added to the list of things to be done in the next increment.

How will this new way of performing acceptance be received by your customers? How will your developers react to it? Take a moment to consider these things and jot down some notes.

The reluctant customer

You have undoubtedly noticed that customers must have a much more active role in an Agile project than in most traditional projects. They are expected to:

> ▸ Participate in project and increment planning (to different extents in different Agile methods);
>
> ▸ Regularly evaluate the interim versions of the product;
>
> ▸ Provide feedback and requirements changes on a regular basis;
>
> ▸ Evaluate and prioritize the expected parade of requirements changes;
>
> ▸ Do other specific things for different Agile methods (for example, XP expects a customer staff member to be on-site with the developers at all times).

These expectations raise the question of how much effort your customers are ready or willing to expend on the projects they hired *you* to do. Most customers expect the contractor to provide the lion's share of the project's effort, and they, as customers, will have to do little other than check its status and do a final acceptance test.

Will your customers accept these new demands on their time? How will this alter the relationships you have built with your clients? Take a moment to consider these things and jot down some notes.

Project course corrections

Traditional projects begin with a Requirements Specification and a plan and schedule. The project is expected to track to those documents and only deviate when something is wrong that requires corrective action. In this environment, most projects progress in a relatively straight-line fashion with a few sometimes-significant course corrections.

Agile methods manage projects the way we drive cars. Kent Beck begins his chapter, "Learning to Drive" with this statement:

> We need to control the development of software by making many small adjustments, not by making a few large adjustments, kind of like driving a

car. This means that we will need the feedback to know when we are a little off, we will need the opportunities to make corrections, and we will have to be able to make those corrections at a reasonable cost [1].

Adopting an Agile method will mean accepting this metaphor of driving your software projects as you drive a car, expecting to use the fast feedback loops to make course corrections on a regular basis. How well will this mode of operation be accepted by your projects' stakeholders? Take a moment to consider these things and jot down some notes.

Contract as a weapon

Contracts are weapons. For some among us they are offensive weapons, for most of us they are defensive. But their role as weapons is clear when you consider that their purpose is to protect and enforce the interests of the parties involved. Perhaps this rather negative image of weapons is the reason why the Agile Manifesto discounts contract negotiation in favor of the more positive value of collaboration.

Agile Manifesto:
We have come to value…
Customer Collaboration
over Contract Negotiation

Although the Agile Manifesto frames the issue as one over the other, in reality you must deal with both. Any project will involve customer collaboration (Agile projects simply require more of it), and so the inevitable contract negotiation must take the expected level of collaboration into account. The challenge is to make the inherently adversarial activity of contract negotiation a tool to achieve the more positive result of collaboration.

The implications of the practices we discussed in this chapter bear directly on your contractual relationships with your clients. Adopting an Agile method will certainly require that your contracts be structured differently in a variety of ways, including definitions of the expected product, cost, and schedule constraints, and the types and levels of interaction that will take place between contractor and client.

Since the Agile methods make the assumption that the details of the expected product cannot be known ahead of time with certainty, the contract for an Agile project must be built on that same assumption. It should identify the broad goals for the project and the success criteria, but it should avoid detailed enumeration of features and functions (or references to documents that do that).

Most contracts establish strict cost and schedule constraints, but this may not be most appropriate in an Agile project. Clearly, the customer's requirements will drive the degree to which these things are constrained, but strict specification of both cost and schedule will circumscribe the degree to which the expected learning about the product can be translated into functionality.

Without cost or schedule flexibility, the only choice available to the customer will be to abandon previously identified features to make room for newly understood functionality.

Whatever Agile method you may choose to adopt, there will be specific expectations about the customer's (or end user's) role in the project. Because of the criticality of these collaborations to the success of an Agile project, they must be identified upfront so clients understand what you will need from them and what they should expect from you.

All of these things mean that negotiating a contract for an Agile project will entail different and new considerations than you or your customer may be used to. Take a moment to consider these things and jot down some notes.

Customer collaboration

Adopting an Agile method will alter the types and amounts of collaboration that will go on between you and your clients. While these new collaborations will likely have positive effects on your projects' ability to produce products that satisfy your clients, the details of those changes may be difficult of adopt. They are also likely to be challenging to formalize in your contracts.

Reference

[1]   Beck, K., *Extreme Programming Explained*, Reading, MA: Addison-Wesley Longman, Inc., 2000, p. 27.

PART

V

Value: "Responding to Change over Following a Plan"

This is the fourth of five parts of this book in which we discuss the implications of the Agile practices. In this part, we examine those practices that support the value, "Responding to change over following a plan." We will begin with a general discussion in Chapter 17, "Understanding Change in Software Projects," about the nature and role of change in software projects. We will then look at the Agile Principle that embodies this value in Chapter 18, "Welcome Changing Requirements."

CHAPTER

17

Contents

Understanding Change in Software Projects

This first chapter of Part V lays the foundation for our exploration of the Agile Principle that embodies the Agile value, "Responding to change over following a plan." Chapter 18 will delve into that principle.

> **Agile Manifesto:**
> We have come to value...
> **Responding to change**
> over Following a plan

The nature of change

Change is generally held to be an impediment to software projects. We specify requirements and estimate and plan carefully. Then, as we are blissfully executing against our plans, something changes. What used to be true is no longer the case, and now all of our well-thought-out plans are worthless. We must replan, and when we do, we discover that the project can no longer meet the original needs for the agreed-upon budget or on the original schedule. We have been foiled by change, yet again.

Why do things always change? Why can't they remain stable long enough for us to follow our plan and produce what we promised? Change should *not* be unexpected. We experience change in all parts of business and have generally learned to adapt to it and even capitalize on it. When the marketplace shifts, we recognize it as an opportunity to gain market share. When new technology comes along, we look for ways to exploit it.

Change is a fact on software projects, just as much as in any other part of business. If we are honest with ourselves, we will see that change has been a factor on almost every project on which we have embarked. The Agile methods recognize the pervasiveness of change. They are designed to change our views about change in the context of software development, to bring them more in line with the ways we view it in other contexts.

Figure 17.1 shows us that changes come from two general directions. The first is from external sources. These would include such things as regulatory changes, economic turmoil, and marketplace shifts. While there is little we can do about those sorts of changes other than react to them or try to anticipate them, we have great latitude to choose how we deal with the other source of change, the learning that goes on among project participants.

External changes

Time passes from the time we contract to develop a system until we deliver it. As that time passes, the world does not remain static; it continues to move forward, to evolve, and to change even as we are focusing on the project at hand. The longer it takes us to complete our project, the greater the likelihood that some change in the environment will impact the system we are building.

There is little or nothing we can do to affect these externally generated changes. They are simply risks that we should identify, monitor, and plan for as part of our project. But how we react to those changes is fully under our control.

If our objective is to produce a system that fully meets our customer's needs, then these environmental changes are important considerations. For example, if new regulatory requirements alter how the customer can use the system, then adapting the system to those changes is critical to its ability to satisfy the customer's needs. Or if some technological advance renders our approach to the project inadequate, then capitalizing on that change will improve the system we build. In other words, reacting in a positive way to external changes can be just as important to project success as is responding to the customer's new understanding of his or her own needs.

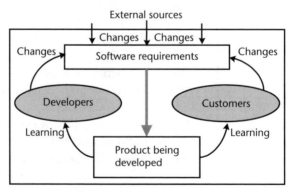

Figure 17.1   External and internal changes.

Internal change: customers learn

Our customers contract with us to develop software for them because they have identified a need. The whole focus of our initial contracting and requirements elicitation activities is to gain insight into exactly what it is that they need so we can structure a project that will produce it. The unarticulated but pervasive assumption in these activities is that customers have a full and complete understanding of their needs, and our job is to draw the requisite information out of them and document it in a way that will allow both parties to understand it and agree on it.

This assumption, however, is only partly true. While customers have quite definite ideas about what they need, they also realize that there are gaps in their understanding. This can lead them to ask for everything they can possibly think of (whether they ultimately need it or not), because they realize that the initial requirements specification is their only opportunity to do so. This can result in bloated requirements that (in spite of their size) are still incomplete and may even include contradictory demands.

The Agile methods seek to change this customer-developer dynamic by allowing the requirements to change throughout the project. Unreasonable expectations about customers' initial understanding of their needs, and the pressure on customers that attend these expectations, are replaced with an acknowledgement that change is expected and should be welcomed. The Agile methods hope to keep customers focused on what they *do* need (as opposed to what they *might* need), so the customer-developer relationship can evolve in a more realistic way.

Even the most technically savvy customers will experience shifts in their understanding of their needs as the project progresses. These shifts are not generally a matter of fickleness or indecision; more often, they are a natural and understandable result of the learning that they experience as the project progresses. With each project activity, the customer learns about the product you are building. Negotiating the requirements specification, reviewing the architectural structure, approving the user interface prototypes, discussing the details of business rules, and many other activities are all two-way interactions. Yes, the customer is providing you with critical information but, at the same time, is gaining new insights into the product.

With these new insights comes a deeper understanding of both the needs themselves and the options for satisfying those needs. So we should expect that as customers interact with us throughout the project, they will continually gain these sorts of insights. And we should further expect that these insights will result in changes to their understanding of the system and, ultimately, to changes in their requirements.

Internal change: developers learn

At the same time that the customer is learning, we are learning too. In fact, every step of the software development process is a learning activity.

Requirements elicitation, architectural design, detailed design, and coding are all step-wise refinements of our understanding of the system being built and the technical details it embodies.

While the focus and intent of this learning is step-wise refinement, the result is not always so orderly. Often we learn something that invalidates our prior assumptions. Architectural analysis may reveal that a set of requirements is mutually exclusive. Detailed design may show that the architecture has unexpected limitations. Prototypes may illuminate complexities that the user interface storyboards could not capture. And at any time, we may discover that a simpler solution will provide more value for the customer while requiring less effort on our part.

So, while the customer's learning is generating new or refined functional requirements, we find that the developer's learning is generating new or refined *technical* requirements. And these changes to technical requirements will often have impacts on the customer's requirements, just as their requirements changes will obviously impact the technical ones. This interplay means that learning on the part of the customer can accelerate the developers' learning, and vice-versa.

Capitalizing on what we learn

The Agile methods all recognize the importance of the learning that both the customer and developers experience. The resulting refinement of customers' understanding of their own needs allows them to express those needs in progressively more concrete ways to developers. And the resulting refinement of developers' understanding of the technical details of the product allows them to guide the customer toward a solution that meets those needs in the most straightforward way possible.

The Agile methods are structured to maximize the learning opportunities for both the customer and developers. This learning then provides the foundation for capitalizing on their growing common understanding about the product to ensure that it provides the greatest possible value for the customer. As the Agile Principle that we will discuss in Chapter 18 says, "Welcome changing requirements..." because they mean you are converging on the final product.

Planning for change

So, if change is a constant, then what should we do about plans? Watts Humphrey tells us, "If you can't plan accurately, then plan often." As Figure 17.2 shows, the Agile methods all take this advice to heart by making incremental planning a part of their incremental life cycles.

Each Agile method begins with an initial planning activity, but none stops there. This initial plan provides a high-level overview of the project as it is expected to unfold, as well as a more detailed plan for the initial

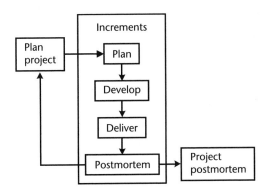

Figure 17.2 Incremental planning.

increment. Each subsequent increment of the project begins by revisiting the project plan. Adjustments are made to the overall project expectations based on what was learned to date, and the detailed plans for the new increment are laid out.

Because the increments in Agile projects are short (2–8 weeks), this planning is most certainly being done often. By revisiting the overall project plan so often, the Agile project avoids the big surprises that are too common on software projects. New understandings and assumptions are discussed on about a monthly basis, and changes to functionality, cost, or schedule are worked out.

If hard decisions must be made, then the stakeholders, including the customer, the development team, and management come together to explore the problem from all sides and adopt a new project plan that best meets all stakeholders' needs. In this way, Agile projects can "welcome changing requirements" while keeping the project as reasonably on track as is possible so it is most likely to result in a product that meets the customer's needs.

Change happens

Far from being unexpected, change on software projects should be expected and anticipated. Just as in the other parts of our businesses, our software development projects must accept that change *will* happen. We must change our attitude toward change; rather than hiding from it and wishing it would go away, we should be looking for opportunities to capitalize on it to make our projects and our businesses more successful.

Welcome Changing Requirements

In this chapter, we will discuss the Agile Principle that supports the fourth Agile value statement.

Agile Manifesto:
We have come to value…
Responding to Change
over Following a Plan

Agile Principle

This fourth Agile value about responding to change is supported by the Agile principle[1] about welcoming change.

Welcome changing requirements

Welcome changing requirements, even late in development. Agile processes harness change for the customer's competitive advantage.

As this principle states, the Agile methods are specifically designed to make the most of change. Since change is a given in our projects, the developers of the Agile methods have taken the stance that it should not just be tolerated or accounted for, but that it should be embraced.

To *welcome* change is a significant departure from the more traditional mode of *controlling* change. It represents a 180-degree shift in our thinking and attitude. Such a shift may be a challenge to make, but according to the Agile methods, it is the key to *harnessing* change for competitive advantage.

---

1. All 12 Agile Principles are quoted and discussed in Appendix B.

Agile practices

All six Agile Methods have practices that directly support this principle. We will look at nine different practices, one method at a time.

Adaptive Software Development (ASD)

ASD's Adaptive Life Cycle practice supports this principle. ASD is described in Appendix C.

Adaptive Life Cycle

The core of ASD is the Adaptive Life Cycle, shown in Figure 18.1. And the core of the Adaptive Life Cycle is the "Learning Loop," which is ASD's mechanism for harnessing change.

During each increment of an ASD project, all stakeholders are learning[2] about the product that is being produced. That learning results in changes to their assumptions and expectations, and especially to the customer's requirements. The Learning Loop feeds all of this information back to the Adaptive Cycle Planning phase that marks the beginning of the project's next increment. In this way, changes are continually being generated, welcomed, and harnessed for the customer's benefit.

Dynamic Systems Development Method (DSDM)

Two of DSDM's Principles deal directly with change. Principle 6 teaches us not to fear change, and principle 7 addresses the requirements baseline. DSDM is described in Appendix D.

All changes are reversible

Principle 6: All changes during development are reversible.

This principle states the obvious (assuming we have a minimally functional code control system). And yet we rarely act as if we believe it. Why are we reticent to make changes to code that works, and even less willing to reverse those changes later?

The primary reason we do not like making or reversing changes is that it seems wasteful of our time. And changes sometimes result in unexpected consequences that require us to "waste" even *more* effort to fix. Would it not be better to spend our effort writing *more* code, rather than changing what is already there?

The Agile methods teach us that code that is implemented well is valuable, whereas code that only marginally meets the need can endanger our project's agility by making it more difficult to do further development. Code

---

2. See Chapter 17 for a more complete discussion of the role of learning in a software project.

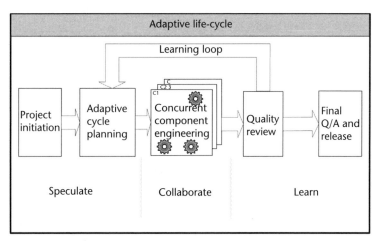

Figure 18.1 Adaptive Life Cycle. (*From:* [1]. © 2000 Dorset House Publishing Co. Inc. Reprinted with permission.)

that works on a marginal level or is not structured appropriately to support development as it moves forward is targeted for rework as a way to ensure that the project's agility is maintained.

If we are learning throughout the project, then we should expect the need to change our code. By giving us permission to make changes and reverse them, DSDM provides an environment that welcomes change rather than shunning it.

Requirements are baselined at a high level

Principle 7: Requirements are baselined at a high level.

This is the only practice among the Agile methods that addresses the question of a requirements baseline. The other Agile methods operate under the assumption that requirements are always in play and are liable to be changed any time during the project.

DSDM circumscribes this idea by calling for a requirements baseline. The baseline's intent is to provide a stable basis for moving forward with project activities. Changes can be made to a baseline, but only with careful deliberation and consensus among stakeholders. Therefore, the baseline is likely to rarely change, resulting in a stable basis for the project.

But DSDM qualifies this statement by saying that the requirements baseline should be "at a high level." That is, the protection from ad-hoc change should be extended only to the overarching ideas that give the requirements their form. The details of how the requirements will look and act in practice should be left for the stakeholders to work out as the project progresses.

Changes to lower-level requirements on a DSDM project can thus be welcomed just as with any other Agile method. But changes to the baselined higher-level requirements will be welcomed less readily and subjected to more traditional control.

Extreme Programming (XP)

Two of XP's practices speak to changing requirements—Metaphor discusses how requirements are managed, and Refactoring discusses changing the program's design. XP is described in Appendix E.

Metaphor

XP projects document requirements in two ways prior to implementation, the Metaphor and Stories. The Metaphor describes (using similes to readily recognizable objects or concepts) the product that the project is expected to create. It describes in broad terms what the project is attempting to achieve. This statement is meant to be broad enough that it will remain consistent throughout the project, even as the details of what is being built evolve.

There is no guarantee that an XP project's metaphor will not change, but it is expected to provide a stable vision for the project. The Metaphor is supposed to be a touchstone for the project stakeholders, to ensure that as they are welcoming changes, the project nonetheless continues to track toward its agreed-upon goal.

The detailed requirements for the project are described in Stories. Each Story describes a single feature of the system in prose that fits on a 3x5-inch card. This level of brevity is designed to provide guidance to the programming pair implementing the Story, while still leaving room for experimentation and innovation. Ultimately, only the on-site customer can determine if the code has actually captured the intent of the Story it implemented.

The Stories are the elements of an XP project designed to welcome change. It is expected that Stories will be added to and deleted from the slate on a regular basis, and that the descriptions of the Stories will change, sometimes even after they have been implemented. As the project progresses, the growing understanding of the ultimate product is documented in the Stories that describe its ultimate functionality.

Refactoring

Refactoring is XP's primary means of encouraging programmers to make changes to code that is already working. Welcoming change (in addition to XP's "Simple Design" practice) can result in the original structural assumptions of a class or method (or even a whole subsystem) being far removed from what it ultimately ends up being. Refactoring is a matter of bringing all the information that has been learned since the code was written to bear on it, and reworking it to best suit its use.

A second effect of Refactoring is to eliminate a phenomenon that we refer to as "brittle code." Code (like metal) becomes "brittle" after it has been changed, bent, and twisted over and over again. After the code has been changed enough times, it becomes subject to breakage from even minor manipulation. (Many of us have observed this phenomenon in systems that have been maintained over a long period of time.) Code that is showing signs of becoming brittle is a prime candidate for refactoring to restore its structural integrity.

In XP projects, Refactoring is a critical part of welcoming change. It encourages programmers to improve the way the code is implemented when they see the opportunity. And it ensures that the system that is ultimately produced remains structurally sound by eliminating "brittle code" along the way.

Feature-Driven Development (FDD)

FDD balances the benefits of a stable basis for the project and welcoming changes through its Domain Object Modeling practice. FDD is described in Appendix F.

Domain Object Modeling

Each FDD project begins with the creation of a Domain Object Model that identifies all the objects the project team expects to build and how they will relate to each other. This up-front analysis seems to contradict the general assumption among the Agile methods that you cannot figure it all out upfront. But in reality, this modeling activity is not done just once; it is revisited regularly throughout the project.

The purpose of the *initial* attempt at modeling the objects is to provoke analysis by the project stakeholders, both the developers and customer. This exercise requires careful thought about the boundaries of the system to be built and the capabilities that are to comprise it. By modeling objects at the beginning of the project, the FDD project team can generate not only an initial conception of the product but also the feature list, which becomes the basis for planning and managing the project.

The project team initiates each project increment by revisiting the Domain Object Model. Like the other Agile methods, FDD expects that development of each increment will result in new insights into the product. So the first step in each increment is to consolidate what has been learned and update the Domain Object Model to reflect the new higher level of understanding.

Thus, the Domain Object Model is a living document that is maintained consistent with the learning that each project stakeholder experiences. And as the project progresses, this model is slowly transformed from an initial approximation into an accurate depiction of the objects in the system.

Lean Software Development (LD)

LD's principle, "Decide as Late as Possible" embodies in its three tools LD's approach to welcoming change. Its Refactoring tool, under "Build Integrity

In," provides a mechanism for accommodating change. LD is described in Appendix G.

Decide as Late as Possible: Tool 7, Options Thinking, Tool 8, The Last Responsible Moment, Tool 9, Making Decisions

This LD principle and the three tools that support it embody LD's method for welcoming change. Essentially, change is destabilizing when it invalidates prior decisions. So, LD seeks to mitigate that risk, not by shunning change but by employing decision-making strategies that make change less disruptive. The principle's wording states the sum total of the three tools: "Decide as late as possible." That is, by postponing decisions, we can avoid having many of them invalidated by changes that may take place in the interim.

LD's Tool 9, "Making Decisions," discusses using appropriate rules to narrow the options in any decision you have to make. It suggests that for an Agile software project, the LD principles provide a good set of rules for making decisions. If decisions are kept consistent with these principles, then the project will progress on a more consistent basis.

But *when* should those decisions be made? LD defines "The Last Responsible Moment" (Tool 8) as that point in time when indecision results in a decision perforce, because one of the alternatives is about to disappear. Delaying a decision until that Last Responsible Moment means that more information will be available to us, and many changes that might have affected the decision will have already occurred. So we can be surer that it will be the correct decision, and it will be less likely to be impacted by changes.

By "Options Thinking" (Tool 7), LD refers to a decision-making mode used in the financial markets to delay the Last Responsible Moment. Besides the obvious choices of "yes" or "no," there is sometimes a third choice available: "decide later." This third choice is often marked by the purchase of the *option* to say "yes" or "no" at some future date. Then, when that future date arrives, the decision-maker can choose to use the option or to *not* use it. He has delayed the decision until that later date. Software development, like financial markets, can sometimes provide this third choice. By making some small investment, we can sometimes hold off on choosing between "yes" and "no" for some period of time. The Last Responsible Moment for making a decision can be delayed by purchasing and exercising options.

So LD's Tools 7, 8, and 9 work together to help Agile projects mitigate the effects of change on their decisions by applying an appropriate set of rules and delaying the ultimate decision until the latest date possible.

Build Integrity In: Tool 19, Refactoring

Like XP, LD uses Refactoring both to encourage regular changing of code and mitigate the effects of it. Please refer to the discussion of Refactoring under XP (earlier in this chapter) for information about how Refactoring can lead to better code.

Scrum

Scrum both welcomes and constrains change through its Sprint Planning Meeting. Scrum is described in Appendix H.

Sprint Planning Meeting

A Scrum project consists of a series of Sprints. Each Sprint is a 30-day increment of development that implements some items from the Product Backlog.

After the Sprint has begun, the development team is protected from external changes. If anyone comes up with new ideas or changes, those items are added to the Product Backlog, but they do not affect the progress of the current Sprint. This allows the team to focus on the Sprint Goal without being distracted by the many changes going on around them.

The team is free to adopt any change they believe will facilitate their achievement of the Sprint Goal. But if a development team member generates an idea for a change that is not relevant to the Sprint Goal, then that idea is added to the Product Backlog, just as anyone else's ideas would be.

So, the Product Backlog is Scrum's parking lot for changes. Then, during the Sprint Planning Meeting, the Product Backlog provides the basis for decisions the stakeholders make about the next Sprint. They agree on a Sprint Goal, and they constitute a Sprint Backlog as the subset of the Product Backlog that will be addressed during the Sprint.

Thus, at the beginning of each Sprint, the stakeholders take stock of their new understanding of the product and project and plan how they should move forward for the next 30 days. In this way, changes are welcomed into the project in a controlled way.

Adoption implications

Welcoming change is a key attribute of Agile projects. Although this welcoming brings with it a number of risks, the Agile methods mitigate those risks both through many of their practices and by changing how change itself is perceived. For example, Refactoring encourages regular changing of code, while at the same time keeping it from becoming brittle. And the customer is encouraged to continually rethink requirements but is also made responsible for reconciling those requirements changes with available resources. What will be the effects of the Agile practices on our projects?

Incremental planning

All of the Agile methods do some form of incremental planning. Figure 18.2 shows that as each increment begins, they revisit their high-level plans for the project, making whatever adjustments may be necessary based on what has been learned to date. Then they do more detailed planning for the upcoming increment.

None of the Agile methods does exhaustive planning at the beginning of the project. Although different methods address high-level planning differently, they share the fact that high-level planning is treated as only a rough estimate, and that the details may end up being different from what was first anticipated. By the same token, even the more detailed plans for the current increment are treated more as targets than guarantees.

Because Agile increments are relatively short (2–8 weeks), the Agile methods update their plans on a regular basis. This has the benefit of keeping the plans in synch with the latest understanding of the project, but it also means that the project plans are a constantly moving target. This could make it difficult to gain and keep sponsors' commitment to the project because of constantly shifting expectations. Would this be an issue in your organization? Take a moment to consider these things and jot down some notes.[3]

Tracking and reporting progress

Short increments have the benefit that everyone can see material progress on the project on a regular basis. Every 2–8 weeks, some material thing (usually functional code) is delivered for evaluation. This gives developers a set of regular victories, and it provides both management and the customer with a concrete sense of progress.

Some Agile methods give us mechanisms for tracking progress *during* an increment. For example, XP tracks the numbers of Stories completed and

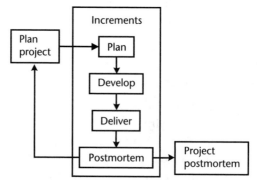

Figure 18.2 Incremental planning.

---

3. You may want to use the "Evaluating Agile Methods Workbook" that is available to support this book. Refer to Chapter 7 for information on obtaining and using this workbook.

waiting for work. And FDD includes a mechanism for tracking each feature as it progresses through the development life cycle.

The real trick to understanding the status of an Agile project comes in dealing with the constant flow of changes that are expected. Progress during an increment, and even delivering code, do not give us a clear understanding of when the project is likely to finish if the backlog of work is expanding at the same time.

Scrum is unique among the Agile methods in that it includes a mechanism for judging progress toward actual completion of the project. Although its Product Backlog is expected to grow in the early Sprints of the project, Scrum expects the growth will soon level off and the backlog will begin to shrink. Once a pattern of backlog shrinkage is established by working off more backlog items than are added in each Sprint, the rate of shrinkage can be projected forward to determine when the backlog will be exhausted. Based on this information, stakeholders can take specific actions to accelerate backlog shrinking, if it is needed.

How well would Agile projects fit into your project tracking and oversight mechanisms? Would the Agile methods' way of tracking progress work in your organization? Take a moment to consider these things and jot down some notes.

When the project deviates from the plan

(That's "when," *not* "if"!) All projects deviate from their plans in some ways. Incremental planning (as previously discussed) is the mechanism used by Agile projects precisely *because* they do not expect to conform to their plans.

The traditional project management methods hold plans to be a goal to be achieved. When a project deviates from its plan, they take corrective action to remedy the problem. At times, that corrective action includes replanning, but more often, it involves some action designed to bring actual performance back in line with the original plan.

The Agile methods take the opposite tack. When actual performance deviates from the plan, they assume that the plan was wrong and simply change it to match "reality." There is no concept of "corrective action" (except for replanning). How would this philosophy work in your organization? Take a moment to consider these things and jot down some notes.

Handling customer change requests

Agile methods expect and even encourage customers to regularly change their expectations for the product being developed. As we have discussed in this chapter and in Chapter 17, the learning that is constantly going on is expected to result in changes to their requirements.

Because of this, the Agile methods do not even have the concept of "change requests." The customer does not request changes (with the concomitant expectation that those requests may or may not be granted). Rather, the customer is anointed with authority to direct what is being developed. As customers' perception of what they need changes, they are expected to articulate those changes and so affect what is being built.

This is not to say that they are given carte blanche to demand what they will. At all points during the project, the development team is responsible for keeping the customer fully apprised of the technical, schedule, and cost implications of those changes. This means that when the customer wants to add a requirement for the project, he or she must decide to cut some other functionality, increase project cost, stretch the schedule, or some combination of these options.

Placing so much authority in the customer's hands is uncommon. Would it work in your organization? How would your customers react to this? Take a moment to consider these things and jot down some notes.

Changes injected by the development team

In addition to the customer, the development team is also expected to regularly adjust the project's technical requirements and make the code better. Again, this is because as they work through more and more details, they learn about the product, and that learning results in a better understanding of the limitations and benefits of the courses taken.

The Agile methods expect the development team to be proactive in changing both the technical requirements and the code as the system progresses. At times this may mean that previously expected functionality cannot be delivered within the planned cost and schedule constraints. When this happens, the results are supposed to be very much like when the customer makes changes. There should be an open discussion between the development team and the customer of the new issues, with the customer deciding whether functionality, cost, or schedule must be sacrificed to account for the new information.

This kind of equal footing between the development team and customer is unique to the Agile methods. How would your developers adapt to such an arrangement? How would your customers react? Take a moment to consider these things and jot down some notes.

Welcoming change

The Agile methods *welcome* changing requirements. This is in stark contrast to the traditional methods, which control change and try to avoid it when possible. Adopting an Agile method will require considerable adjustment in your people's thinking about change. It will also alter the balance of power within your projects, empowering both the customer and technical team to take actions they deem appropriate.

The effects of constant change in projects are many, and the Agile methods include many practices designed to mitigate those effects. These include incremental planning, refactoring, and delaying decisions to the Last Responsible Moment. All of these practices may present challenges to any organization.

But the benefits of embracing change include an increased likelihood that the final product will indeed satisfy the customer's needs and be fit for the business purpose to which it will be put.

Reference

[1]   Highsmith, J. A., III, *Adaptive Software Development, A Collaborative Approach to Managing Complex Systems*, New York: Dorset House, 2000, p. 84.

PART

VI

The Unstated Value: Keeping the Process Agile

This is the last of five parts in which we discuss the implications of the Agile practices. In this part, we examine those practices not directly related to any of the four values of the Agile Manifesto but nonetheless important to the Agile methods. The three Agile principles we will discuss and the practices that underlie them are all focused on ensuring that the processes that Agile projects use support the goal of Agility.

We will begin with a general discussion in Chapter 19, "Maintaining the Process," about the fact that all methods, especially Agile ones, rely on processes. We will then look at three Agile Principles:

- Chapter 20: "Technical Excellence" discusses the importance of high-quality work on Agile projects.

- Chapter 21: "Simplicity: Maximize Work Not Done" discusses the Agile methods' quest to avoid unnecessary (wasteful) work.

- Chapter 22: "Regular Team Retrospectives" discusses how the Agile methods have adopted and changed the project postmortem.

Maintaining the Process

This first chapter in Part VI lays the foundation for our exploration of the Agile Principles that focus on maintaining the agility of software development processes. Chapters 20, 21, and 22 will discuss each of those three Principles and the Agile practices that underlie them.

Agile is not antiprocess

"We don't need no stinkin' process!"
—Anonymous software developer

There is a common misconception within the software development community that the Agile methods are antiprocess. Many developers, like the one quoted above, push for adopting Agile methods because they believe these methods will free them from the constraints of following a defined process. And many in the process community *disparage* the Agile methods for exactly the same reason.

To be sure, most Agile methods do not use the word "process" (except when they complain about the evils of process-for-process's-sake). Books and articles about the Agile methods tend to make a habit out of depreciating disciplined process, but when you pay attention to their tirades, it becomes clear that they are really complaining about the *abuse* of process. For example:

▸ Process that does not support people in doing good and efficient work.

▸ Process that drains the organization of enthusiasm and excitement.

▸ Process that gobbles up more value than it will ever return to the organization.

These things represent *un*disciplined process — process that is out of control and not performing its vital role of supporting the development work. We in the disciplined process community aught join the chorus and rail against such abuses!

The analysis we have been doing in this book should make it clear that, far from being antiprocess, each Agile method prescribes its own process. In fact, as you read the books about each Agile method, you will find not only explicit processes, procedures, inputs, and outputs but also dire warnings that if the benefits of that particular method are to be realized, you must follow the prescribed process faithfully!

You are using a process

The fact is we all use processes for anything we do on a regular basis. What is *your* process for reading this kind of a book?

- Did you start at the beginning and work straight through to this point?
- Did you skip the front matter but otherwise read the book in order?
- Did you go directly to the table of contents and select this, among other parts of the book, to read?
- Or did you just happen to flip the book open to this spot and start reading?

Process is important shorthand that frees us from paying attention to the mundane or repetitive so we can focus on the important things. Our morning process gets us from the pillow to the coffee pot so we can get started with actually living out our day. In the same way, the process your organization uses to develop software (hopefully) frees your developers to focus on the truly interesting and demanding work of designing solutions and reducing them to working code.

The question is not whether or not you should follow a software development process, but whether or not the process you *do* follow serves your needs.

Process efficiency and effectiveness

To be worth following, processes must be both efficient and effective.

- Your processes are *effective* when they ensure that you do the right things. They are *in*effective when they add little or no discernable value toward achieving the organization's goals.
- Your processes are *efficient* when they prompt you to do the right things in ways that are as unobtrusive and effortless as possible. They

are *in*efficient when they require inordinate amounts of effort to follow, so that their cost rivals their value to the organization.

People chafe against processes that are either inefficient or ineffective, or both. On the other hand, processes that are both efficient *and* effective tend to become invisible; we follow them automatically without thinking about them and can even be unaware of the processes themselves.

Efficient and effective processes do not happen automatically. They require care in their establishment and regular tuning to ensure that their value to the organization grows over time. And they may need to be eliminated, replaced, or changed after a time, as the organization's needs change.

Mary, Mary, quite contrary, how does your [process] grow?

Processes, like gardens, tend to grow in one of four ways, and the way that processes grow in any particular organization is a direct result of the actions (or inactions) of the people tending them. Some gardens are carefully tended on a regular basis, others receive occasional new plantings and maybe some water or fertilizer every once in a while but little else, a few are overplanted and become overgrown, and the rest are left to grow wild.

Most of us have not thought critically about the processes that have evolved in our organizations. Our process garden has essentially grown wild. Seeds of new processes blow in on the wind, sometimes from a neighbor's beautiful flowers, sometimes from a briar patch. These seeds may or may not take root. And those that do take root might last only for a season, they might grow alongside our other processes, or they might take over the whole garden, choking out everything else. While natural selection has a certain logical elegance to it, an untended garden rarely produces beautiful flowers or healthy vegetables, just as untended processes are rarely efficient and effective.

Many of us attend to our processes only when things go wrong. When there is a crisis, we examine the problem to determine where the fault lies. Then we dig around our process garden, remove the dead processes, plant new ones, pull those obnoxious weeds, till in some fertilizer, and water it … for a while. Once the crisis is past, our attention turns elsewhere, and our garden is left to fend for itself. The new processes may bloom, or they may not. And the weeds are certain to make a comeback sooner or later. While irregular tending may result in some of the processes we need actually taking root, it is unlikely to produce processes that are healthy, beautiful, effective, or efficient.

Some organizations hire gardeners and give them the tools and supplies they need. But if the gardeners do not have a firm grasp of the organization's needs and constraints, they may view the processes themselves as being their goal. So they plant processes in every available space, pull every weed, and fertilize and water them copiously. Without thinning or pruning, the processes become overgrown and choke the garden, making it neither efficient nor effective.

A few organizations carefully tend their processes. They hire gardeners and give them the tools and supplies as well as the perspective they need to keep their processes efficient and effective. And they plant processes that will protect their other processes from their natural enemies, much as marigolds among the tomatoes may protect them from certain bugs. The right amount of appropriate attention will ensure that your garden blooms with efficient, effective processes.

Continuous process improvement

Continuous process improvement is the term that we in the process community use to denote a well-tended process garden. As the term implies, maintaining efficient, effective processes requires continuous attention to them, along with adopting changes when opportunities for improvement are identified.

The essence of continuous process improvement is to explicitly evaluate your processes on some regular basis. If a process has become ineffective (that is, it no longer produces the desired result or it has some unintended side effect), then you might search for an alternative process that will produce the desired results while avoiding the undesirable ones. If a process has become inefficient (that is, it requires a disproportionate amount of time or effort when compared with the benefit it produces), then you might seek ways to streamline it so you can realize the benefits without undue investment.

While all of this is very much a part of the disciplined process world, you may be surprised to learn that it is also a key part of the Agile methods. As we will see in this part of the book, all of the Agile methods include practices specifically designed to ensure that their processes remains Agile.

20

Contents

Technical Excellence

In this chapter, we will discuss the first of three Agile Principles directed at keeping the process Agile.

Agile Principle

The first Agile Principle[1] that deals with keeping the process Agile is about technical excellence.

Continuous attention to technical excellence and good design

Continuous attention to technical excellence and good design enhances agility.

This principle states that technical excellence is a prerequisite to agility. That is, in order for a project to be able to move quickly and react to change, it must produce technically excellent products. At first blush, this may sound exactly backward. We tend to equate technical excellence with excessive cost and time. After all, improving quality usually requires more reviews, more testing, more analysis, more, more, and more. So how can these things be said to result in *agility*?

But the Agile methods take a different route to technical excellence. Instead of taking what the programmers produce and trying to *make* it excellent, they focus on programming practices that will result in higher quality code in the first place. If they can achieve that end, then the project will require much less rework, including *less* retesting and *fewer* re-reviews. And when changes *are* required (for example, incorporating a new

---

1. All 12 Agile Principles are quoted and discussed in Appendix B.

requirement), well structured, cleanly implemented programs will be easier to change.

At the same time, the practices that the Agile methods use to focus on technical excellence have tremendous potential for upgrading each programmer's capability to do excellent work. We will see as we examine the practices in this chapter that each of them sets the stage for programmers to learn while they improve product quality. This will result not only in technically excellent products but also in an ever-increasing capability of the development team to do even better work for the remainder of this project, and in the future. This is technical excellence breeding technical excellence.

So we see that technical excellence is a key part of all Agile methods and part of the reason why they are able to be as agile as they are.

Agile practices

All six Agile Methods have practices that directly support this principle of technical excellence. We will look at nine different practices, one method at a time.

Adaptive Software Development (ASD)

ASD's Quality Review practice supports this principle. ASD is described in Appendix B.

Learn: Quality Review: Software inspections

ASD's Quality Review practice includes three separate facets. The one that supports technical excellence, software inspections, is a relatively rigorous method for software developers to review each other's work, similar to formal "Fagan" inspections mentioned in an earlier chapter.

The primary reason for software inspections is to find defects in designs or code so they can be corrected before they can cause other problems. By doing these inspections at the end of each increment, ASD ensures that the code base on which the next increment will be built is a clean as it can possibly be.

However, an inspection has other benefits besides this primary one.

- First, it is an opportunity for every development team member to gain familiarity with code on which he or she has not worked. This is good for a variety of reasons. For example, writing code that must interface with code you have inspected is easier because you have a much better understanding of that code's capabilities and how it must be used.

- Another benefit of inspections is that more experienced team members may identify design or coding inefficiencies. This allows all code that is produced by the team to benefit from the expertise of those members without making them a bottleneck on the project.

> Related to that benefit is the fact that all team members will learn from more experienced ones. When they have the opportunity to review code written by more experienced people, they can see how a truly expert person approaches the problem at hand. And when a more experienced person reviews their code, the less-experienced people will see the kinds of concerns that an expert has and what he or she looks for.

So, we can see that software inspections improve the technical excellence of the team's work in several different but related ways, improving not just the designs and code themselves but also the technical capabilities of the team as a whole.

Dynamic Systems Development Method (DSDM)

DSDM's Principle 8 deals directly with technical excellence. DSDM is described in Appendix D.

Testing throughout the life cycle

Principle 8: Testing is integrated throughout the life cycle.

DSDM (like many people in the software industry) uses the word "testing" to refer to *any* verification or validation activity, not just to the execution of a program to see if it works properly. So this principle says that verification or validation is done during each step of the development process.

We usually think of V&V as a series of activities that take place at the end of the project, for example, unit test, integration, and acceptance. But in reality, V&V can (and should) take place at every phase of a project. Figure 20.1 shows how this can work.

> Plan—After planning the project and after planning each increment:
> > Verify: Is the plan consistent with itself and with the team's capability?
> > Validate: Are we planning to achieve the objectives for the project or increment?
> Requirements—After both high-level and detailed requirements activities:
> > Verify: Are the requirements complete, consistent, achievable?
> > Validate: Do the requirements reflect what the customer wants and needs?
> Design and develop—After each development activity:

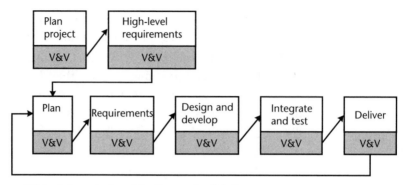

Figure 20.1 Integrated verification and validation.

> ▸ Verify: Is the component complete, self-consistent, defect-free?
>
> ▸ Validate: Does the component accurately implement the requirements?

▸ Integrate and test—After each integration and test activity:

> ▸ Verify: Were all tests run and all defects corrected?
>
> ▸ Validate: Do the tests verify all requirements (business and technical)?

▸ Deliver—After delivering an increment (or the whole system) to the customer:

> ▸ Verify: Is the software complete, self-consistent, defect-free?
>
> ▸ Validate: Does the software do what the customer wants and needs?

By working in this rather mature way, DSDM ensures that the highest-quality work has been done at each step of the project.

Extreme Programming (XP)

Two of XP's practices speak to technical excellence. Test First places the responsibility for code quality squarely on the shoulders of each programming pair, and Coding Standards provide guidelines for producing quality code. XP is described in Appendix E.

Test First

In most organizations, programmers are responsible for producing code, and the QA people are responsible for ensuring that code's quality. This is an unfortunate division of labor, because it has allowed the programming community to come to regard quality as not part of their responsibility. But the QA people cannot produce high-quality code; they can only measure the quality of what was already produced. If programmers have not built high-quality code in the first place, it will still be no better than mediocre quality after testing (because even the best tests catch and remove only about half of the defects that exist in a program).

XP turns the tables by placing the primary responsibility for quality squarely on the shoulders of the pair of programmers writing the code. This is not to say that there is no place for independent testing in XP, only that testing by developers takes on much greater importance.

XP's "Test First" adds a unique twist to the testing equation. It forces programmers to think about quality by having them write all the tests for the Story they are implementing *before* they write any code. This means programmers must think about how the code can break *before* they begin to think about how to make it work. This twist gives them special insights into the code they are about to write that naturally results in better code that is freer of defects in the first place.

Then, as they are writing the code, the pair member who is not typing is (among other things) watching what is written to be sure that the tests they developed will fully test what they are writing. If not, then they stop and add the required tests to their test suite before continuing with the coding task. Finally, the pair uses the test suite to determine when they are finished with their programming tasks. If any of the tests fails, they have more work to do. When all their tests pass, they are ready for integration.

But Test First does not stop there. It is the driving factor during integration as well. When the pair adds their code to the growing baseline, they also add their tests to the testing baseline, which includes all the tests for each Story that has already been integrated. If *all* the tests (their own and all the others) run with no problems, then the integration was successful. If not, they must back their code and tests out of the baseline and continue working.

XP's strong quality focus gives it good mechanisms for ensuring the technical excellence of the system, whether any independent testing is done or not.

Coding Standards

XP also establishes Coding Standards to keep the technical excellence of the code high. Coding Standards are important because they facilitate many of the quality-related XP practices. For example:

- Pair Programming will only work well when both members of every pair share a common approach to coding. (Pair Programming is essentially a continuous real-time peer review, making it a strong quality-related activity.)

- Collective ownership requires that any pair be able to pick up code that is written by any other pair and quickly understand it to the point that they can make changes to it. (Collective ownership is designed to give each pair full ownership of any code they touch, encouraging the highest-quality work.)

- Refactoring (redesign of already-implemented code) will work best if the pair that is doing the refactoring can understand the existing code with ease and make changes to it with confidence. (Refactoring supports quality by encouraging programmers to improve on their work and by keeping code from becoming brittle due to continuous change.)

Although Coding Standards are a good addition to ensure technical excellence with *any* development method, they are especially important to XP because they support several of XP's other practices.

Feature-Driven Development (FDD)

FDD enhances technical excellence through inspections. FDD is described in Appendix F.

Inspections

FDD's Inspection practice is similar to ASD's Quality Review practice. They are both similar to Fagan inspections and provide significant benefits in achieving technical excellence. (Please refer to ASD's Quality Reviews, discussed earlier in this chapter, for more information on this topic.)

Lean Software Development (LD)

Four of LD's tools deal with technical excellence: Set-Based Development, Leadership, Expertise, and Testing. LD is described in Appendix G.

Amplify Learning: Tool 6, Set-Based Development

Set-Based Development is a unique way to identify the best options for solving the hard technical challenges presented by system development. This method postpones the decision, focusing instead on identifying and analyzing the set of solution options that may be applicable. The team brainstorms as many solutions to the problem as they can. They then analyze each option to see how well it suits the problem at hand as well as the system as a whole. Only after all the relevant information has been considered is the optimal solution selected for implementation.

This approach is superior to standard practice because it abrogates our tendency to commit to the first solution we think of. It replaces that tendency with a mechanism to engage the entire team in identifying the most technically excellent solution, resulting in a higher-quality system.

Empower the Team: Tool 15, Leadership

LD makes an important distinction that is often overlooked in business—that management and leadership are two distinct activities that require different skill sets. We often expect leaders to manage and managers to lead and are often disappointed because it is a rare individual who can excel at both tasks.

Management is a matter of ensuring that all of the project's pieces are in place. Managers ensure that resources are obtained and deployed at the right times and in the right amounts. They make sure that the supporting structures (like finance, human resources, and information technology) provide the required services to the project. They document plans, produce budgets, report status, and initiate corrective actions when things are not going as planned.

Leadership, on the other hand, keeps the project moving in the right direction. Leaders develop a vision of the result they hope to achieve, and they communicate that vision in a way that makes it real in the team members' imaginations. They inspire loyalty to the project and create an environment of teamwork. And they remain out front, showing the team not just by word and vision but also by their actions that they are committed to the project's success.

In short, the leader blazes the trail, and the manager paves it.

LD focuses on the important role of Leadership to make sure that the project is not just progressing, but that it is indeed progressing in the correct direction.

Empower the Team: Tool 16, Expertise

Just as Leadership and Management are important roles in the project, there are also a variety of technical roles that vary depending on the project's demands. And just as it is important that the leader and manager both have the requisite expertise, LD stresses that each of these other roles requires special expertise.

Therefore, LD urges that the project identify all the different types of expertise required to produce a technically excellent product and ensure that each of them is available to the project in one way or another (e.g., by adding full- or part-time team members or through training and mentoring existing members).

With all the required expertise available to the team, the project is much more likely to produce a technically excellent product.

Build Integrity In: Tool 20, Testing

Like DSDM's Principle 8, LD's Tool 20 puts a strong focus on verification and validation during each and every step of development. And like DSDM, LD uses the word "testing" to refer to all of the many V&V activities in which we might engage. By engaging in V&V throughout the life of the project instead of just at the end, the team will be more likely to build technical excellence into the product. (Please refer to DSDM's Principle 8 earlier in this chapter for a complete discussion of this topic.)

Scrum

Scrum addresses technical excellence through the role of the Scrum Master. Scrum is described in Appendix H.

Scrum Master

Scrum attempts to ensure technical excellence through the unique role of the Scrum Master. Although similar to LD's Leadership tool (see LD Tool 15, earlier in this chapter), the Scrum Master has a slightly different focus. Scrum states, "The Scrum Master is responsible for the success of Scrum" [1]. This is clearly a leadership role but with a strong focus on process.

When you investigate the specific things the Scrum Master is expected to do, you find that he or she mainly focuses on keeping the Scrum process tuned so it is effective and efficient for the project and on keeping all the project stakeholders faithfully following the Scrum practices. This includes the technical team, as well as management and the customer. The other main focus is communication among all stakeholders. The Scrum Master ensures that all information that should be shared among project participants is in fact shared.

Scrum ensures technical excellence by assigning this special kind of process leadership to the Scrum Master, operating on the assumption that if the project follows the Scrum process, they *will* be successful!

Adoption implications

Who can be against technical excellence? It is something to which we all aspire, and none of us is likely to want to avoid. Our question is not, "Should we seek excellence?" It is more likely to be, "How much excellence can we afford?" But even *that* is not the right question. That question is based on the assumption that producing technical excellence will result in higher costs; the more excellent the results we seek, the higher the costs we expect.

The Agile methods are based on a reality that the quality and process communities have been preaching for decades: That many of the quality-improvement activities we can engage in, far from increasing costs, will actually result in projects that are more efficient, both with money and time. As we observed while exploring the Agile practices in the first half of this chapter:

- Focusing the programmers' attention on excellence results in better code in the first place.
- Testing (V&V) at every step of the process corrects problems early and efficiently.
- Inspections improve the code upon which future increments will be built.

- Leaders keep the project moving toward its goals.
- And all these things build the team's capability for producing even more excellent work.

So, rather than asking yourself if you can afford to seek technical excellence as the Agile methods propose, ask rather if you want to experience the quality *and* time *and* money benefits that some of these practices will provide. Take a moment to consider these things and jot down some notes.

Project roles

In addition to the roles we usually expect on software projects (project manager, software developers, and testers), the Agile methods urge us to involve others. These include the customer, end user, special technical experts, a project leader (as opposed to a manager), and, in the case of Scrum, a process leader.

While the addition of each role represents some incremental cost to the project, that cost must be weighed against the benefit that each should be expected to generate for the project.

- Involving a *customer* or *end user can* mean building a product that thrills the customer, leading to repeat business. It will also likely significantly reduce the amount of rework that must be done during the project's Acceptance phase and will almost certainly avoid the worst case of litigation over project results.

- Having appropriate *technical experts* available to the team can help them avoid costly implementation errors. It can also mean that the product is structured in a more elegant way, leading to easier development and lower maintenance costs later.

- A *project leader* (distinct from the project manager) will keep the whole team inspired and focused on reaching the project goals. This will undoubtedly mean that the project will progress more rapidly toward its objectives as each team member works more effectively with his or her peers.

- And including a *process leader* on the team will ensure that the team is making the best use of the practices they adopted and that they are tuning them to their needs. This will result in a smoother project that progresses more rapidly toward successful completion.

How might you implement each of these roles on your projects to increase its technical excellence? And if you do that, then what significant savings can you expect, either by doing things correctly the first time or by avoiding the high cost of rework? Will there be people in your organization who might resist establishing any of these new roles? Will anyone rejoice? Take a moment to consider these things and jot down some notes.

Developers' attention to quality

All the Agile methods bring a new quality focus to the software developers themselves. Besides just designing and coding, each Agile method includes practices that have developers reviewing or inspecting each other's work, developing test cases for their own code, and doing a significant amount of testing (much more than most programmers generally do).

These methods seek to redefine the programmers' idea about when they have finished their work. Instead of defining their jobs in terms of coding and compiling, the Agile methods place specific requirements on programmers to produce code that does the right things in customers' eyes (validation) and to ensure that the code operates correctly (verification).

This may seem like a semantic difference, but for most programmers, it is very real. When programmers are measured by the amount of code they produce and how quickly they can get it into test (read, "throw it over the wall to the testers"), then the quality of that code becomes of secondary importance to them. But when programmers are measured by how well they satisfy the customer, quality becomes their primary goal. Fewer defects and oversights will remain after programmers are finished, avoiding much of the rework and wasted effort common on traditional projects. This means that the project can progress more quickly and costs will actually be reduced, even as quality improves!

Although none of the Agile methods addresses the subject of independent testers, there is no reason why those professionals could not still be included in your projects. The expectation, however, should be that because they will find fewer defects, they will be able to do a better and more complete job of testing, allowing you to have greater confidence in the products you ship to your customers.

Consider how the practices of the Agile methods will alter how your developers think about their jobs and their responsibility toward quality. How would this affect the quality of their code, and how might that affect your project schedule and costs? How would the adoption of an Agile method affect your testers? Take a moment to consider these things and jot down some notes.

Technical excellence

The first and most important Agile Principle that serves to keep the process Agile is that of technical excellence. Each Agile method includes practices that are aimed at excellence, and as we have discussed, when they are implemented properly, they will indeed result in more benefits beyond the technical excellence itself. They will also result in improving the team's capability to build excellent products and, at the same time, ensure that the project progresses more quickly toward its goal, and likely at lower cost.

Technical excellence does indeed enhance Agility.

Reference

[1]   Schwaber, K., and M. Beedle, *Agile Software Development with Scrum*, Upper
       Saddle River, NJ: Prentice-Hall, 2002, p. 31.

CHAPTER

21

Contents

Simplicity

In this chapter, we will discuss the second of three Agile Principles directed at keeping the process Agile.

Agile Principle

The second Agile Principle[1] that deals with keeping the process Agile is about simplicity.

Simplicity: Maximizing work not done

Simplicity—the art of maximizing the amount of work not done—is essential.

In addition to technical excellence (discussed in Chapter 20), the Agile methods avoid waste by adopting a philosophy of simplicity. As this principle states, simplicity means "maximizing the amount of work not done."

It seems obvious that you can improve your projects' performance by avoiding doing unnecessary work. But the trick lies in identifying activity that can be safely eliminated and differentiating it from activities that add value, either by directly contributing to achieving the project's goals or by mitigating project risks.

Agile practices

Although simplicity is a general theme of all Agile Methods, only two have practices that directly support this principle. We will look at three different practices, one method at a time.

1. All 12 Agile Principles are quoted and discussed in Appendix B.

Extreme Programming (XP)

XP's Simple Design practice addresses the Agile principle of Simplicity. XP is described in Appendix E.

Simple Design

Kent Beck, the author of XP, tells us, "If you believe that the future is uncertain, and you believe that you can cheaply change your mind, then putting in functionality on speculation is crazy" [1].

On an XP project, each pair of programmers implements one Story at a time. The Simple Design practice dictates that the pair must avoid taking anything into consideration that is not part of the Story they are implementing. Even if they "know" that some other Stories that will be implemented later will require a certain design, they are expected *not* to act on that information. They design their code in the simplest way possible to meet the requirements of only the current Story. They use the simplest design that will satisfy the immediate requirements.

This rule may seem wasteful. After all, why implement something with full knowledge that it will have to be changed later? Is it not always better to "do it right the first time"?

But XP's philosophy is that this rule saves far more effort than it wastes, because our anticipation of future needs is quite often inaccurate. Even when we "know" that a future Story will require a certain design, later when we are implementing that other Story, we are likely to find that our prior assumptions about the design had been inaccurate in one way or another. That will necessitate making changes to the code we wrote, and possibly to other code that has been written since that time. This kind of rework can be expensive, as it involves changing how an existing structure works.

But if XP's rule prevailed and we did *not* implement the faulty design we thought was needed, then we have avoided most of that rework. Yes, implementing the new Story may involve some rework of existing code, but in all likelihood, that rework will be less extensive, since it will be a matter of adding capability, not changing existing capability.

Because of this philosophy that it saves more effort than it spends, XP highlights Simple Design as a key practice for keeping the process Agile.

Lean Software Development (LD)

LD's first principle and first two tools deal with simplicity: The principle is "Eliminate Waste" and the tools are Seeing Waste and Value Stream Mapping. LD is described in Appendix G.

Eliminate Waste: Tool 1, Seeing Waste and Tool 2, Value Stream Mapping

This LD principle and these two tools come directly from LD's roots in lean manufacturing. LD instructs us to look for waste in each and every step of our processes and to seek more efficient ways to do the work. These tools prompt us to look in several specific places for the waste in our processes.

- *Partially Done Work*—This is very similar to XP's Simple Design practice previously discussed. When applied to software development, partially done work is usually found in the form of unimplemented or partially implemented designs. And the source of these designs is often anticipation of features we expect to implement later. Like XP, LD cautions us not to engage in such behavior.

- *Extra Processes*—This caution links directly to Tool 2, Value Stream Mapping. It leads us to identify all the steps in our processes that actually add value; that is, they directly contribute to production of the final product. The steps that do not add value should be considered for elimination. This is not to say that they *should* be eliminated, because some of these non-value-added steps are included in the process to mitigate risks. But you should consciously decide if these sorts of steps are really warranted or if they are merely wasteful.

- *Extra Features*—We in software development often provide things that the customer did not ask for. In our zeal to please the customer, we substitute our judgment for their specifications and deliver functionality they never wanted and will not use. This is wasteful, not just because of the effort we put into these useless features but also because of the increased complexity of the product and the testing and debugging it requires.

- *Task Switching*—People in software development are often assigned to multiple projects. Management does this in many cases because there is more work to do than people to do it, so rather than making the hard decision *not* to do some of the work, they spread existing people out over too much work. Often this results in overloading these people, which has negative impacts on their productivity. But even when that is not the case, such multitasking of people is still wasteful.

    When a computer switches tasks, it is simply a matter of moving data in and out of memory, resulting in a small overhead cost. But task switching is much more disruptive for people. Each time people switch tasks, they must not only shuffle papers but also must rebuild the context of what they are working on in their own memory. Not only does this result in a sizable overhead cost, it often results in mistakes and oversights due to errors in rebuilding that context.

- *Waiting*—Software projects are just like any other activity in that much time can be wasted while people wait for others to provide the necessary inputs. While it is most likely that a person will have other work they can do in the mean time, this will require task switching, the wastefulness of which we discussed in the prior bullet.

▸ *Motion*—This is somewhat related to the second bullet (about extra processes) but is aimed more at how individual tasks are carried out. Do some of the tasks your people do require extra steps that do not add value? Can some of that motion be automated? (For example, instead of the engineer printing a report, walking to the printer to fetch it, then delivering it to the reviewer's mailbox, could the system detect that the report has been generated and automatically e-mail it to the reviewer?)

▸ *Defects*—The biggest waster of time and effort in software development, as with many activities, is defects. Each and every defect must be recognized, logged, managed and tracked, corrected, closed out, and the corrected product delivered. Every defect incurs significant cost, and that cost escalates as the development life cycle progresses. It is always worthwhile to avoid generating defects. But those defects that cannot be avoided need to be caught and corrected as soon as possible, before major waste has been incurred.

Eliminating waste from your development processes will directly contribute to achieving an Agile process.

Adoption implications

Adopting the philosophy of Simplicity is not simple.

Object-Orientation

All the Agile methods assume the use of Object-Oriented (OO) design and construction. This is an important part of their focus on Simplicity because OO, when done well, results in code that is modularized and compartmentalized in ways that facilitate programmers' ability to easily use it and modify it as the system grows.

By Object-Orientation, we do not mean merely using an OO programming language (although that is critical). We mean actually understanding and using the *principles* of Object-Oriented design to build Classes and Methods that truly stand on their own. Too often, people call what they are doing "Object-Oriented" when in reality they are using an OO language to implement a nonobject design. (How many programs that were written in C++ could have been written in C just as easily?) True OO design includes the use of concepts such as information hiding and cohesiveness in identifying and building Classes.

Becoming proficient with Object-Oriented design takes more than going to a class on an OO programming language. It requires education in the principles behind OO design and mentoring by professionals who have already mastered this technology. To make the best use of any Agile method, you will need to ensure that your programmers are fully versed in true OO design and that you have at least one expert in OO on your team.

Does your staff make good use of OO design? Or do they need training and mentoring to become proficient? How well would their current level of expertise with OO support the adoption of an Agile method? Take a moment to consider these things and jot down some notes.[2]

Identifying the expendable

We all want to embrace activities that produce value and avoid wastefulness. But identifying those activities that can be eliminated without danger can be a challenge.

Value Stream Mapping (as described by LD) can be a good way to identify those activities that add value to your product and determine if the value added is worth the effort expended in those activities. But should you really eliminate an activity just because it does not show up in your value stream? Is there such a thing as an activity that does not directly add value to the product but is critically important?

Clearly, we must do many things that do not directly add value. Here are some examples of activities that do not directly add value, and yet many of them are expected by the Agile methods, not to mention being common practice on most projects.

- Planning the project;
- Updating the project plan at the beginning of each project increment;
- Establishing and maintaining a code control system;
- Reporting status to management and the customer;
- Managing risks and mitigating them;
- Defining project processes and ensuring that they are effective.

These and many other kinds of activities, though they do not add value, are important to the health of our projects, and so we do not hesitate to do them. Some keep important stakeholders informed about project progress. Others help us keep the project moving forward. And still others serve as insurance against things going wrong.

So, how can we identify activities that are truly expendable? What activities on our projects neither add direct value nor provide sufficient indirect value to justify doing them? This, of course, becomes a judgment call. And this question is at the heart of most of the arguments between the proponents of Agile methods and the proponents of traditional methods.

For many project activities, strong arguments can be made for either side. And the final decision about whether they are expendable or not will

---

2. You may want to use the "Evaluating Agile Methods Workbook" that is available to support this book. Refer to Chapter 7 for information on obtaining and using this workbook.

hinge more on the strength of the proponents' arguments and the predisposition of the decision makers than on any specific facts.

But the degree to which the decision is arguable does not mean it is unimportant. Indeed, just as there is waste involved in unnecessary activity, there is danger in not performing activities that actually are important. Are there activities on your projects that are clearly expendable? Are there others that are arguable? Take a moment to consider these things and jot down some notes.

Simplicity

Simplicity is a laudable goal. But it is not easy to identify those activities that are truly expendable. Careful consideration must be given to each activity that you may contemplate doing away with. What will be the ramifications of eliminating such an activity? Is the savings you realize from not doing it worth the cost or risk you incur?

Reference

[1]   Beck, K., *Extreme Programming Explained*, Reading, MA: Addison-Wesley Longman, 2000, p. 57.

CHAPTER

22

Contents

Retrospectives

In this chapter, we will discuss the last of three Agile Principles directed at keeping the process Agile.

Agile Principle

The last Agile Principle[1] that deals with keeping the process Agile is about retrospectives.

Regular team retrospectives

At regular intervals, the team reflects on how to become more effective, then tunes and adjusts its behavior accordingly.

Project retrospectives, also known as "postmortems" and by a few other names, have been well known but little used in software projects. A retrospective is a meeting of all project participants to consider how well the project's processes worked. Retrospectives are designed to answer the following questions:

- What worked particularly well in this project? What do we want to ensure that we replicate the next time?
- What did we try that did not work at all? What should we avoid next time?
- What risks were realized on this project? How could we have been better prepared for them?
- How were we inefficient on this project? What changes would make the next project more efficient?
- What made this project enjoyable? How can we keep morale high on future projects?

1. All 12 Agile Principles are quoted and discussed in Appendix B.

> ▸ What made this project burdensome to work on? How can we make future projects more attractive to participants?

It is generally recognized that a retrospective can provide valuable insight into what worked well and what did not on a project. But we find it difficult to take the time to do them amid all the other priorities.

Generally, the end of a project is a sprint toward the goal, and the frenetic pace of activity squeezes out anything that does not directly contribute to delivering the software. Also, it makes the most sense to hold the retrospective *after* this critical project phase so its lessons can be collected along with others. But after the product has been delivered, stakeholders are immediately drawn off into other projects. Getting everyone together for a retrospective meeting after product delivery becomes a logistical impossibility as project participants scatter to their new work.

The Agile principle that is the subject of this chapter, and the one practice of an Agile method that implements it, solve this problem in an innovative way. The principle refers to holding retrospectives "at regular intervals" and ASD is more specific than that.

Agile practice

Of the Agile Methods, only ASD has a practice that supports this Agile principle about retrospectives.

Adaptive Software Development (ASD)

ASD's Postmortems practice supports this principle about retrospectives. ASD is described in Appendix C.

Learn: Quality Review: Postmortems

ASD defines "at regular intervals" to be at the end of each increment. This solves both of the scheduling problems previously sighted by making retrospectives a regular project activity, rather than a one-time thing that is really unrelated to the project itself. And since they happen at the end of each increment, this analysis is going on approximately monthly!

Besides ensuring that the retrospectives are actually held, timing them this way has a second benefit. Project members can learn from their own experiences and make changes to their processes while those changes can still have a positive impact on the project itself. They are no longer forced to wait until the next project to try doing things differently. The retrospectives become very relevant to project participants because they are their opportunity to correct problems they are currently experiencing.

When a single retrospective meeting is held at the end of a project, it is generally a half- or full-day workshop. But when they are held often (as in

ASD), the time required for each one is generally much less. When things are going well on the project, the retrospective could be a half-hour or less, just enough time to brainstorm why things are going well.

Even when there are problems, it is unlikely that more than an hour will be required to identify them and brainstorm potential fixes. Lengthy deliberations are not really necessary, as any potential fix for a problem can be tried out in the project's next increment. If it works, the next retrospective will show that. If not, the team can seek other fixes for that problem with the additional information gained in the intervening increment.

Examining the effectiveness of the project's practices at the end of each project increment (every 2–8 weeks), rather than once at the end of the project provides a variety of benefits, including the increased likelihood that retrospectives will actually take place and the opportunity for project stakeholders to benefit from adjustments to their processes during the current project.

Adoption implications

Project retrospectives do not generally have any negative sides. Even from the most routine projects, there are plenty of things that can be learned and many opportunities for improving processes' effectiveness and efficiency. The difficulty, as discussed at the beginning of this chapter, is in deciding when to hold retrospectives so that they actually take place and can provide significant benefits.

When to hold a retrospective

To be effective, a retrospective must take place (as the name implies) after the fact. Therefore, they should be scheduled to coincide with a natural break point in the project. This allows project participants to look back over a specific time period and consider how well things worked during the activities they just completed.

While a retrospective can review activities of almost any length, one should keep in mind the natural limitations of human memory. If a retrospective is held once at the end of an 18-month project, participants are much more likely to remember and discuss things that happened recently than those that took place a year or more in the past. While it would be difficult to set a particular limit on the length of time a retrospective should cover, it seems clear that the shorter the period, the more complete people's memories will be.

This leads us to see that ASD's practice of holding a retrospective at the end of each increment (every 2–8 weeks) has the effect of ensuring that people's memories are fresh. When you are discussing things that have gone on in the past month or so, you will be unlikely to forget about anything that was particularly good or bad about how the work was done.

Have your projects held retrospectives? Would your staff embrace retrospectives, especially if they are done on a regular basis throughout the project? Take a moment to consider these things and jot down some notes.

How to capitalize on a retrospective

Often, a company will try holding project retrospectives, then abandon the practice because they see little benefit from them. Causal analysis will generally reveal that the information from the retrospectives that were held was rarely taken into consideration when new projects were being formed. When retrospectives are done only after a project is finished, there must be mechanisms in place to ensure that others (who may not have been involved in the first project) will consider the information.

ASD's practice of doing retrospectives throughout the project solves a big part of this problem. Because the project will continue after the retrospective, ideas for improvements can be easily incorporated into the project's processes. If the fixes work, then project members will be likely to continue to use the new practices on their next project, simply because they have actual experience with them, as opposed to having just thought about them.

This does not solve the problem of sharing the learning of one group of people with other groups within the organization. But that problem will be more tractable because as each project finishes, personnel will shift to other projects. People will take their experiences with them, and when their new project experiences similar problems as their old one, they will remember how that problem was solved last time. In this way, the information will be likely to diffuse through the organization. Even so, it makes sense for you to identify ways to encourage cross-pollination of process improvement ideas among project teams.

What opportunities are there for your project teams to learn from one another? What would it take to put the right mechanisms in place to ensure that process improvement information is shared readily? Take a moment to consider these things and jot down some notes.

Process change in mid-project

This entire discussion and ASD's practice make the assumption that adopting improvements to the project's processes is always a good idea. While improvement generally *is* good, one must keep in mind the fact that any change can disrupt project activities. One must consider if the disruption that is caused by the process change is worth the benefit it will bring.

Clearly, making a few minor adjustments from time to time will not be of any concern. But if the project is grappling with any significant issues, or if a proposed process change is significant, then it will be worthwhile to consciously compare the costs of making the changes with the benefits that are expected to accrue. For example, you may want to think about these sorts of questions:

- Will the process change require rework to already completed work products? If so, how much effort will that rework consume?

- Will the process change require significant behavior change for one or more people? If so, how adaptable are those people? And how willing are they to adopt these changes?

- Have you already made significant process changes on the project? If so, will the requirement for more change be a burden to the team members?

- Will the benefit you expect from the process change be significant? Is there a clear benefit to making people change right now?

Process change is always a two-edged sword. While it may provide significant benefit, it will also undoubtedly incur some cost. How accepting is your organization toward changes in process? How difficult would it be for your projects to make process adjustments in mid-project? Take a moment to consider these things and jot down some notes.

Conclusion

An important part of keeping your process Agile is to regularly take a critical look at how well that process is working and make adjustments to make it more effective. As suggested by the Agile principle about retrospectives, this is best done regularly throughout the project, rather than once at the end. This allows not only for maximum learning but also for the opportunity to tune the processes while the project is ongoing. While mid-project process changes may not *always* be optimal, there will be many cases when they are an appropriate step to take.

The Adoption Decision

In this last part of the book, we will finish up with a discussion about using what you learned as you read this book to make the right decision about the Agile methods for your organization.

In Chapter 23, "Making the Adoption Decision," we walk through the process of compiling the information you collected as you have been reading this book. We show how to use the "Evaluating Agile Methods Workbook" (if you have been recording your observations there) to roll up your collected data. And we discuss working with others in your organization to get their perspectives on this decision and lay the groundwork for the successful adoption of an Agile method.

In Chapter 24, "Adopting the New Practices," we walk through the adoption process itself. This includes customizing an Agile method to your organization's specific needs, training people in how to use it, pilot testing the method, and rolling it out to the whole organization.

Finally, in Chapter 25, "Evaluating the Effects of Your Agile Method," we discuss how to evaluate the results of adopting an Agile method. This includes both how well your projects perform using the new method and how well all the various players have adapted to their new roles.

CHAPTER

23

Contents

Making the Adoption Decision

Now that you have read about all the ways in which the Agile methods will affect your organization, it is time to compile all the information you have gathered and make some sense out of it. Because there are so many things to consider and so many ways in which the uniqueness of your organization comes into play, it is important that you take a careful approach to this decision.

Like a family deciding to adopt a child, an organization will do well to carefully consider the implications of adopting a new way of working. It *will* result in some degree of disruption for everyone in the organization, and it will require each person to make changes that they may or may not be ready to make. Your job is to weigh all the advantages you hope to realize from the adoption against the costs of making it work, and make the decision that is best for the organization's future projects.

In this chapter, we will walk through the steps you should take in making this important decision for your organization. These steps include doing your analysis, drawing conclusions, seeking the opinions of other key individuals in your organization, and creating an action plan for success.

Compiling your "Evaluating Agile Methods" workbook data

This section makes the assumption that you have been using the "Evaluating Agile Methods Workbook" introduced in Chapter 7. If you have *not* been using that tool, it may make sense for you to download the workbook and use it as you consider all the information you have collected and make your adoption decision. (Refer to Chapter 7 for instructions on downloading the workbook from the author's Web site.)

Refer to the Instructions page of the workbook for more detailed information on how to use it. If you need more help, send e-mail to EvalAgile@ASKProcess.com.

Before you begin to draw conclusions from your data, check each of the five pages of the workbook that correspond to Parts II–VI (i.e., Individuals, WorkingSW, CustCollab, RespChange, and Unstated). Make sure that the data are complete and correct, and that they reflect your appraisal after reading the prior parts of this book.

- For each practice, have you rated all the considerations about which you are able to make reasonable judgments? (Leave any consideration rating blank if you feel you cannot or should not make a judgment about it.)

- Are all the consideration ratings digits between zero and five? (If not, are you purposely using the workbook in a way that is different from its designed intent?)

- Do the consideration ratings for each practice agree with any notes you have made about it?

- Do the Practice Summaries reflect the individual Consideration ratings from which they are derived? And do they reflect how well you believe the practices would work in your organization?

- Do the Principle Summaries reflect the individual Consideration ratings from which they are derived? And do they reflect how well you believe the Agile Principles would fit into your organization?

- Does the Value Summary reflect the Principle Summaries from which it is derived? And does it reflect how well you believe the Agile Value would fit into your organization?

Do *not* move ahead with drawing conclusions until you are sure that all the data you have entered in the first five pages of the workbook are complete and correct and that they reflect your appraisal after reading this book.

Conclusions about Agile Values and Principles

The ValueSum page of your workbook is designed to help you draw conclusions about the Agile Values and Principles from the data you entered, so they can guide you in making your adoption decision. That page copies the Principle Summaries and Value Summaries from the first five pages of the workbook into one place and provides places for you to make notes about each Principle and Value, and about all of them in general.

We will now take one last look at each Principle and Value so you can review each of your ratings to draw conclusions about how well they would work in your organization.

We have come to value individuals and interactions over processes and tools

Build projects around motivated individuals. Give them the environment and support they need, and trust them to get the job done.

We discussed this Principle in Part II, Chapter 9. It speaks to building teams of professionals who have the requisite technical strength and providing an environment for them that motivates them to their best work. The point behind this Principle is that it enables the next one: Good people and a motivating environment are prerequisites for a team to begin to self-organize and produce the best possible software.

What would it take in your organization to motivate software professionals to this sort of activity? What changes in management (yourself and others) would be required? And how difficult might it be to make those changes? How well does this principle fit with your organization?

The best architectures, requirements, and designs emerge from self-organizing teams.

We discussed this Principle in Part II, Chapter 9. The various Agile methods use a variety of terms to describe this phenomenon, including "independent agents," "self-determination," and "empowered teams." ASD even includes a management model for this environment called "leadership-collaboration." The essence of this model is that self-organizing teams do not need to be managed (in the classic command-and-control sense). Rather, they need leadership and an environment that encourages collaboration among all the players, including the technical team, management, and the customer.

How much of a challenge would it be to establish the "leadership-collaboration" management model in your organization? What would it take for your management team to adapt to this totally new way of interacting with their project teams? And how would technical team members react to this new environment? How well does this principle fit with your organization?

The most efficient and effective method of conveying information to and within a development team is face-to-face conversation.

We discussed this Principle in Part II, Chapter 10. Its essence is that the richest form of communication takes place face to face, and so your projects should have a strong bias to that mode. But we also discussed the drawbacks to this communication mode, the most serious of which is that it is not persistent. And we discussed the importance of supplementing face-to-face communication with persistent records of those exchanges.

To what degree is communication in your organization face to face, as opposed to telephone, e-mail, written, and other less rich modes? To what degree can the Agile ideal of face-to-face communication be realized in your environment? And to what degree are persistent records of interactions used in your organization? How well does this principle fit with your organization?

Agile processes promote sustainable development. The sponsors, developers, and users should be able to maintain a constant pace indefinitely.

We discussed this Principle in Part II, Chapter 11. This principle is aimed at avoiding the all-too-common fact of burnout among technical staff due to the overuse of overtime. But our examination of this principle showed us that the Agile methods tend to achieve this result because of their leveling effect on the demands on project team members.

The Agile methods tend to include analysis, design, coding, testing, and, sometimes, even acceptance and delivery in each increment. Therefore, they ramp up to full force in a matter of a week or two and then continue at a steady pace through final delivery. The projects do not include the relatively slow analysis phase at the beginning or the frenetic testing phase at the end, so the pace becomes much more stable and sustainable.

What benefits would maintaining a sustainable pace bring to your organization? Would it bring any negative effects? For instance, is significant overtime considered by some people in your organization to be a badge of importance or loyalty? Are there factors in your organization that might make it difficult to cultivate or achieve the ideal of a sustainable pace? How well does this principle fit with your organization?

The unstated principle: Appropriate processes and tools

We discussed this unstated principle in Part II, Chapter 12. In spite of the fact that the first Agile Value downplays the value of processes and tools, all the Agile methods assume the support of appropriate processes and tools. The most important of these for the Agile methods are CM and automation of the build and testing processes. In Chapter 12, we discussed a variety of processes and tools that the Agile methods assume are in place.

To what degree will the processes and tools being used in your organization support an Agile method? Are there processes or tools that would have to be significantly altered or eliminated to accommodate an Agile method? And are there processes or tools that you would need to adopt to make an Agile method work well in your organization? How well does this unstated principle fit with your organization?

We have come to value individuals and interactions over processes and tools.

We discussed the relative importance of people, processes, and tools in Part II, Chapter 8. In doing so, we saw that although people are our organizations' most important assets, processes and tools are no less important.

This is true because people need the support of the appropriate processes and tools to do their best work. Therefore, we concluded that people, processes, and tools are all equally important.

After considering the four Agile Principles (and the one unstated principle) that support this first Agile Value, to what degree do you believe it could become a guiding value in your organization?

We have come to value working software over comprehensive documentation

Our highest priority is to satisfy the customer through early and continuous delivery of valuable software.

We discussed this Principle in Part III, Chapter 14. Its focus is on satisfying customers, and the chosen mechanism for doing so is to deliver software to them. What makes the Agile methods unique is their time frame for delivery "early and continuous."

The Agile methods are all built on the assumption that the best way to ensure that customers will be satisfied is to deliver increments to them often. This provides customers with the opportunity to provide feedback to the project team, and thus to direct them toward a final product that will indeed satisfy their needs.

How would the "early and continuous delivery of valuable software" work in your projects? How would you have to change the structure of your projects to do this? And what would be the effect of such a change on your relationships with your customers? How well does this principle fit with your organization?

Deliver working software frequently, from a couple of weeks to a couple of months, with a preference to the shorter time scale.

We discussed this Principle in Part III, Chapter 14. It amplifies the prior Principle by specifying how short the development cycles are expected to be. At approximately one month, Agile project cycles are significantly shorter than most of us are used to seeing. But at the same time, such short cycles would enhance our ability to manage Agile development, because they would allow us to take corrective actions on approximately a monthly basis.

What effect would such very short cycles have on your projects? What adjustments would this mode of operation require, both within your organization's management and in your relationship with your customers? How well does this principle fit with your organization?

Working software is the primary measure of progress.

We discussed this Principle in Part III, Chapter 14. We use many indirect measures on our software projects to judge our progress toward our true

e

objective of achieving working software. We need to do this because, on traditional projects, we do not deliver software often enough to use the primary objective as our measure of regular progress.

But the prior Principle corrects that problem. Since an Agile project delivers software approximately monthly, it would allow us to dispense with the indirect measures we generally use and simply track our primary objective: the software itself.

What would it take to change the way your organization thinks about progress on software projects? What impediments would there be to abandoning indirect measures of progress in favor of the direct objective itself? Can you identify any negative effects such a change would cause, either within your organization or in your relationship with your customer? How well does this principle fit with your organization?

We have come to value working software over comprehensive documentation.

We discussed the role of documents in software projects in Part III, Chapter 13. We saw that although the software itself *is* our primary objective, there are important roles that documentation plays. Depending on the nature of the project and the expected longevity of the software being built, some types of documentation may be nearly as important as "working software."

After considering the three Agile Principles that support this second Agile Value, to what degree do you believe it could become a guiding value in your organization?

We have come to value customer collaboration over contract negotiation

Business people and developers must work together daily throughout the project.

We discussed this Principle in Part IV, Chapter 16. We observed that the term "business people" is used broadly in this principle to refer to everyone outside of the technical team itself. The effect of this is that this principle calls for the technical team to interact "daily" with management, the customer, and any other stakeholder on the project. Essentially, it calls for open and regular communications on an ongoing basis.

The main way in which the Agile methods implement this is through soliciting feedback from the stakeholders (especially the customer) on every increment of software that is built. At a minimum, this would result in formal feedback no less often than bimonthly. Some Agile methods prescribe interaction much more frequently, with XP taking the extreme position of requiring a customer representative to be colocated with the development team continuously throughout the project.

How different would this level of collaboration be from your software projects' normal mode of operation? How willing would various stakeholders (especially your customers) be to invest in significantly more interaction than they have in the past? What costs would this principle incur for each stake-holder? How well does this principle fit with your organization?

We have come to value customer collaboration over contract negotiation.

We discussed the roles of customers, contracts, and collaboration in Part IV, Chapter 15. We first explored the different types of customers you may be working for. We observed that different customers may have different levels of toleration for running a project on the basis of collaboration versus contracts. Then we explored the relative roles of collaboration versus contracts in software projects and different ways in which the two must be balanced for success in any environment.

After considering the Agile Principle that supports this third Agile Value, to what degree do you believe it could become a guiding value in your organization?

We have come to value responding to change over following a plan

Welcome changing requirements, even late in development. Agile processes harness change for the customer's competitive advantage.

We discussed this Principle in Part V, Chapter 18. We observed that the Agile methods are structured with this specific thought in mind: Changes are to be expected on a software project, so the methods we use should make responding to those changes as easy as possible.

Each Agile method approaches the subject of requirements incrementally. That is, they define overall requirements only at a very broad level, with additional detail to be provided later. The details of a particular requirement are either worked out when planning the increment in which it will be implemented or left to the programmers who develop it. No matter how the requirements are defined, customers always have the sole authority to decide if the software meets their needs of not.

To what degree are the requirements for the software your projects develop identified in detail at the beginning of the project? And to what degree do those requirements tend to change over the life of the project? Would this sort of clear acceptance of change make sense in your projects? How would your customers react to projects with only high-level requirements defined upfront? How well does this principle fit with your organization?

We have come to value responding to change over following a plan.

We discussed the nature of change in software projects in Part V, Chapter 17. We determined that the most common root source of change on software projects is the learning that takes place as the project progresses.

As customers see the increments of software, they gain a stronger understanding of their own needs and what it will take to satisfy them, and they grow in their understanding of what can and should be done with the software. By the same token, developers also learn as they go through the work of building each increment. They learn about what will and will not work and which things satisfy the customer's needs. They gain insight into the ramifications of their own decisions, and they discover assumptions that have turned out to be incorrect.

This learning is a natural part of the intellectual work of developing software. And ideas for changes to be made are a natural outgrowth of this learning.

After considering the Agile Principle that supports this fourth Agile Value, to what degree do you believe it could become a guiding value in your organization?

The unstated value: Keeping the process agile

Continuous attention to technical excellence and good design enhances agility.

We discussed this Principle in Part VI, Chapter 20. All Agile methods put a high premium on ensuring the technical excellence of the software they produce. This is done through a variety of practices, including reviews and inspections, rigorous testing by developers, and leadership roles of professional experts.

The unique feature of a number of Agile methods is the degree to which developers are made responsible for the quality of their software. Rather than being responsible merely for writing software and delivering it to independent testers, Agile developers are responsible for delivering *high-quality* software. (Although none of the Agile methods provides explicitly for independent verification and validation, there is no reason why they cannot be used in that kind of an environment.)

How radical will be the shift in your developers' responsibilities if you adopt an Agile method? What will it take for them to adopt a new quality ethic in their work and not count on someone else to find problems with their software? How would this change developers' relationships with testers or other supporting groups? How well does this principle fit with your organization?

Simplicity — the art of maximizing the amount of work not done — is essential.

We discussed this Principle in Part VI, Chapter 21. We observed that the concept of avoiding wasteful activity makes perfect sense but identifying activities that are expendable is problematic. The activities we include in our development process are all there because someone at some point believed they added value.

Before eliminating any particular activity, we must take care to understand why it is there and what will be the ramification of eliminating it. We must take care to realize that while some activities directly contribute to producing software, other equally important activities serve insurance purposes. That is, they are designed to mitigate either the probability of something going wrong or the impact to the project if something *does* go wrong. (For example, most configuration management activities guard against lost work in one way or another.)

How can your projects simplify (that is, maximize the amount of work *not* done)? Are there obviously wasteful activities on your projects? Are there activities that some people would classify as being wasteful but that serve some important purpose? How difficult would it be to put simplicity into practice? How well does this principle fit with your organization?

At regular intervals, the team reflects on how to become more effective, then tunes and adjusts its behavior accordingly.

We discussed this Principle in Part VI, Chapter 22. Project retrospectives are generally embraced in theory but rarely are they actually held for software projects. The key problem tends to be related to timing: After the project is finished, when a retrospective makes the most sense, many of the project's participants have already moved on to other projects and are not available for a workshop.

The Agile methods correct this problem by calling for retrospectives "regularly" throughout the project. The easiest way to implement this would be to hold a retrospective at the end of each increment (approximately monthly). Besides ensuring that project participants are available for meetings, this schedule has the added benefit of producing process improvement ideas while the project can still benefit from them.

Does your organization currently hold project retrospectives? Would the Agile recommendation of holding retrospectives "regularly" throughout the project work in your organization? How well does this principle fit with your organization?

The unstated value: Keeping the process agile.

We discussed maintaining the effectiveness of our processes in Part VI, Chapter 19. We observed that we are usually following processes. The only question is whether we are thinking about them consciously and if they are serving our needs as well as they should. Keeping our processes effective requires some level of attention to them, which is why the Agile methods take steps to keep their processes Agile (in spite of the fact that the first Agile Value downplays the importance of process).

After considering the three Agile Principles that support this unstated Agile Value, to what degree do you believe it could become a guiding value in your organization?

Agile Values in your organization

We have just stepped through the four Agile Values (and the one unstated value) and examined the extent to which you believe each would work in your organization. What conclusion does this bring you to?

▶ Does it seem that the Agile Values and Principles can be made to work in your organization?

▶ Will any one of those Values or Principles be particularly troublesome?

▶ If you see challenges in any of them, can you envision how they can be overcome?

If it seems reasonable to adopt some form of an Agile Method in your organization, then you should continue with the next section to decide *which* Agile method you should embrace.

Conclusions about the Agile Methods and Practices

The last six pages of your workbook are designed to help you draw conclusions about each Agile Method from the data you entered. Each page copies your individual Practice ratings for a particular Agile Method from the first five pages of the workbook into one place and provides a place for you to make notes about that method.

We will now take one last look at each Agile Method so you can review each of your ratings to draw conclusions about how well they would work in your organization.

Adaptive Software Development (ASD)

Your ratings for the practices of Adaptive Software Development are compiled on the ASD page of your workbook. ASD is described in Appendix C.

Project Stakeholders as Independent Agents—On an ASD project, there is no hierarchy. The development team, management, and customer are treated as peers.

Adaptive (Leadership-Collaboration) Management Model—Because of the independent agent practice (just described), management of an ASD project is a matter of leadership and collaboration, as opposed to the more traditional command and control.

Adaptive Life Cycle—ASD's incremental development process is characterized by the Learning Loop, which cycles through the Speculate, Collaborate, and Learn phases.

Speculate: Project Initiation and Adaptive Cycle Planning—ASD calls planning "Speculation." Initial planning involves setting the project mission and vision and then each increment of the project begins with "speculation" about what will be done during that increment.

Learn: Quality Review: Customer Focus Group Reviews—The first step in the Quality Review phase of each increment of an ASD project is this review, during which the customer determines what of value has been developed during the just-finished increment of the project.

Learn: Quality Review: Software Inspections—The second step in the Quality Review phase of each increment of an ASD project is this review, during which the development team inspects each other's work.

Learn: Quality Review: Postmortems—The last step in the Quality Review phase of each increment of an ASD project is this review, during which stakeholders discuss the process they are using and determine how it may be improved.

After considering ASD's practices, how appropriate do you believe this Agile method would be for your organization?

Dynamic Systems Development Method (DSDM)

Your ratings for the practices of Dynamic Systems Development Method are compiled on the DSDM page of your workbook. DSDM is described in Appendix D.

Principle 1: Active user involvement is imperative.—DSDM projects require more involvement by the true end users of the system being developed than do most traditional projects.

Principle 2: DSDM teams must be empowered to make decisions.—The DSDM development team is given broad authority to make the day-to-day decisions on the project.

Principle 3: The focus is on frequent delivery of products.—Delivering product to the customer on a regular basis is a key part of DSDM.

Principle 4: Fitness for business purpose is the essential criterion for acceptance of deliverables.—The customer is the final authority on whether or not the product as it was delivered is appropriate to his or her needs.

Principle 5: Iterative and incremental development is necessary to converge on an accurate business solution.—Because it assumes that system details cannot be known upfront, DSDM uses incremental development as the means for developers and the customer to arrive at a satisfactory product.

Principle 6: All changes during development are reversible.—DSDM encourages developers to improve code at any time by reminding them that changes can always be backed out.

Principle 7: Requirements are baselined at a high level.—DSDM is the only Agile method that establishes a requirements baseline, but that baseline consists only of a broad description of the project's goals. The detailed requirements are left for the customer and developers to work out during incremental development.

Principle 8: Testing is integrated throughout the life cycle.—Verification and validation should take place during all phases of a DSDM project, not just at the end.

Principle 9: A collaborative and cooperative approach between all stakeholders is essential.—In order for DSDM to work as designed, the development team, customer, and management must collaborate closely.

After considering DSDM's practices, how appropriate do you believe this Agile method would be for your organization?

Extreme Programming (XP)

Your ratings for the practices of Extreme Programming are compiled on the XP page of your workbook. XP is described in Appendix E.

The Planning Game—The development team, customer, and management collaborate at the beginning of each increment of development to plan that increment.

Small Releases—Each increment of an XP project should be small, delivering a little functionality and taking as short a period of time as possible (2–8 weeks).

Metaphor—This overall idea of what the system under development will be like is as close to a requirements statement as XP gets. Each feature is described by a Story that fits on a 3x5-inch card.

Simple Design—XP requires programmers to use the simplest possible design that will meet the current need. They should not account for future needs.

Test First—Before a pair of programmers writes any code, they must first write the automated tests that will be required to verify it.

Refactoring—XP encourages programmers to redesign programs any time they recognize an opportunity to improve them.

Pair Programming—All technical work is done by two people working together.

Collective Ownership—Individuals do not own code, rather all team members change any code they believe they need to change when implementing a Story.

Continuous Integration—As each pair of programmers completes work on each Story, they integrate it into the growing system, so integration is going on almost continuously.

40-Hour Week—Overtime should be rare and can never happen two weeks in a row.

On-Site Customer—A customer representative who is authorized to make decisions about the project must be on-site with the development team at all times.

Coding Standards—The XP team should adopt coding standards to facilitate other practices (e.g., Pair Programming, collective ownership).

Facilities Strategy—The XP team should be located together in a single room with appropriate spaces for Pair Programming and regular interaction among team members.

After considering XP's practices, how appropriate do you believe this Agile method would be for your organization?

Feature-Driven Development (FDD)

Your ratings for the practices of Feature-Driven Development are compiled on the FDD page of your workbook. FDD is described in Appendix F.

Domain Object Modeling—An FDD project begins with the construction of a model of the objects in the system to be built, then each increment of development revisits the model and updates it based on what has been learned.

Developing by Feature—Development is done one feature at a time. Each increment of development is defined by the list of features to be included in that increment.

Class (Code) Ownership—A single programmer owns each class, and that person is the only one who is allowed to change it.

Feature Teams—Each feature is developed by the owners of all the classes that will be affected by implementation of that feature.

Inspections—All development work products are inspected by other team members.

Regular Build Schedule—Builds of the growing system are done on a regular basis (though FDD does not prescribe how often that should be).

Configuration Management—FDD reminds us that good CM tools and processes are important to project success.

Reporting/Visibility of Results—An FDD team reports progress as the number of features completed versus the number remaining and objectively computes percent-complete for partially-completed features.

After considering FDD's practices, how appropriate do you believe this Agile method would be for your organization?

Lean Software Development (LD)

Your ratings for the practices of Lean Software Development are compiled on the LD page of your workbook. LD is described in Appendix G.

Eliminate Waste

Tool 1: Seeing Waste—Look for waste in all parts of your development process.

Tool 2: Value Stream Mapping—Identify all the steps in your process that add value to the product (and those that do not).

Amplify Learning

Tool 3: Feedback—Design your process to provide feedback as often as possible.

Tool 4: Iterations—Use iterative time-boxed development.

Tool 5: Synchronization—Use appropriate mechanisms to synchronize people's work.

Tool 6: Set-Based Development—When dealing with a problem, think about the solution *space* instead of specific solutions.

Decide as Late as Possible

Tool 7: Options Thinking—By incurring some added cost, you can sometimes delay making decisions.

Tool 8: The Last Responsible Moment—Delay commitment to a decision until the moment at which failing to make a decision eliminates an important alternative.

Tool 9: Making Decisions—Make decisions by applying an appropriate set of rules.

Deliver as Fast as Possible

Tool 10: Pull Systems—Establish an environment that provides automatic prompting for what people should do.

Tool 11: Queuing Theory—Use queuing theory to analyze all bottlenecks in your software process and determine ways to minimize the cycle time.

Tool 12: Cost of Delay—Use financial models to allow all stakeholders to make appropriate trade-off decisions.

Empower the Team

Tool 13: Self-Determination—The people who do the work are in the best position to improve their processes and eliminate waste.

Tool 14: Motivation—Motivating a project team to perform well has many dimensions.

Tool 15: Leadership—A successful team needs both project management and technical leadership.

Tool 16: Expertise—Every software project requires a variety of expertise.

Build Integrity In

Tool 17: Perceived Integrity—Does the customer perceive the system to be useful and well designed?

Tool 18: Conceptual Integrity—An important component of Perceived Integrity. Was the system built correctly?

Tool 19: Refactoring—Redesign of the system to improve its structure and avoid brittle code.

Tool 20: Testing—Both validation (ensuring the right system is built) and verification (ensuring the system is built right) must be done throughout the development process.

See the Whole

Tool 21: Measurements—Avoid measurement dysfunction and focus measurement at higher-level aggregations of data.

Tool 22: Contracts—A variety of contractual arrangements are possible, and each has good and bad points.

After considering LD's practices, how appropriate do you believe this Agile method would be for your organization?

Scrum

Your ratings for the practices of Scrum are compiled on the Scrum page of your workbook. Scrum is described in Appendix H.

The Scrum Master—This individual has a leadership role in ensuring that the team is making the best use of Scrum and that the processes are tailored to the team's needs.

Product Backlog—The list of features waiting to be implemented is a good measure of progress as it grows and shrinks during the project.

Scrum Teams—The development team freely commits to the goals of the project and to the goal of each Sprint.

Daily Scrum Meetings—Short (15 minute) stand-up team meetings to synchronize everyone's work are held each day.

Sprint Planning Meeting—A meeting of all stakeholders to establish the goal and backlog for a Sprint is the first step of each Sprint.

Sprint—A 30-day increment of the project that has a goal and a backlog of features to be implemented.

Sprint Review—A meeting of the project stakeholders to examine and discuss the results of a Sprint is the last step of each Sprint.

After considering Scrum's practices, how appropriate do you believe this Agile method would be for your organization?

The Agile Methods in your organization

We have just stepped through the six Agile Methods and examined the extent to which you believe each would work in your organization. What final conclusion does this bring you to?

- Are you ready to adopt one of the Agile methods?
- Have you identified a specific Agile Method that would be best for your organization?
- Do you need to customize one of the Agile methods to meet your organization's constraints and needs?
- Would you have to "roll your own" Agile method by choosing from the Practices of the various Agile methods we have explored?
- Would an Agile method not make sense for your organization at this time?

The decision about adopting an Agile method is not an easy one because there are so many variables to consider and there is a wide spectrum of options available to you. Take your time to settle on a decision that you believe is best for your organization.

Marketing your conclusions in your organization

Although making your adoption decision is difficult, it is not the end of the matter. You will need to get input and support for your decision from the knowledgeable and influential people in your organization. This includes the managers above and below you in the hierarchy, your peer managers (to the extent they are affected by the changes), and members of your technical teams.

Changing the way an organization works is never as straightforward as we expect it to be. Even if you are the most senior executive in the company, simply decreeing "thou shalt" goes only so far. People will raise concerns and questions that you have not yet considered. And there will be resistance to the change from people whom you expected would embrace it. For these reasons (and many more), our first step is to "market" our decision to everyone in the organization.

Just as with marketing a new product, marketing a change to an organization involves identifying who is the "buyer" and what is the "value proposition."

> ▸ The "buyer" in any organizational change effort is each and every person who must change his or her behavior as a result of the change. Adopting an Agile method will result in a large number of "buyers," including members of management, the technical staff, and even some individuals at your customers' organizations. You must take care to address each buyer in a way that will generate interest in and support for the new Agile method.

> ▸ The "value proposition" describes the way in which each buyer will derive value from adopting the change. You can postulate the value that you *expect* each buyer will derive, but only each person can decide what is of value to him or her. So identifying the true value proposition for each person will involve a bit of "market research."

This "market research" takes the form of seeking their input on the decision. Even if you already have made up your mind, the best approach is to present the decision as a work-in-progress. "I believe this is what we should do. This is why I believe this. What do you think about it? Did I miss anything in my analysis?"

By asking for their input in this way, you will do several things.

> ▸ First, you will give them a stake in the decision. Rather than something that was forced on them, it is now a decision into which they had input. (You do not have to do what they say for them to feel that they had input.)

> ▸ Second, you will undoubtedly learn a lot. It is unlikely that you have thought of everything in your analysis, so the questions and concerns people raise could be important points for you to consider. You may even find that you will change your decision in some way due to this

input. (This is good, because it results in a better decision for the organization!)

> Third, you will learn about each person's value proposition. You will see if your assumptions about what is of value to them is correct, and, if not, you will get important insight into their values.

> Then, because of the first three points, you will gain more of their support for the decision. Because they felt involved, provided input that you found valuable, and gave you an understanding of how they might find value in it, they will embrace the change more readily than might have been the case.

This "marketing" of your decision is not magic. It will not prevent problems or resistance to the changes that must be made. But it *will* result in a much higher likelihood that your decision will be the right one and that it will be accepted in the organization.

Agreeing together on an action plan

The final step is to create an action plan for adopting the new Agile method. This plan fleshes out all the steps you must take to move from where you are (having just made a decision) to successful implementation of an Agile method. As with "marketing" the change to the organization, this plan is best created with the participation and input of the people who will be implementing it.

Refer to Chapters 24 and 25 for suggestions about all the things that this plan should take into consideration. Then work with all the stakeholders in the organization to come up with an action plan that they can support and execute against. Then all of you can work together to make your vision of adopting an Agile method a reality.

CHAPTER

24

Contents

Adopting New Practices

Once the decision to adopt a new way of working has been made, all that is left is to "just do it," right? Yes, but this phase of your journey may turn out to be the most challenging of all. At this point, you will move beyond words and ideas and concepts, to begin to change what people actually *do* on a daily basis. Even when support for such a change is strong, actually following through with it can still be difficult.

In this chapter, we discuss all the activities that will be required to be successful in making the changes you have decided to make. We will discuss customizing your chosen Agile method to the specific needs of your organization, training the people who will be affected by the change, running pilot tests to determine how well the new method performs, and finally rolling the change out to your entire organization. But first, we will address an overarching topic, probably the single most important activity of them all: communication.

Three critical things to do: communicate, communicate, communicate

With all the activity that will be going on, and with so many people being affected in one way or another, the success of your change effort will hinge on how well, and how often, you share information with everyone who eventually will be affected by it. People need to know that the effort is real, what it is all about, why it is happening, and how it will affect them. In addition, they will need to hear about it again and again so that they remember it is happening, see that progress is being made, see the benefits that have accrued so far, and anticipate how they will next be affected.

1. Communicate while making the decision.

The first phase of communication was discussed in Chapter 23, when we talked about marketing the decision to the organization by soliciting people's input to it. This phase is critical to the organization's initial acceptance of the change because it gives everyone a sense of ownership in the decision. When I have been asked to provide my opinion on something, I am more likely to support the resulting decision, even if some of my suggestions were ultimately not used.

This phase of communication lays the groundwork for successful implementation by providing two key ingredients:

▸ Information you may not have considered (resulting in a better decision;

▸ Buy-in to the decision by the people who were involved in making it (the people who will be key in making it work).

2. Communicate about the decision you made.

The second phase of communication is to announce that the decision has been made. This works best as a big splashy event, much like the announcement you might make about a product your company will soon put on the market. Like a big marketing splash, the purpose of such an event is to generate buzz within the organization and get everyone excited about the change. To achieve this, you may want to include in the event things such as these:

▸ *Make it special.* If your company has a way of celebrating special events, then use a similar mechanism for this announcement. If you have no such traditions, then develop a unique approach, something that the organization has never done before. Maybe hold a two-hour picnic lunch in the parking lot (provide the food from company funds and count the extra hour as regular work time for everyone who attends).

▸ *Include everyone.* Anyone who will be even marginally affected by the change *must* be invited. And since it may be difficult to imagine all the secondary impacts of the change, you should err on the side of inviting people who will actually not be affected by it. It may even make sense to invite *everyone* in the department, the division, or the company. That way you will not miss anyone, and everyone will know that this really *is* a big deal!

▸ *Express enthusiasm.* You have made this decision because you believe it is important to the organization. Wear your enthusiasm on your sleeve. Let your excitement show. Talk about it, both in your formal address to the staff and in your casual conversations with them. Try to excite enthusiasm for the change in everyone else.

 ‣ *Explain why.* You have just spent significant effort coming to a well-reasoned conclusion. Make it clear to everyone what your reasoning was, so they can join you in supporting the decision. Will it solve problems? Will it make the company more competitive? Will it shorten development time? Will it reduce overtime? Will it improve profitability? Will it provide competitive advantage? Will it please shareholders? Is it responsive to the staff's suggestions? Will it make their jobs more secure? Will it keep the company in business? Provide them with as many reasons as possible to evoke their support for the decision.

 ‣ *Tell them what to expect.* Outline the plan to the extent that it is known, and explain what you expect will happen as the effort progresses. Provide a reasonable level of detail as it is currently known, and if you have yet to complete the detailed planning, tell them when the plan will finally be available. Do not get bogged down in excessive detail; provide a general picture of the effort and let them know where they can get more detail if they so desire.

 ‣ *Allay their fears.* Making any significant change will raise questions and fears in people's minds. You may already know what some of those fears are, so directly address them now. But you most assuredly *do not* know about all of them, so tell them how they will be involved in the change process, where they can get more information, where to express their fears, and how to provide suggestions for the effort. Most critically, make it clear that you intend for this change to be beneficial for everyone, and you want to address all concerns they might have about it.

 ‣ *Celebrate.* Make the event fun and memorable for everyone. You want them to have a positive impression of the change that will be taking place, so start it off with a positive experience.

 ‣ *Document the event.* Create a lasting record of the announcement event. (An intranet Web page with pictures and the text of all speeches would be a great way to do this!) This will provide a touchstone for those who attended — a place to which they can return whenever they want to relive the event and remind themselves about why the change effort is being done. But this also provides a way for those who could not attend the event to experience some of the celebration and read about what is happening and why. This will be invaluable for those who were traveling or out sick the day of the event, or for people who are hired after it takes place.

3. Communicate regularly about the status of the change effort.

If you allow any significant period of time to pass without talking about the change effort, people will either forget about it altogether or begin to wonder if it has been dropped or if some other priority has overtaken it in your mind. Therefore, you should establish a schedule (e.g., monthly) and provide status updates on that regular schedule.

These status updates need not be elaborate. They should communicate where the effort stands against the plan. And if the plan or any other significant element of the effort has been revised, the pertinent information should be shared.

You should post the status information along with any new plans or other updates in the same way you documented the original announcement. Provide a place where any interested person can go to find the most current information about the effort.

When something important takes place in the change effort, do not wait until the next scheduled status update to tell everyone about it. Celebrate every victory and savor every step forward. And by all means, praise the effort that each contributor has made, and thank key individuals for their actions. If the progress is significant, show your excitement and seek to rekindle that excitement among the staff.

When you achieve a critical milestone (and especially at the end of the effort), celebrate again. Hold an event like the original announcement and thank all the contributors for their contributions to the effort's success. Be liberal in your praise for work well done, and make it clear that you are celebrating a significant milestone for the organization.

Crafting your custom Agile Method

Even if you decide to implement one of the Agile methods "off the shelf," there will still be ways you will have to customize it to meet your organization's needs. This customization must be done carefully to enhance the method's likelihood of success in your organization.

Customization will require the participation of a number of key players.

> ▸ *An expert.* You will want to involve someone who has experience with applying the method you have chosen in a real organization. This person will bring his or her prior experience to the project and provide a perspective that most of those who are involved will lack. Whether this person is an external consultant, a newly hired person, or an existing employee, his or her active participation in the effort is critical.

> ▸ *Management.* Both you as the sponsoring manager and the other affected managers will need to be involved to ensure that the customizations that are implemented will work with the organization's constraints. In addition, each of you must verify that he or she is ready and able to change the management activities as required by the new way of working. (This is not an insignificant point, so all the managers must consider it carefully!)

▸ *Technical staff.* Naturally, the people who will be most strongly affected by an Agile method will be the teams of technical people who develop the software. Appropriate members and opinion leaders must be involved in ensuring that development projects will operate as efficiently as you hope they will.

▸ *Customer.* It is unusual to include any customer personnel in an internal change effort. But in this case, a customer representative must be involved because adopting an Agile method will affect them as well. You need to be sure that the ways in which your relationship and interactions with your customers will change will be acceptable to them.

Although the customization step is important, everyone who is involved must keep in mind that it represents only the beginning of the process. The Agile method as you decide to implement it will be pilot tested (see the next section), and many changes will likely be adopted as a result of what is learned. The purpose of the customization step is merely to provide a viable method to pilot test.

When the customization step is complete, celebrate the milestone by announcing to the organization that this important activity was successful and that the pilot test will soon begin. Identify the pilot group(s) and give them credit for the effort they will expend in this test of the new method. You are making progress; celebrate this first significant step!

Training those who will be affected

Before the pilot test can begin, all the individuals who will be involved must be trained in the new method. Although the details of the training will differ depending on each person's role in the Agile method, this training should follow a similar pattern for everyone:

1. Reiterate a summary of the information from the initial announcement (discussed at the beginning of this chapter). Provide context for what they are about to learn, and show where the change effort stands against the plan. Make it clear that the training is for a pilot test, and that you expect the participants to make suggestions for improvements as a part of that test.

2. Provide a high-level overview of the development process that will be used. Contrast it to the existing process, and highlight what will change and what will remain the same.

3. Point out where the people who perform each role are involved in the new process. What will they do? What information will they handle? What are their responsibilities and authority? With whom will they interact in doing these things?

4.   Instruct each person in the details of his or her new responsibilities. Give them step-by-step instructions, explain why each step is important, and answer every question they may have.

5.   Assure them that an appropriately knowledgeable individual will be available to answer their inevitable questions and provide guidance as they perform their new tasks the first few times.

6.   Give everyone a written copy of all that they have learned in the training. Provide reference materials that will help them become proficient in their new tasks as quickly as possible.

Then, begin to use the new method immediately after the training. Allow people to gain practical experience with using the information they received before they can forget it.

Pilot testing the new method

A successful pilot test will involve many activities.

Just-in-time training

It is often best to provide "just-in-time" training in conjunction with the first trial of an activity. For example, if you are adopting XP, then the training session on the Planning Game may be done as part of the first Planning Game that the pilot team holds. The trainer would begin by providing detailed explanations about what the team will be doing, and then he or she might observe or actively coach the Planning Game meeting. Finally, the trainer could provide feedback about the parts of the meeting that went well and those that could be improved the next time.

Expert on call

As the organization uses the new method, a knowledgeable person should regularly touch base with all those involved to see how the method is working out, provide encouragement in its use, and answer questions and provide pointers on its use. This person should also encourage individuals to think about ways in which the method could be improved and submit any such ideas for consideration. A key source of these improvement ideas would be the retrospectives or postmortem reviews that the Agile projects should be holding on a regular basis.

Celebrate project milestones

As each pilot project achieves a milestone in using the new method, celebrate their achievement. Tell the organization about the progress they are making and discuss any benefits they have experienced. Use each success to reinforce the organization's commitment to the new method.

Improving the Agile Method

As suggestions for improvements are made, be sure they are captured and recorded. On some regular basis, a group of people should deliberate about each one and select those that merit implementation. Some changes should be tried out on the ongoing pilot projects. But others (the more major ones) should wait until the pilot is finished to avoid disrupting the project.

At the end of the pilot test, the organization must decide on the next steps to take, based on the experiences of the pilot project(s). Refer to Chapter 25 for suggestions about the things you may want to consider in making this decision. You may decide to take actions like these:

› Roll the new method out to the whole organization as it was tested, or with minor changes.

› Make some major changes to the method and run another pilot test (after the necessary re-training).

› Change direction (e.g., switching to a different Agile method) and backtrack to the customization phase.

› Abandon the change effort altogether.

Rolling it out to the whole organization

Successful completion of the pilot test phase means you are ready to use the new method in all the organization's software projects. This calls for celebration of yet another important milestone! All the preliminary work is done; we are ready to embrace our new method completely!

This rollout phase looks very much like the training and pilot test phases we just discussed, but it is done on a much larger scale and may have to be phased over time (depending on the size and scope of the organization). The first step is to plan the rollout. It is unlikely that all your software groups will be ready and able to adopt a new method at the same time, so you must establish a schedule for when the method will be rolled out to each group. This plan must provide for training, coaching, and all the other support that each project will require in a way that will avoid overloading those who provide these services.

The next job is to rework the training from the training phase. The first part of the training (setting the context for it) should be retained, but, naturally, it should be updated to indicate the actual status of the change effort. (After the rollout phase is complete, this part of the training can be removed or significantly modified to provide the appropriate context for new employees joining an organization that uses an Agile method.) The remainder of the training may need to be revised to make it more effective or accommodate changes to the method.

As each software group is ready to switch to the new method, they must be trained, coached, and supported in much the same way as the pilot projects were (described in the previous section). As with the pilot projects, these groups should also be encouraged to think about how the method can be improved to better meet their needs. As we will discuss at the end of Chapter 25, continuously improving your Agile method will be the key to ensuring that is remains effective.

Finally, when all the projects have adopted the new method and are using it to develop software, you are ready for your final celebration. As we said in step 3 of the Communication section, this is a time for *real* celebration. The organization took on an important and difficult project to change the way it works, and that project has now come to fruition. Celebrate this major success. You and your entire staff deserve it!

CHAPTER

25

Contents

Evaluating the Effects of Your Agile Method

This final chapter discusses the things you should take into consideration as you evaluate the effectiveness of the Agile method you have adopted. As suggested in Chapter 24, you may want to use these criteria at the end of the pilot test phase to decide if you will go forward with rolling the new method out to the whole organization. But you should also perform this evaluation after the Agile method has been integrated into how your organization works, as well as on a regular basis thereafter.

Project performance

The most important criterion for success is the new method's effect on how well your projects perform. There are a variety of ways in which project performance can be measured, and for each organization, each one holds a different significance. You must decide which of these performance questions is most important in your organization.

How has your adoption of an Agile method affected these measures?

- *Schedule performance.* (See equation in Figure 25.1.) Has your Agile method helped your projects deliver software more in line with scheduled expectations? If you adopted time boxing, has this mechanism worked well for you? Have any of the Agile practices been particularly helpful or problematic from a schedule perspective?

- *Budget performance.* (See equation in Figure 25.2.) Has your Agile method helped your projects stay within their budget constraints? Have any of the Agile practices been particularly helpful or problematic from a budget perspective?

Schedule performance

$$SP = \frac{\text{Actual project length in weeks}}{\text{Planned project length in weeks}}$$

SP > 1.00 – Schedule overrun
SP = 1.00 – Exactly on schedule
SP < 1.00 – Schedule underrun

Figure 25.1   Schedule performance equation.

Budget performance

$$BP = \frac{\text{Actual project cost}}{\text{Planned project cost}}$$

BP > 1.00 – Cost overrun
BP = 1.00 – Exactly on budget
BP < 1.00 – Cost underrun

Figure 25.2   Budget performance equation.

‣ *Quality performance.* (See equation in Figure 25.3.) Has your Agile method improved the quality of the software your projects produce? Has independent testing (or customer acceptance testing) encountered fewer or less serious problems? Have problem reports from the field been reduced in number or severity? Have any of the Agile practices been particularly helpful or problematic from a quality perspective?

‣ *Cycle time.* (See equation in Figure 25.4.) Has your Agile method reduced the time your projects require to transform a concept into delivered software? Are your projects able to move quickly toward a good solution? Have any of the Agile practices been particularly helpful or problematic from a cycle-time perspective?

‣ *Productivity.* (See equation in Figure 25.5.) Has your Agile method improved productivity on your projects? Are your technical staff members wasting less time in administrative work and rework? Are

Quality performance

$$QP = \frac{\text{Defects reported in 1st year of use}}{\text{Size of product*}}$$

*Possible size measurements:
-Lines of code
-Function points
-Web pages

Figure 25.3   Quality performance equation.

Cycle time

$$CT = \frac{\text{Actual project length in weeks}}{\text{Size of product*}}$$

*Possible size measurements:
-Lines of code
-Function points
-Web pages

Figure 25.4   Cycle time equation.

Productivity

$$Pr = \frac{\text{Actual project effort in person-weeks}}{\text{Size of product*}}$$

*Possible size measurements:
-Lines of code
-Function points
-Web pages

Figure 25.5   Productivity equation.

they able to produce more software with the same resources? Have any of the Agile practices been particularly helpful or problematic from a productivity perspective?

Which measures of project performance are most important in your organization? Have those particular measures benefited from your Agile method? If not, are there actions you can take to bring your projects' performance more in line with your expectations and the organization's needs?

Management acceptance

How well have you and the rest of the management team adjusted to the new way of running projects? Are you and they able to understand the status of projects on a timely basis? And is appropriate information available to be able to take corrective action when things are going wrong?

- Have project teams embraced their new empowerment and shown the ability to self-organize and self-manage?
- Have managers been willing to cede authority to project teams and allow them to self-manage?
- How well has incremental planning worked? Do project plans evolve appropriately over time?

- Does defining requirements only at a high level provide an appropriate basis for managing the project? Have requirements changes been a destabilizing factor?

- Has incremental development worked well? What has been the effect of the short cycles or time-boxing on your ability to manage projects?

- Has the bias toward face-to-face communication and away from documents had a positive or negative impact on project management?

- Are staffing levels easier to manage? Has project demand for staff effort leveled off? Are your people working less overtime?

- Have your management tools and processes worked well with the new methods? If you eliminated or reworked some of them, have there been any negative effects?

- Have regular project retrospectives or postmortems provided insights into how management practices can be improved?

Have the new management structure and mechanisms produced the benefits that had been anticipated? Are there ways in which they can be made more effective in the organization?

Customer relationship

How have your organization's relationships with customers changed? Has the Agile method resulted in better working relationships?

- Have your customers been willing to engage in the additional interaction with the projects that may have been required? Have they experienced benefits from doing so?

- How comfortable are your customers with the idea of defining requirements only at a high level, and then working out the details during the project?

- How have your customers reacted to the changes in your organization's willingness to embrace requirements changes throughout the life of the project? Have you seen an increase in the volume of changes?

- Have your customers accepted the incremental planning model? Are they comfortable with the level of planning being done on your projects?

- Has incremental development, short development cycles, or time-boxing provided benefits to your customers?

- Do your customers like being able to view and provide feedback on product increments so often?

- Have your customers noticed improvements in the quality of the programs you deliver to them?

> ▸ Have regular project retrospectives or postmortems provided insights into how your customer relationships can be improved?

Have the changes you made resulted in happier customers and better customer satisfaction?

Team satisfaction

How have your technical personnel adapted to the new working environment?

> ▸ Have they embraced the opportunity to self-organize and self-manage? Have they done a good job of taking control of their projects and making them work well?
>
> ▸ Has your more collaborative management model motivated them to greater ownership of their projects? (This assumes your managers have successfully adopted such a model!)
>
> ▸ Has incremental planning helped them maintain control over their projects?
>
> ▸ Have they embraced incremental development, short cycles, time-boxing, and continuous integration and exploited them for their projects' benefit?
>
> ▸ Do they find that closer interaction with the customer has helped them do a better job?
>
> ▸ Does the customer's evaluation of each increment help the team produce a product that satisfies the customer?
>
> ▸ Has defining requirements only at a high level, then working out the details during the project proven to be effective for them?
>
> ▸ Has more face-to-face communication and fewer documents helped them be more efficient?
>
> ▸ Have they worked less overtime?
>
> ▸ Have the tool and process changes (e.g., CM) been helpful to them?
>
> ▸ If they have used Pair Programming or a new code ownership model, have these things worked well?
>
> ▸ Has refactoring been used effectively? Has it resulted in better software?
>
> ▸ Have they accepted greater responsibility for the quality of their software? Have they become effective testers of their own code?
>
> ▸ Have regular project retrospectives or postmortems provided insights into how your teams can become more effective?

Have all these things contributed to greater job satisfaction among your technical staff?

Continuously improving your Agile Method

Adopting a new Agile method has (hopefully) produced many benefits for your organization. But those benefits do not mark the end of the road. Regardless of how positive your experience has been, there remain ways in which your development processes can be improved. There are opportunities to improve the satisfaction of your customers, managers, and staff. You can improve the quality of the software you produce. And there are many ways that you can reduce costs and improve schedule performance.

Establishing a culture of continuous process improvement is not difficult. Holding retrospectives on your projects on a regular basis is an important start, because they tend to lead your staff to think about the processes they use, and how to make them better. But you must build on that start by embracing what you learn through them. Retrospectives that result in no improvements will become extinct very quickly. But using them to make life better for your project teams will ensure that they continue to be a source of great ideas.

The other part of a culture of continuous improvement lies in how you react to disasters. Our normal reaction is to try to find out who was at fault, assign blame, and fix the person (or fire them). A different approach will yield much sweeter fruit. In this approach, you focus not on the people, but on the processes. Find out which process was at fault and fix the process. This way, each disaster will result in a smoother-operating organization with fewer opportunities for things to go wrong.

Whether you have adopted a new Agile method, decided to adopt a more traditional method, or even stay with what you currently use, the attention you have paid to the questions raised in this book will yield big returns. And as you continue to pay attention to these things, your software development projects will grow more and more effective.

APPENDIX

Introduction

These appendixes provide information about each of the Agile Methods that the reader may find useful.

The first two appendixes provide the full text of the Agile Manifesto and its underlying principles. They include some clarifying commentary on those topics, along with references where the interested reader may find additional information.

- Appendix A: The Agile Manifesto.
- Appendix B: The 12 Principles of Agile Methods.

Each of the remaining appendixes provides a high-level description of one of the Agile Methods. These descriptions are designed to provide a broad understanding of each method and the practices that comprise it. Each appendix also includes references where the interested reader may find additional information.

- Appendix C: Adaptive Software Development.
- Appendix D: Dynamic Systems Development Method.
- Appendix E: Extreme Programming.
- Appendix F: Feature-Driven Development.
- Appendix G: Lean Software Development.
- Appendix H: Scrum.

The Agile Manifesto

This appendix provides the full text of the Agile Manifesto along with some commentary and references where the interested reader may find additional information.

The Agile Manifesto
We are uncovering better ways of developing software
by doing it and helping others to do it.
Through this work we have come to value:
Individuals and interactions over processes and tools.
Working software over comprehensive documentation.
Customer collaboration over contract negotiation.
Responding to change over following a plan.
That is, while there is value in the items on the right,
we value the items on the left more.

The Agile Manifesto provides a good focal point for examining the Agile methods and understanding the basis on which they were built. It was developed in February 2001 by 17[1] of the leading developers and users of Agile methods.[2] These people met, according to Alistair Cockburn, "to see whether there was anything in common among the various light methodologies" [1]. The Manifesto documents the common values that those people identified.

The concluding sentence in the Manifesto is important. The authors of the Manifesto were *not* saying that processes, tools, documentation, contracts, and plans are worthless. To the contrary, each Agile method addresses these items (with the

---

1. The 17 people were Kent Beck, Mike Beedle, Arie van Bennekum, Alistair Cockburn, Ward Cunningham, Martin Fowler, James Grenning, Jim Highsmith, Andrew Hunt, Ron Jeffries, Jon Kern, Brian Marick, Robert C. Martin, Stephen J. Mellor, Ken Schwaber, Jeff Sutherland, and Dave Thomas.

2. The Agile methods represented were ASD, Crystal, DSDM, XP, FDD, Scrum, and "pragmatic programming."

exception of contracts) and specifies how they should be managed and used. Rather than discounting the value of those items, the Manifesto attempts to elevate the value of other things, which the authors felt are important but overlooked.

The four statements of the Agile Manifesto are simple (if not overstated). The first and third are about communication. They focus on the fact that because *people* develop software, communication among those people is a primary success factor. The second and fourth statements are pragmatic views of what constitutes success in a software project; it must produce software that meets the (changing) needs of the ultimate users.

The four statements of the Agile Manifesto are quite high level and abstract. They leave a lot of room for interpretation and do not provide much in the way of guidance. The 12 principles (enumerated and discussed in Appendix B) flesh out the ideas expressed in the Manifesto. They provide a much more concrete view of the types of activities that comprise the various Agile software development methods.

For more information about the Agile Manifesto, visit www.Agile Alliance.org.

Reference

[1]   Cockburn, A., *Agile Software Development*, Boston, MA: Pearson Education, Inc., 2002, p. 215.

Appendix

B

Contents

The 12 Principles of Agile Methods

This appendix provides the full text of the 12 Principles of Agile Methods, along with some commentary and references where the interested reader may find additional information.

These 12 principles were documented during the February 2001 meeting during which the Agile Manifesto was written. (Refer to Appendix A for more information on that meeting.)

The Agile Manifesto (quoted and discussed in Appendix A) is quite high level and abstract. It leaves a lot of room for interpretation and does not provide much in the way of guidance. The 12 principles discussed in this appendix flesh out the ideas expressed in the Manifesto. They provide a much more concrete view of the types of activities that comprise the various Agile software development methods.

The 12 Principles of Agile Methods

Our highest priority is to satisfy the customer through early and continuous delivery of valuable software.

Welcome changing requirements, even late in development. Agile processes harness change for the customer's competitive advantage.

Deliver working software frequently, from a couple of weeks to a couple of months, with a preference to the shorter time scale.

Business people and developers must work together daily throughout the project.

Build projects around motivated individuals. Give them the environment and support they need, and trust them to get the job done.

The most efficient and effective method of conveying information to and within a development team is face-to-face conversation.

Working software is the primary measure of progress.

Agile processes promote sustainable development. The sponsors, developers, and users should be able to maintain a constant pace indefinitely.

Continuous attention to technical excellence and good design enhances agility.

Simplicity — the art of maximizing the amount of work not done — is essential.

The best architectures, requirements, and designs emerge from self-organizing teams.

At regular intervals, the team reflects on how to become more effective, then tunes and adjusts its behavior accordingly.

Our highest priority is to satisfy the customer through early and continuous delivery of valuable software.

Few of us would argue that satisfying the customer is unimportant. The distinctive feature of this principle is the means by which the Agile methods pursue that goal.

"… through *early* … delivery of … software." Agile methods tend to shun long upfront requirements development and design activities. Rather, after laying an appropriate foundation ("appropriate" being defined differently for each method), they seek to develop working software as quickly as possible. In essence, these methods replace the traditional requirements and design phases of development with early proof-of-concept activities. The Agile methods look very much like prototyping projects but with the distinction that the resulting product is delivered for use, instead of being thrown away.

"… through … *continuous* delivery of … software." Agile methods all assume an incremental development strategy. They seek to mitigate risk by delivering increments quickly and often (every couple of weeks to every couple of months) so that the customer can validate the project's decisions and assumptions and verify the utility of the resulting software.

"… through … delivery of *valuable* software." Most Agile methods allow the customer to define what is most valuable and give the customer a significant role in establishing the order in which features are delivered.

Welcome changing requirements, even late in development. Agile processes harness change for the customer's competitive advantage.

This is the core principle on which the Agile methods are built and the reason why the name "Agile" was adopted. This principle acknowledges the fact that change is inevitable and establishes the philosophy that encouraging regular change is an advantage of the Agile methods for their customers. Rather than trying to suppress or control change, the Agile Methods are designed to allow—even encourage—change throughout the project's life.

Deliver working software frequently, from a couple of weeks to a couple of months, with a preference to the shorter time scale.

This principle expands on the "continuous delivery" phrase from the first principle. It is explicit that the increments on Agile projects should be as short as possible and goes so far as to say that a week or two is *not* too short for an increment. It also sets an upper limit that might be surprising to many, since development phases of fewer than three months are generally not seen.

Business people and developers must work together daily throughout the project.

The Agile methods all require collaboration between the development team and the other stakeholders in the project. A most crucial role in Agile projects is given to the customer (or the ultimate user of the system being developed). But all other stakeholders (identified by these technophiles as "business people") have important roles and are expected to interact with the team on a regular basis.

Build projects around motivated individuals. Give them the environment and support they need, and trust them to get the job done.

The Agile methods are all built on the assumption that development team members are all competent, motivated, supported by the organization, and empowered to do their jobs. At the same time, each method builds an environment that is intrinsically motivating to the technical staff and has the natural effect of building each staff member's capability to self-motivate and self-manage.

The most efficient and effective method of conveying information to and within a development team is face-to-face conversation.

This is the principle that explains why the Agile methods tend to have few written documents. They all favor face-to-face communication as the primary means of sharing information, often supplementing it with tools such as whiteboards. The results of communication are often documented in the form of "information radiators," which are visually available postings of information to which people can refer whenever it is needed.

Working software is the primary measure of progress.

This principle is another way in which the Agile methods strike against documentation. Most software projects will identify the acceptance of a requirements or design specification as a milestone showing significant progress. Many Agile methods (though not all) reject that idea. They tend to place little value on the project's interim products and focus almost entirely on the resulting software. Of course, since working software is delivered so often on an Agile project (see the third principle), it becomes a reasonable measure of progress.

Agile processes promote sustainable development. The sponsors, developers, and users should be able to maintain a constant pace indefinitely.

In many organizations, overtime is the norm, and in some it is routinely required. The Agile methods rebel against those norms and argue instead for "sustainable" schedules (generally meaning something in the vicinity of 40 hours per week). And by this they do not mean to plan for 40 hours per week, then work 80; rather, they mean to change the expectation of what can be accomplished so that overtime is rare. But as this principle states, the nature of the Agile methods tends to level out the demands on the project team so that a more sustainable pace is naturally maintained.

Continuous attention to technical excellence and good design enhances agility.

This is perhaps the most valuable principle of the Agile methods. Each Agile method has a strong focus on ensuring that the quality of the technical work is maintained at a high level. The different methods do this in different ways, but each has a strong quality component.

This principle provides a refreshing counterpoint to the all-too-common perception that the developers' job is to write the software and someone else is responsible for making sure it works. In the Agile methods, development teams take on the primary responsibility to be sure that what is delivered is correct and that the software satisfies the customer's needs.

This focus does not mean that independent verification and validation is unnecessary; rather, it means that the software that is delivered for IV&V will be of higher quality and generally more ready for final testing.

Simplicity—the art of maximizing the amount of work not done —is essential.

Before the Agile Manifesto was written, the methods that fall under the "Agile" umbrella were generally referred to as "light" methods. The term "light" was dropped out of recognition that certain application domains require heavier processes (e.g., developing software for safety-critical systems). Even so, the Agile methods always stress using the lightest possible processes.

The best architectures, requirements, and designs emerge from self-organizing teams.

Self-management is a hallmark of Agile methods and a backlash against the command-and-control methods used to manage many software projects. There is growing evidence that self-managed teams are in fact quite effective.

But moving toward self-managed teams requires significant changes throughout the organization. The most significant change occurs in the ranks of management, where managers' roles must evolve toward coaching and leading, as engineers' roles grow to include self-management. These changes are difficult to effect and require that many people learn new skills and behaviors, but they can have significant positive results.

At regular intervals, the team reflects on how to become more effective, then tunes and adjusts its behavior accordingly.

The concept of retrospective or postmortem analysis is well known in the industry (if not widely practiced). The Agile methods adopt this important activity as their primary means of improving their processes. Some Agile methods take this to an extreme by doing these analyses at the end of each increment of development, resulting in lessons learned and process improvements many times each year.

Agile Principles

The 12 Principles of Agile Methods provide a much more concrete picture of the shared intent of those methods than one can gain from the Manifesto alone. From these principles we can see that Agile methods embrace a number of ideas that are significantly different from those embodied by more traditional methods.

How well each of these principles fits into the context of your organization is an important decision for you to make. It seems clear that some principles would be worth the effort and organizational pain required for adoption. Others may be of more questionable utility. These adoption decisions must be based on the needs and constraints of your organization, and making the decision is the focus of this book.

For more information about the 12 Principles of Agile Methods, visit http://www.AgileAlliance.org.

Appendix

C

Contents

Adaptive Software Development

Jim Highsmith's ASD arose out of his understanding of Complex Adaptive Systems theory. He views a software project team as a complex adaptive system that consists of agents (team members and other stakeholders), environments (organizational, technological, process), and emergent outcomes (the product being developed).

At the highest level, ASD is based on a collaborative learning cycle, as shown in Figure C.1. While most of us would label the three components of this model "Plan," "Build," and "Review," Highsmith chose words that fit more closely with his understanding of how Complex Adaptive Systems emerge: "Speculate," "Collaborate," and "Learn."

The Adaptive Life Cycle

In Highsmith's Adaptive Life Cycle (shown in Figure C.2), we see how his Adaptive Development Model expands into a software development life cycle.

ASD's Adaptive Life Cycle is composed of five steps. The initial step of "project initiation" is done once at the beginning of the project, and the final step of "final Q/A and release" is done once at the end.

The other three steps (adaptive cycle planning, concurrent component engineering and Quality Review) form the "Learning Loop" or "Adaptive Cycles" that are the heart of ASD. These Adaptive Cycles are described as:

- Mission-driven—each cycle must make progress toward the project mission;

- Component-based—more centrally focused on building things than on performing tasks;

- Iterative—going through the learning loop repeatedly is the key to progress;

233

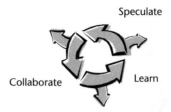

Figure C.1 Adaptive Development Model. (*From:* [1]. © 2000 Dorset House Publishing Co. Inc. Reprinted with permission.)

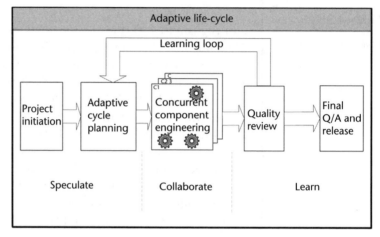

Figure C.2 Adaptive Life Cycle. (*From:* [2]. © 2000 Dorset House Publishing Co. Inc. Reprinted with permission.)

- Time-boxed—the entire project as well as each cycle of the project is completed within a prescribed time period (with the developed functionality expanding or contracting to fit);
- Risk-driven—focusing on the highest-risk items first;
- Change-tolerant—designed to accommodate changes in each cycle.

Speculate: Project initiation

The project's first step in speculation is an initiation workshop, from a few days to a few weeks in length, depending on the project's size and scope. During initiation, the entire project team and the project sponsor or customer determine the project's guiding parameters, including the project mission, objectives and constraints, the organization for the project, the system requirements, initial estimates of product size and scope, and key risks to the project.

Learning Loop

The initiation practice lays the groundwork for the project's "Learning Loop." This loop sees the project continually cycling from speculation to collaboration, to learning as the product emerges incrementally from the adaptive cycles (an iterative approach).

Speculate: Adaptive Cycle Planning

The first cycle of the project begins with the speculative practice we normally call "planning." This includes these steps:

- Determine the project time-box.
- Determine the optimal number of cycles and the time-box for each. (Each cycle is usually established to be from a couple of weeks to a couple of months in length.)
- Write an objective statement for each cycle.
- Assign primary components to cycles.
- Assign technology and support components to cycles.
- Develop a project task list.

In each successive project cycle, Adaptive Cycle Planning consists of revisiting and revising these things as necessary, based on progress to date and what has been learned in earlier cycles.

Collaborate: Concurrent component engineering

This is where the real work gets done. The content of this phase of each cycle is planned in the Adaptive Cycle Planning phase and done to the extent possible within the planned time-box. Trade-offs may have to be made as the end of the time-box constrains what can be accomplished. This phase is shown as multiple boxes because team members or subteams are generally working concurrently and integrating their work products.

Learn: Quality Review

The end of each cycle is marked by learning activities, where the project team gains insight into progress to date and collects the information they need to perform any replanning at the start of the next cycle. Highsmith specifically recommends three learning activities:

Customer Focus Group Reviews—Because the objective of an ASD project is to converge on a system that meets its business purpose, evaluating the results of each cycle by the ultimate users is a critical learning activity. Highsmith recommends using a joint application development (JAD)-style facilitated workshop to collect input from the user community at the end of each cycle. During this workshop, developers would demonstrate and explain what has been built so far. Then users would try using the software and give developers their reactions to it.

Software Inspections—By this, Highsmith does not necessarily mean formal Fagan inspections (although the process he recommends is very similar to

Fagan's). The primary objective of these inspections is to detect defects in the work products of the cycle, but they have a secondary benefit of ensuring that each team member is familiar with all the code that has been written.

Postmortems—The final step in each cycle is the postmortem, where team members evaluate the effectiveness of the processes they have been using as well as the project's performance against its plan. If they identify problems, they also brainstorm ideas for solving those problems. The results of the postmortem are fed back (via the Learning Loop) to the planning phase for the next cycle.

Learn: Final Q/A and release

This phase is the final hand-off to the customer. Its focus is to put both the product and all pertinent information about it into the customer's hands before disbanding the project team.

ASD's conceptual framework

The steps in the Adaptive Life Cycle are relatively obvious. But the key to understanding ASD lies in the conceptual framework on which it is built.

Project stakeholders as independent agents

Highsmith describes the participants in an ASD project not as managers, employees, customers, and the like (which would connote a structure or hierarchy), but as a collection of independent agents who collaborate to facilitate the emergence of the ultimate product. He paints this picture for us:
"… an ensemble of independent agents:

- Who interact to create an ecosystem;
- Whose interaction is defined by the exchange of information;
- Whose individual actions are based on some system of internal rules;
- Who self-organize in nonlinear ways to produce emergent results;
- Who exhibit characteristics of both order and chaos;
- Who evolve over time" [3].

The unique effect of this view of a project is that it establishes the technical team, management, and customer as peers to one another. Each brings unique knowledge and perspective to the project, and none of them is "over" the others.

The Adaptive (Leadership-Collaboration) Management Model

ASD projects are not managed; they are led. Because the project team operates as an organism, and the project results emerge in an organic way, the project cannot be managed in the traditional "command and control" sense. Rather, the project manager's role is to set the direction for the project (lead) and provide the environment in which the various agents can collaborate.

Highsmith's management philosophy is best understood by contrasting the two diagrams in Figure C.3. On the top is his view of how a traditional "mechanistic system" is managed, and on the bottom an "organic system," such as an ASD project.

Although the structure of these two models is almost the same, many labels have changed, indicating a shift in the focus of activities.

‣ Along with "expected inputs," there are also "unexpected inputs."

‣ The system follows a "pattern" (person-oriented) rather than a "process" (mechanistic).

‣ Along with "expected results," there are also "emergent results."

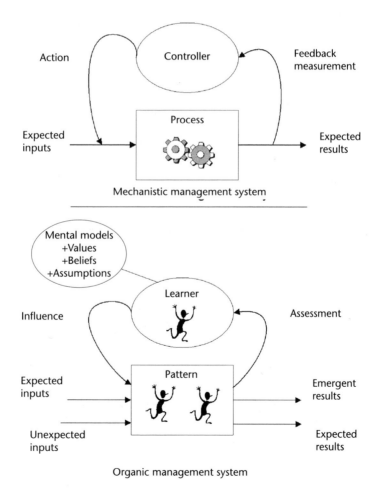

Figure C.3 Adaptive Management Model. (*From:* [4]. © 2000 Dorset House Publishing Co. Inc. Reprinted with permission.)

> The "controller" is reclassified as a "learner" (a person).

> The learner's information comes from "assessment" as opposed to "measurement."

> The learner applies "mental models (values + beliefs + assumptions)."

> The learner exercises "influence" rather than taking "action."

While these changes appear to be mainly semantic, their intent is to highlight the different kind of management model that ASD advocates.

ASD

Although ASD includes a development life cycle with clearly described steps, it seems clear that adopting ASD would require far more than merely following those steps. Adopting ASD would require substantial learning about the conceptual basis Highsmith has built around his understanding of Complex Adaptive Systems theory and adoption of his Leadership-Collaboration Management Model.

References

[1] Highsmith, J. A., III, *Adaptive Software Development, A Collaborative Approach to Managing Complex Systems*, New York: Dorset House Publishing, 2000, p. 41.

[2] Highsmith, J. A., III, *Adaptive Software Development, A Collaborative Approach to Managing Complex Systems*, New York: Dorset House Publishing, 2000, p. 84.

[3] Highsmith, J. A., III, *Adaptive Software Development, A Collaborative Approach to Managing Complex Systems*, New York: Dorset House Publishing, 2000, p. 15.

[4] Highsmith, J. A., III, *Adaptive Software Development, A Collaborative Approach to Managing Complex Systems*, New York: Dorset House Publishing, 2000, p. 230.

Appendix

D

Contents

Dynamic Systems Development Method

DSDM is not specifically about software. Unlike some other Agile methods (most notably XP), DSDM leaves the details of software writing relatively undefined and instead focuses on system development. As we can see in Figure D.1, the DSDM process includes steps for assessing feasibility, studying the business needs, and functional modeling. Programming is buried in the "Design and Build" step.

The DSDM process

Like other Agile methods, DSDM assumes an iterative life cycle. But the DSDM process diagram in Figure D.1 can leave one wondering exactly what is included in each iteration. The "Functional Model Iteration" phase is pictured as four steps that are iterated, as are the Design and Build Iteration" and "Implementation" phases. But the Feasibility and Business Study phases are not shown that way, and the feed-forward (black) and feedback (gray) arrows make it unclear how the smaller iterative phases fit into the larger picture of an iterative system development life cycle.

The answer to this riddle is that Figure D.1 is *designed* to leave these questions unanswered. The intent of DSDM is for *each project* to define how the iterating will be done so that the needs of the project are met. Presumably, the three iterative wheels would generally be turning concurrently (though not necessarily at the same rates), and feedback from "Implementation" and "Design and Build Iteration" to the other phases could happen during any iteration.

The DSDM process provides a structured set of activities with feed-forward and feedback loops, but it allows a large

239

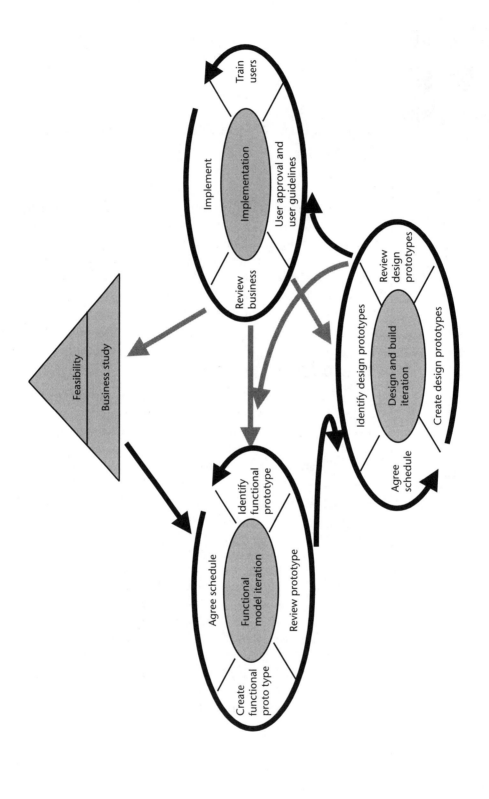

Figure D.1 DSDM process diagram. (*From:* [1]. © 2003 Pearson Education. Reprinted with permission.)

degree of freedom for any particular project to define exactly how those activities are assembled to define the project's life cycle.

Nine principles of DSDM

For purposes of the analysis we are doing in this book, the important part of DSDM is not the process flow itself but the set of nine principles on which that process was built. These nine principles, more than anything else, define the impact that this method would have on an organization that adopts it.

Principle 1: Active user involvement is imperative.

DSDM's strong focus on the business purpose of the system being developed (refer to principles 4 and 5) requires that the ultimate users of the system be involved throughout the development project. This is because the system attributes that will make it fit for its purpose cannot be understood well enough in the project's early stages to commit them to a detailed specification (see principle 7). Therefore, the only way to make appropriate detailed decisions and know that the evolving system is converging on the ideal of "fitness" is to fully involve the users throughout the project.

Principle 2: DSDM teams must be empowered to make decisions.

This principle does not give the team free reign to do whatever they wish. Rather, it advocates that the team be delegated the authority to make most of the day-to-day decisions as the project progresses. With active user involvement (see principle 1), such delegation can result in the team being able to move quickly and steadily toward system delivery. However, when a decision that must be made falls outside the team's authority (e.g., cost overruns), DSDM recognizes the importance of raising such decisions to the appropriate authority.

Principle 3: The focus is on frequent delivery of products.

This principle means that the project's progress should be measured by the production of tangible products, rather than by mere activity. The phrase "delivery of products" does *not* refer only to the incremental delivery of a working system to an end user (though that is included). Products in this sense include any sort of work product that may be produced as the project moves forward (e.g., a specification, a throwaway prototype, a design document); and delivery could be simply within the project team. DSDM requires that as the project moves forward, it must produce artifacts that prove that progress is being made.

Principle 4: Fitness for business purpose is the essential criterion for acceptance of deliverables.

This principle (along with principle 7) is the practical manifestation of DSDM's belief that specifying detailed requirements upfront is not helpful. By placing fitness for purpose above satisfaction of requirements, and by involving users consistently (refer to principle 1), DSDM zeroes in on the end user as the only one who can say whether or not the system as it is evolving is acceptable.

Principle 5: Iterative and incremental development is necessary to converge on an accurate business solution.

In an environment where it is assumed that the project's end result cannot be foreseen in great detail, incremental development is the best insurance against the project going terribly awry. Incremental development is essentially an exercise in trial and error, where each new increment is presented to the user who validates (or invalidates) the direction the team has taken. "Converge" is the key word in the principle. It is assumed that the most direct path to the end product is not likely to be known, so DSDM engages in constant checking and correcting of the path to bring the project to a satisfactory end as quickly as is reasonably possible.

Principle 6: All changes during development are reversible.

This principle goes hand-in-hand with principle 5. If we agree that the project is practicing trial and error, then we must expect that there will indeed be errors from time to time. This principle gives us permission to discard erroneous work when necessary. Surely, we will try to salvage the good from a mistake, but we must recognize that there will be times when the most efficient path is to discard some work and try again.

Principle 7: Requirements are baselined at a high level.

The first three words of this principle, "Requirements are baselined," represent a departure of DSDM from some other Agile methods. DSDM recognizes the importance to the project of stability in scope and direction. By baselining (freezing) the requirements at some level, stakeholders are establishing a stable basis for the team's work. This does not mean that this baseline will not change; rather, it requires that serious deliberation precede any such change so that all stakeholders understand and agree to what would become the new requirements baseline.

The last four words, "at a high level," is the part of this principle that makes it agile. It leaves the details of what the requirements mean to be worked out between the team and user (see principles 1 and 4).

Principle 8: Testing is integrated throughout the life cycle.

Testing does not show up as a step in the DSDM life cycle because, like other Agile methods, DSDM promotes a strong quality-consciousness by all team members. Every task should include an appropriate verification or validation step like a review or test by a team member or user. This principle works together with principles 1, 4, and 5 to continually check the project's progress toward its goal of a system fit for its business purpose.

Principle 9: A collaborative and cooperative approach between all stakeholders is essential.

This last principle is little more than the sum of the first eight. The only way that principles 1–8 can be applied successfully on a project is if all stakeholders accept DSDM and their roles as DSDM defines them. If any stakeholder does *not* agree (especially an influential stakeholder), then DSDM cannot work in that environment.

Reference

[1]   Stapleton, J., *DSDM: Business Focused Development*, London, England: Pearson Education, 2003, p. 4.

Extreme Programming

XP is probably the most widely recognized of the Agile methods. Since Kent Beck first publicized it, XP has been talked about consistently and has come to embody the Agile methods in many people's minds.

XP's 12 practices

XP's 12 practices are its defining features. Organizations that implement XP are adopting these 12 practices as their way of developing software.

The Planning Game

In XP, planning (characterized as "The Planning Game") is both iterative and collaborative. It is iterative in that the "game is played" at the beginning of each increment of development. It is collaborative in that it is played among the technical team members and the customer and management (referred to as the business people).

During the Planning Game for each increment, the business people and the technical people negotiate to establish an achievable plan that best meets the business needs. During this negotiation, the customer identifies what system features would be most valuable to develop next, the technical team determines the feasibility and effort for developing that functionality, and management ensures that the project stays within any relevant parameters (e.g., cost).

Small releases

An XP project team develops the system in the smallest reasonable chunks that provide demonstrable value for the customer. Because each increment should take only a few weeks to develop, the functionality that can be developed in that time is very constrained. But even when it is not feasible to actually release an increment for use, that increment is still demonstrated for customers so they can verify that it is progressing toward meeting their needs and appears to be usable.

Metaphor

An XP project's Metaphor is the overall concept of the system that the team will build. The Metaphor uses similes to describe what the system will be like, in terms that are readily recognizable to both the development team and customer. This very high-level vision is the XP project's overall requirement, and there is an expectation that it will remain relatively stable throughout the project.

The actual descriptions of the system features are documented separately in "Stories." Each feature is documented in a separate Story that describes the feature's essential attributes and actions. These descriptions are also quite brief, comprising only the text that can be written on a 3x5-inch card. The stories on an XP project tend to change dynamically as the development team and customer learn about the product they are building and gain a better understanding of the customer's needs.

The Stories, taken together with the project's Metaphor, form the requirements from which the system is planned and developed.

Simple design

This practice is the heart of XP's value of "Simplicity." It advises that programmers avoid designing for the features that they "know" are coming (even if they will be implemented within the current increment). Instead, they must use the simplest possible design that will allow the current Story to be implemented.

XP is based on the philosophy that this "simple design" practice will result in less rework than designing for the future. This is because we are often wrong when we design for the future, and when we are, the rework can be significant. Beck sums up this practice: "If you believe that the future is uncertain, and you believe that you can cheaply change your mind, then putting in functionality on speculation is crazy" [1].

Test First

One of XP's defining philosophies is "Test First." This philosophy states that before a pair of programmers writes a single line of code, they must implement the automated tests that will be required to verify the Story they are about to write. In addition, customers also develop a set of functional tests to verify the Story according to their own needs.

Coding the XP way consists of code a little, test a little, code a little, test a little—with the test results being the programmers' measure of progress on the Story at hand. Work on the Story is not complete until all the tests run

100% clean. Successful integration is also defined in terms of these automated tests. (See "Continuous Integration" below.)

Refactoring

XP's Refactoring practice prompts each pair of programmers to ask themselves before they begin work on a Story if there is a way to redesign the system so that the final result "is the simplest thing that could possibly work" [2]. Then, after they have completed work on the Story, Refactoring prompts them to ask the same question again. In either case, if the answer is, "Yes," then the redesign is implemented as part of the work on that Story. Refactoring is used to ensure that the "simple" designs that programmers start with do not grow into needless complexity as more Stories are added.

Pair Programming

The most visible practice of XP is Pair Programming. This practice calls for all technical work (from design to coding to test) to be done by a pair of programmers working together at a single workstation. Pairs form and change dynamically throughout the project according to the needs of each story.

The member of each pair who is *not* typing has a very special job. That person is to be thinking about the wider impacts of what is being implemented—to be continuously asking questions like, "Is there a simpler way to do this?" "Do we need tests that we did not yet create?" "Are there defects in this code?" "Will this strategy work?"

Pair Programming has been called the ultimate in peer reviews, because it entails a continuous, real-time review of everything that is done. This is one more example of XP's strong emphasis on technical excellence.

Collective ownership

XP takes a position on code ownership that is quite different from the standard model of assigning responsibility for each code module to a specific person. XP goes to the opposite extreme—stating that code should never be "owned" by any individual. When anyone identifies a need to change any code, it is that pair's responsibility to implement that change. Every member of the team owns all code collectively.

Continuous integration

XP goes beyond the concept of daily builds to require that integration of the product being built goes on continuously. As a pair completes each Story, their last step is to integrate their new and changed code (along with their automated tests) into the baseline system. They then run the entire test suite — all of their own automated tests, as well as those for all the Stories that are already part of the system. If any test fails, the new Story and tests are backed out, and the pair must resolve the problems before they can try again. When all the tests run 100% clean, the Story has been successfully integrated and becomes part of the project baseline. Because there are several pairs of programmers working on different Stories at all times, this practice results in someone integrating something almost all the time.

40-hour week

XP calls for overtime to be rare. It explicitly suggests that overtime should not be worked 2 weeks in a row. The intention with this practice is to keep everyone fresh so they can continue indefinitely on an aggressive but sustainable pace.

On-site customer

One of the key members of an XP project team is the on-site customer. This is a person who will be a real user of the system being built, or some other person who can authoritatively stand in for the customer/user. This practice ensures that an appropriately knowledgeable person is continuously available to the team to review work, try things out, answer questions, and make implementation decisions when they are needed.

Coding standards

Several other XP practices (most notably Pair Programming and collective ownership) give rise to the importance of good coding standards. In a team that is collaborating this closely, appropriate standards are the only way to maintain order.

The XP Facilities Strategy

While it is not one of its 12 practices, XP's Facilities Strategy is illuminating. Because XP is designed to make optimal use of face-to-face communication, it recommends that all project members work together in a single room. There should be no doors, no offices, and not even separate cubicles. In his book *Extreme Programming Explained*, Kent Beck describes the optimal XP workspace to facilitate collaboration among team members. Refer to Figure 10.1 and the accompanying descriptions in Chapter 10 for more information about XP's Facilities Strategy.

References

[1]   Beck, K., *Extreme Programming Explained*, Reading, MA: Addison-Wesley Longman, Inc., 2000, p. 57.

[2]   Beck, K., *Extreme Programming Explained*, Reading, MA: Addison-Wesley Longman, Inc., 2000, p. 30.

Appendix

Contents

Feature-Driven Development

FDD differs from other Agile methods in its focus on upfront design and planning. As can be seen from the FDD process diagram in Figure F.1, the Object Model, feature list, and planning are done once at the beginning of the project, and iterations are essentially an incremental building of identified features. This is not to say that the model, feature list, and plans never change; rather, it indicates that evolution of those items is not an inherent part of this method.

FDD practices

Like other Agile methods, the impact of FDD on an organization is better gauged from its practices than its process flow. FDD is defined by these eight practices.

Domain Object Modeling

FDD begins with the construction of a relatively detailed object model for the system to be built. This model is not intended to provide all the design details for the features. Rather, its intention is to force all stakeholders' assumptions out into the open and provide a road map for the project.

Although the initial Object Model is built at the beginning of the project, each increment of development results in updates to it as details are filled in and corrections are made. Thus, the Object Model is a continually evolving picture of the product, as it is currently understood.

Developing by feature

The Object Model identifies all the expected classes in the system, but development is not done class by class. Rather FDD requires that development be done a feature at a time. FDD

249

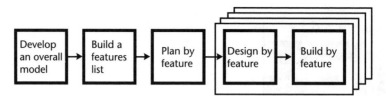

Figure F.1   FDD process diagram. (*From:* [1]. © 2002 Pearson Education. Reprinted with permission.)

defines a feature this way. "A feature is a small, client-valued function expressed in the form: <action><result> <object> with the appropriate prepositions between the action, result, or object" [2]. An example of a feature might be, "Retrieve the medical records of a patient."

As can be seen from the example, a feature is small and can normally be developed in a few hours or days. FDD defines the upper limit on feature size at 2 weeks.

Because developing a feature can require additions or changes to several classes, the next two practices are included in FDD to define how this activity is managed.

Class (code) ownership

FDD prescribes that a single developer owns each class. This is diametrically opposed to XP's practice of "collective ownership" and grows from a different philosophical basis. FDD depends on the class owner to have a full and detailed understanding of all that his or her class does and contains. The philosophy is that such an individual will be more efficient at making changes to a class than anyone else on the project team. Of course, the danger in this practice is that the loss of a team member can be catastrophic. (To see how FDD mitigates this risk, refer to the "Inspections" section later in this appendix.)

This class ownership practice essentially requires that the class owner be directly involved in the development of each feature that affects his or her class. The next practice (feature teams) defines how this requirement is managed.

Feature teams

Each feature is implemented by a team of project members, consisting of the feature owner (a Chief Programmer) and the owners of all the classes affected by the feature. With direct participation of the expert on each class involved in the feature, that feature should be implemented not only very quickly but also in the most effective way. If, during a feature implementation, the team determines that another class must change, the owner of that class is simply added to the feature team.

Thus, feature teams are a dynamic part of FDD, forming and disbanding on a daily or weekly basis as the development of each feature is undertaken and completed. Multiple feature teams will likely be operating at any one point in time, and each individual may be operating on more than one feature team at a time. A feature team has not completed its work until it has verified its feature and integrated it into the current product baseline. (See the "Inspections," "Regular build schedule," and "Reporting/Visibility of results" sections later in this appendix.)

Inspections

FDD makes heavy use of Inspections to ensure the quality of the designs and code that are built. Although FDD does not specify formal Fagan inspections, the rigor described in the guidelines for feature team members is similar to that of formal inspections.

The primary purpose of an inspection is to detect defects in designs and code, but FDD identifies two other critical results of inspections. First, it mitigates the risks involved in the class ownership practice by ensuring that many team members have a good understanding of each class. And second, it is a forcing function to ensure that the project's coding standards are adhered to consistently.

Regular build schedule

FDD does not prescribe any particular timing for builds, only that they be "regular." How often builds are done must be defined for each project based on the project's needs and constraints and the environment. Even so, FDD envisions that builds are done no less often than weekly, and possibly daily or continuously.

Regular builds are done to maintain an up-to-date system comprised of all the features that have been developed to date. This current system then can be used as the baseline for testing each new feature, as a basis for writers to develop documentation, and as a continually available demonstration for customers and project sponsors.

Configuration Management

This FDD practice acknowledges the importance of good CM to the success of an FDD project. The dynamism of the feature teams and regular build schedule make it critical that the project carefully manage its artifacts. But FDD does not prescribe any specifics about CM. It simply directs that the project team practice a level of CM rigor that is appropriate to the project size, complexity, and scope.

Reporting/Visibility of results

FDD uses a unique mechanism for tracking and reporting the project's status so that the common "90% complete" syndrome is avoided. This

Feature value = Sum(weights of completed milestones)

Value of a Feature not yet worked on = 0.00 Value of a Feature that is complete = 1.00 Value of a Feature in progress is between 0 and 1

$$\text{Project status} = \frac{\text{Sum(Feature Value) for all features}}{\text{Total \# features in the product}}$$

Figure F.2   Project status equation.

mechanism uses the project's feature list and feature development milestones along with some weighting factors for those milestones.

FDD defines the milestones for each feature to be:

- Domain walkthrough—complete;
- Design—ready for inspection;
- Design inspection—and any rework and reinspection complete;
- Code—ready for inspection;
- Code inspection—and any rework and reinspection complete;
- Promote to build—all feature code checked in and ready for the next build.

Each FDD project team uses its historical data to assign a weight to each milestone. For example, if their data shows that they average 4% of their time in design walkthroughs, then that milestone is given a weight of 0.04 for every feature in the project.

Figure F.2 shows that the project status becomes both objective and easy to compute. It is simply the sum of the weights of every milestone that has been reached, divided by the number of features. On a project with 285 features, if the sum of the completed milestone weights is 201, then the project is 70.5% complete.

References

[1]   Palmer, S. R., and J. M. Felsing, *A Practical Guide to Feature-Driven Development*, Upper Saddle River, NJ: Prentice-Hall, 2002, p. 57.

[2]   Palmer, S. R., and J. M. Felsing, *A Practical Guide to Feature-Driven Development*, Upper Saddle River, NJ: Prentice-Hall, p. 41.

Appendix

G

Lean Software Development

Lean Software Development is not a software development method. Rather, it is a set of principles and tools that an organization can employ in making its software development projects more lean. The principles behind LD are drawn from the world of lean manufacturing, and although some LD tools relate directly to lean manufacturing principles, many do not.

Lean Software Development principles and tools

LD is characterized by seven lean principles that are elaborated into 22 Lean Software Development tools.

Eliminate Waste

Tool 1: Seeing Waste—The authors suggest looking for waste in these parts of your development process:

- Partially done work (e.g., unimplemented designs);
- Extra processes (steps in your process that do not add value);
- Extra features (things for which the customer did not ask);
- Task switching (people assigned to multiple projects);
- Waiting (for hand-offs);
- Motion (hand-offs);
- Defects.

Tool 2: Value Stream Mapping—Identify all the steps in your process that add value to the product, and for each of those steps, identify how much time is required to add the value and how much time is wasted in waiting. Note that some steps that do not directly add value are necessary (e.g., Configuration Management mitigates risks).

Amplify Learning

Tool 3: Feedback—Design your process so that participants receive feedback as often as possible. For example:

- Test early and often;
- Show users the evolving system;
- Prototype instead of analyzing.

Tool 4: Iterations—Iterative time-boxed development is the best way to converge on the ultimate solution. Often this results in negotiation of project scope or duration. But such negotiation is good if done early in the project, when adjustments are less painful.

Tool 5: Synchronization—Every development method results in synchronization problems (e.g., collective code ownership can result in multiple people changing the same program at the same time.) The authors recommend several synchronization mechanisms for software projects.

Tool 6: Set-Based Development—When faced with a difficult problem, it is often good to think about the solution *space* instead of specific solutions. The authors recommend these steps:

- Develop multiple options (e.g., brainstorming ideas);
- Communicate constraints;
- Let the solution emerge.

Decide as Late as Possible

Tool 7: Options Thinking—In financial markets, you can purchase options that, for a price, allow you to delay making a decision until a later date. The same model can be used in Agile software development. By incurring some added cost, options can be held open, allowing decisions to be delayed until more information is available.

Tool 8: The Last Responsible Moment—Options Thinking (Tool 7) delays commitment to a decision until the last *responsible* moment. The authors define that as "the moment at which failing to make a decision eliminates an important alternative" [1].

Tool 9: Making Decisions—Good decisions are more likely to be made when the options can be narrowed by the application of a set of rules. The authors recommend that decisions in software development always be made in light of the seven lean principles (the major headings in this appendix).

Deliver as Fast as Possible

Tool 10: Pull Systems—The best way to ensure that each team member knows exactly what he or she should do each day is to ensure that the environment provides automatic prompting. For example:

> • Short iterations with well-defined deliverables provide near-term targets for people to work toward.

> • Daily stand-up meetings keep everyone aware of progress toward that target.

> • Information radiators [2] (publicly posted charts) keep everyone aware of the big picture.

Tool 11: Queuing Theory—Much waste can be attributed to people waiting for constrained resources. The authors suggest using queuing theory to analyze all bottlenecks in your software process and determine ways to minimize the cycle time.

Tool 12: Cost of Delay—In many software projects, the cost of delaying delivery (even when it is significant) is often invisible to the project team and sometimes to managers. The authors recommend developing a financial model for the project that will allow all stakeholders to make appropriate trade-off decisions, especially when cost and delivery date are in conflict.

Empower the Team

Tool 13: Self-Determination—The people who do the work are in the best position to improve their processes and eliminate waste. Although Quality Circles have fallen out of favor, this philosophy still has value in guiding process improvement efforts.

Tool 14: Motivation—Motivating a project team to perform well has many dimensions. The authors stress that the team must have:

> • *Purpose*—A shared goal that they all believe in.

> • *Belonging*—They feel that each person is a part of the team.

> • *Safety*—Mistakes are corrected without punishing people.

> • *Competence*—The team feels they able to complete their tasks.

> • *Progress*—Each person can see regular progress on the project.

Tool 15: Leadership—Project management and technical leadership are two distinct skill sets. A successful team needs both, and it is rare for those two attributes to exist in the same person.

Tool 16: Expertise—Every software project requires a variety of expertise (e.g., domain, user interface, database, project management, writing). This tool is about identifying communities of expertise and ensuring that they are available to the project.

Build Integrity In

Tool 17: Perceived Integrity—Perceived Integrity is the system's integrity from customers' viewpoint. Do they perceive it to be useful and well designed? With appropriate interaction between the team and customer, the team can be sure they build the right system.

Tool 18: Conceptual Integrity—Conceptual Integrity is an important component of Perceived Integrity (Tool 17). Building the system right (as differentiated from building the right system) involves such concepts as architecture, consistency, and elegance. (See Tool 19, Refactoring.)

Tool 19: Refactoring—Programmers should improve the software any time they see the opportunity to do so. Refactoring refers to redesign of the system to improve the program's Perceived and Conceptual Integrity (Tools 17 and 18).

Also, after many changes have been made to software, it tends to become brittle. (That is, over time, it becomes more and more difficult to make any changes to the software without breaking it in unforeseen ways.) Brittle code is a Conceptual Integrity problem that Refactoring remedies.

Tool 20: Testing—Testing provides an important feedback mechanism. (See Tool 3.) Both validation (ensuring the right system is built) and verification (ensuring the system is built right) must be done throughout the development process, not just at the end. That way, the team gets the feedback they need to ensure their system's integrity, both Perceived (Tool 17) and Conceptual (Tool 18).

See the Whole

Tool 21: Measurements—The authors focus on the various problems associated with measurement (e.g., suboptimization) and their sources. In essence, this tool is about focusing measurement where it is effective: at higher-level aggregations of data. This focus has the dual benefit of protecting individual engineers from management's abuse of their personal data and focusing attention on data that is useful to the organization as a whole.

Tool 22: Contracts—Contracts are a fact any time the supplier and customer are different companies. Because these relationships can be so complex and varied, the authors discuss a variety of contractual arrangements and the positive and negative effects of each.

References

[1]   Poppendieck, M., and T. Poppendieck, *Lean Software Development: An Agile Toolkit*, Reading, MA: Addison-Wesley, Inc., 2003, p. 57.

[2]   Cockburn, A., *Agile Software Development*, Reading, MA: Addison- Wesley, Inc., 2002, pp 84–88.

Appendix

H

Contents

Scrum

Scrum is not primarily about software development. It is a method for managing product development that can be wrapped around any specific technology, including software. Scrum as it exists today grew from its beginnings in Japan in the mid-1980s [1]. The name "Scrum" is from the game of rugby and refers to a strategy used to get a ball back into play.

The Scrum process, shown in Figure H.1, is incremental, just as with other Agile methods.

Scrum practices

As with other Agile methods, Scrum is defined not so much by its process as by the practices that comprise it. Each practice is described here.

The Scrum Master

"The Scrum Master is responsible for the success of Scrum" [3]. Although Scrum defines this as a new role, in traditional projects its responsibilities are often taken on by an existing position such as project manager or team leader. The primary responsibilities of the Scrum Master are to:

- Ensure that the Scrum practices are followed and that the values behind Scrum drive enactment of the process.
- Work with management and the customer to identify the individual who will take on the role of "Product Owner." (Refer to the Product Owner's role under the "Product Backlog," "Sprint Planning," and "Sprint Review" practices, later in this appendix.)

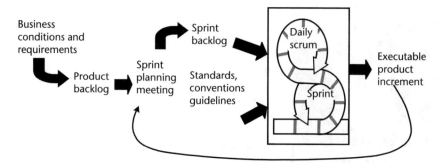

Figure H.1 Scrum process diagram. (From: [2].© 2002 Pearson Education. Reprinted with permission.)

> • Facilitate each of the other practices, as described later in this appendix.
>
> • Be the interface point among management, the customer, and the Scrum team. Of primary importance are:
>
>> • Communicating project status;
>>
>> • Removing impediments to progress (see "Daily Scrum Meetings" later in this appendix).

Product Backlog

"Product Backlog is an evolving, prioritized queue of business and technical functionality that needs to be developed into a system" [4]. The Product Backlog is the sum total of the work that remains to be done on the project and includes everything from major features to bug fixes. (Contrast this with the "Sprint Backlog" described in the "Sprint Planning" and "Sprint" practices, later in this appendix.) Any stakeholder in the project can contribute to the Product Backlog at any time, but it is the Product Owner who has the primary responsibility for determining the priority of backlog items.

The primary measure of progress in a Scrum project is the change in the number of items in the Product Backlog over time. It may grow in early Sprints as stakeholders gain an understanding of the system being built, but ultimately, a pattern of steady decrease in the size of the Product Backlog is expected. If this does not materialize, or if it is not fast enough, then hard decisions must be made about the project's scope.

Scrum Teams

"A team commits to achieving a Sprint goal. The team is accorded full authority to do whatever it decides is necessary to achieve the goal" [5]. Almost all software development involves teams. The key difference with Scrum is that the team freely commits to what they believe they can produce during each Sprint, and they are empowered to make whatever decisions they must to fulfill those commitments. (Refer to "Sprint Planning Meeting" and "Sprint," below.) This level of autonomy is foreign to most organizations.

Daily Scrum Meetings

"Software development is a complex process that requires lots of communications. The Daily Scrum meeting is where the team comes to communicate" [6]. The Daily Scrum (the defining feature of Scrum) is a short 15-minute meeting that takes place every working day. It is the forum where team members exchange information and others may come to listen —but not speak. To keep the meeting short, all deliberation and discussion is relegated to meetings of interested people after the Daily Scrum. During the Daily Scrum, each team member answers three questions:

- What have you done since the last Scrum?
- What will you do between now and the next Scrum?
- What got in your way of doing work?

The third question provides the Scrum Master with the information he or she needs to be effective in removing impediments to progress and ensuring the team continues to be productive.

Sprint Planning Meeting

"Customers, users, management, the Product Owner, and the Scrum Team determine the next Sprint goal and functionality at the Sprint Planning meeting. The team then devises the individual tasks that must be performed to build the product increment" [7].

Each 30-day Sprint begins with this planning meeting. The critical outputs of this meeting are:

- Sprint Goal—The objective that is to be achieved during this Sprint.
- Sprint Backlog—The subset of the Product Backlog that will be completed during the Sprint.

The Product Owner is the sole arbiter of the priority of the Product Backlog items. But only the Scrum Team can commit themselves to completing specific work. The Sprint Planning meeting is the forum where lobbying and negotiation take place. At its conclusion, all stakeholders will have agreed to a Sprint Goal and Sprint Backlog to which the Team is willing to commit.

Sprint

"The team works for a fixed period of time called a Sprint" [8]. After the negotiations of the Sprint Planning meeting, the Scrum Team has full authority to complete the 30-day Sprint by doing whatever they feel is necessary. During the Sprint, the team self-organizes and self-directs, and their authority even extends to being able to:

- Change the functionality to be delivered by the Sprint — as long as the Sprint Goal is still achieved.

▸ Abort the Sprint if new information leads them to believe its Goal or Backlog is no longer achievable or relevant.

Assuming the team does not abort the Sprint, it ends with the delivery of the promised executable product increment.

Sprint Review

"The Sprint Review meeting is a four-hour informational meeting. During this meeting, the team presents to management, customers, users, and the Product Owner the product increment that it has built during the Sprint" [9]. This meeting provides a concrete picture of the progress achieved during the Sprint and lays the foundation for the next Sprint Planning meeting.

References

[1]   Takeuchi, H., and I. Nonaka, "The New New Product Development Game," *Harvard Business Review*, January 1986, pp. 137–146.

[2]   Schwaber, K., and M. Beedle, *Agile Software Development with Scrum*, Upper Saddle River, NJ: Prentice-Hall, 2002, p. 8.

[3]   Schwaber, K., and M. Beedle, *Agile Software Development with Scrum*, Upper Saddle River, NJ: Prentice-Hall, 2002, p. 31.

[4]   Schwaber, K., and M. Beedle, *Agile Software Development with Scrum*, Upper Saddle River, NJ: Prentice-Hall, 2002, pp. 32.

[5]   Schwaber, K., and M. Beedle, *Agile Software Development with Scrum*, Upper Saddle River, NJ: Prentice-Hall, 2002, p. 35.

[6]   Schwaber, K., and M. Beedle, *Agile Software Development with Scrum*, Upper Saddle River, NJ: Prentice-Hall, 2002, p. 40.

[7]   Schwaber, K., and M. Beedle, *Agile Software Development with Scrum*, Upper Saddle River, NJ: Prentice-Hall, 2002, p. 47.

[8]   Schwaber, K., and M. Beedle, *Agile Software Development with Scrum*, Upper Saddle River, NJ: Prentice-Hall, 2002, p. 50.

[9]   Schwaber, K., and M. Beedle, *Agile Software Development with Scrum*, Upper Saddle River, NJ: Prentice-Hall, 2002, p. 54.

Glossary

Acceptance   A review or test that is done by customers or system end users to determine if the system meets their needs

Adaptive Software Development   One of the Agile Methods (see Appendix C)

Agile   Able to think and act quickly and in a well-coordinated way

Agile Alliance   A loose on-line federation of practitioners of the Agile Methods who share their experiences in an attempt to promote the use of those methods (refer to www.AgileAlliance.org)

Agile Manifesto   A set of four statements that reflect the core values on which each Agile Method is based (see Appendix A)

Agile Method   Any development method characterized by the Agile Manifesto and its 12 Agile Principles (see Appendices C–H)

Agile Principles   Twelve statements that provide concrete interpretation of the meaning of the Agile Manifesto (see Appendix B)

Agilists   People who promote and use the Agile Methods

ASD   See Adaptive Software Development

Baseline   "A specification or product that has been formally reviewed and agreed upon, that thereafter serves as the basis for further development, and that can be changed only through formal change control procedures." (IEEE-STD-610)

Brainstorming   Listing as many ideas as a group can generate without assessing the validity or goodness of each idea. (This mechanism is designed to generate as many ideas as possible and is always followed by an evaluation exercise in which the ideas are screened and prioritized.)

Business People   Everyone outside of the Agile software development team with whom the team interacts (e.g., managers, human resources, information technology, the customer, end users)

CCB   See Configuration Control Board

Change Request   A document that records a suggestion for some manner of change (e.g., to correct a defect, enhance system capability, or change a requirement)

CI   See Configuration Item

Colocated Team   A team in which all members are located in the same place (usually in the same part of a single building, sometimes in the same room)

Configuration Control Board   A formal group that is empowered with the authority to manage configurations for a project or organization. This authority includes:

- Approving the establishment or updating of baselines;
- Assuring the integrity of baselines (including acting on the results of Baseline audits);
- Approving or disapproving proposed changes to baselined CIs;
- Approving the release of CIs outside of the project.

Configuration Item   "An aggregation of hardware, software, or both that is designated for configuration management and treated as a single entity in the configuration management process." (IEEE-STD-610) Examples of configuration items are:

- A single source code file;
- A single program consisting of multiple source files and includes;
- A completed increment consisting of multiple programs and their related specifications;
- A finished system consisting of operational software, user documentation, and specifications.

Configuration Management   "A discipline applying technical and administrative direction and surveillance to identify and document the functional and physical characteristics of a configuration item, control changes to those characteristics, record and report change processing and implementation status, and verify compliance with specified requirements." (IEEE-STD-610)

Convergence   Movement of various entities toward a common result or conclusion. (Dynamic Systems Development Method uses this term to describe how the stakeholders in a software project arrive at the system that is ultimately delivered.)

Cooperative Organization   An organization characterized by people working or acting together willingly for a common purpose and without regard for rank or position (contrast with Hierarchical Organization)

Corrective Action   Any action initiated to remediate an undesirable state (e.g., project performance deviating from the plan)

CR   See Change Request

Culture   The sum total of the ways of working and interacting with each other built up by an organization over time and informally transmitted to new employees during their indoctrination

Cycle Time   The total time it takes to go through a complete development project (from concept to deployment)

Documentation   Any written form of communication. (Agile methods tend to prefer simple documentation like information radiators and multiple-use documents like self-documenting code.)

DSDM   See Dynamic Systems Development Method

Dynamic Systems Development Method   One of the Agile Methods (see Appendix D)

Entity-Relation Diagram   A diagram that shows all the tables and columns that exist in a relational database and uses lines and notations to indicate the relationships among them

Extreme Programming   One of the Agile Methods (see Appendix E)

FDD   See Feature-Driven Development

Feature-Driven Development   One of the Agile Methods (see Appendix F)

Ghant Chart   A graphical representation of a project schedule that shows each task and the dependencies among tasks using boxes and arrows.

Harness   A stand-in for an entire system. (It has functioning interfaces for one or more components but does not actually do anything and is usually used to allow testing of a component before the rest of the system is available.)

Hierarchical Organization   An organization characterized by a system of persons or roles ranked one above another (contrast with Cooperative Organization)

Incremental Development   To develop a system in stages, extending the functionality of each installment to form the next one

Independent Verification and Validation   Verification and validation performed by a group or individual that is independent of and separate from the development team

Information Radiator   A publicly posted document that can generally be read from a distance to be used by the team as reference (e.g., status of work being done)

Inspection   See Software Inspection

IV&V   See Independent Verification and Validation

LD   See Lean Software Development

Lean Software Development   One of the Agile Methods (see Appendix G)

Life cycle   The steps or phases through which a project progresses

Manifesto   A public declaration of intentions, opinions, objectives, or motives (see Agile Manifesto in Appendix A)

Object-Oriented   A method for designing and implementing programs

OO   See Object-Oriented

Pilot Test   To test something in a limited environment. (When implementing any significant process change, it is best to use the change on one or two projects before introducing it to an entire organization.)

Postmortem   See Retrospective

Process   "A sequence of steps performed for a given purpose, for example, the software development process." (IEEE-STD-610)

Program Office   The group that manages the overall project when that project consists of multiple development teams (for example, when both hardware and software development is involved)

Refactoring   Redesigning software after it has been partially developed

Regression Test   A test that is performed after a change (fix or enhancement) has been implemented to ensure that the system has not regressed. (It ensures that previously working functionality still works.)

Retrospective   A meeting in which participants in a project review how the project's processes and methods have been working to identify opportunities to improve them. (The Agile Methods promote holding retrospectives regularly throughout the project, instead of once at the end, as is common practice.)

Rollout   Introducing something that is new to a large context. (After the Pilot Test is completed, the process change can be rolled out to the entire organization.)

Scope-Creep   The tendency of a software project's scope (e.g., functionality to be delivered) to expand as the project progresses

Scrum   One of the Agile Methods (see Appendix H)

Self-Documenting Code   Program code that is written in such a way that it also serves to describe its own requirements, design, and implementation (as opposed to recording those things in separate documents)

Smoke Test   Simple tests that are run to ensure that the software will work at some basic level. (This term comes from the hardware practice of leaving a device turned on for some period of time to see if it starts smoking.)

Software Inspection   A relatively rigorous peer review activity undertaken to detect and correct defects in the software. (Michael Fagan, while he was at IBM in the 1970s, developed a rigorous formal software inspection method that has come to be known by his name and has been written about extensively. Although this inspection method is more expensive than any other peer review method, including those advocated by the Agile methods, many studies have concluded that the return on this extra investment is substantial because of the high proportion of defects it can remove before testing begins.)

Stub   A stand-in for a system component. (It has a functioning interface but does not actually do anything and is usually used to allow testing of a system before the stubbed-out component has been developed.)

Testing   See Verification and Validation. (Agile methods use this term to refer to any V&V activities like reviews, not just the manual or automated execution of a program to see how well it works.)

Time-boxing   A method for managing projects that sets hard begin and end dates for the project or project iterations and allows the delivered functionality to change in order to complete work within the specified period (e.g., refer to Scrum in Appendix H)

Validation   Checking (usually by testing or review) to ensure that the system as built or specified is appropriate to the need (contrast with Verification)

Verification   Checking (usually by testing or review) to ensure that the system has been built or specified accurately and with integrity (contrast with Validation)

V&V   See Verification and Validation

XP   See Extreme Programming

About the Author

Alan S. Koch PMP, is a speaker and writer on effective project managment methods. He is a certified project management professional and presiden of ASK Process, Inc. ASK Process helps companies improve the return on their software investment by focusing on the quality of both their software products and the processes they use to develop them. ASK Process provides consulting, training, coaching, and mentoring services related to both Agile Methods and disciplined processes (including CMMI®, PSP/TSP^{SM}, PMBOK®, the Software Engineering Body of Knowledge (SWEBOK), and IEEE standards).

Mr. Koch consults with a variety of software organizations in their process improvement programs, has contributed to the accomplishment of several successful process improvement efforts, speaks in numerous venues on process, quality, and related topics, has written many articles on software development processes and software quality, has taught as an adjunct professor of computer science, and has mentored students in Carnegie Mellon University's Master of Software Engineering Program. He is also a member of the Project Management Institute, has developed and maintained numerous software systems, has performed software QA and testing, established and managed a QA department, and was a member of the technical staff at the Software Engineering Institute at Carnegie Mellon University.

Mr. Koch welcomes your questions and comments about this book or other related topics. He can be contacted through http://www. ASKProcess.com.

Index

A

Acceptance, 134
Accidental communication, 75
Action plan, 207
Adaptive software development (ASD), 7, 200, 233
Adaptive management model, 64, 129, 200, 236
    Adaptive life cycle, 107, 148, 200, 233
        Collaborate: concurrent component engineering, 235
        Conceptual framework, 236
        Independent agents, 63, 129, 200, 236
        Leadership-collaboration. *See* Adaptive management model
        Learn
            Final Q/A and release, 236
            Quality review, 235
            Customer focus-group reviews, 109, 201, 235
            Postmortems, 108, 184, 201, 236
            Software inspections, 108, 166, 201, 235
            Project mission, 63
        Speculate
            Adaptive cycle planning, 63, 200, 235
            Project initiation, 63, 200, 234
Agile alliance, 4, 21
Agile manifesto, 3, 225
See Agile values
Agile methods, history, 3
Agile principles, 4, 227
    Deliver working software frequently, 106, 195, 229
    Early and continuous delivery, 105, 195, 228
    Face-to-face conversation, 73, 193, 229
    Motivated individuals, 61, 68, 193, 229
    Regular team retrospectives, 183, 199, 231
    Self-organizing teams, 62, 193, 231
    Simplicity, maximizing work not done, 177, 198, 230
    Stakeholders collaborate daily, 123, 127, 196, 229
    Sustainable pace, 83, 194, 230
    Technical excellence, 165, 171, 198, 230
    Unstated principle: appropriate processes and tools, 161, 194
    Welcome changing requirements, 147, 197, 228
    Working software: primary measure of progress, 107, 195, 230
Agile values. *See* agile manifesto
    Customer collaboration over contract negotiation, 196
    Individuals and interactions over processes and tools, 193
    Responding to change over following a plan, 197
    Unstated value: keeping the process agile, 198
    Working software over comprehensive documentation, 195
Agility, defined, 5
Agreements, 15
ASD. *See* Adaptive software development

B

Balance
    Contracts and collaboration, 124
    People, processes and tools, 53
Baseline. *See* Configuration management, baselines
Beck, Kent, 245
Build process, 91
    Automation, 96
Business people, definition, 128
Buy-in for a new method, building, 40, 206, 209

269

Process (continued)
   Project success factor, 55
Program office, 25
Project
   Corrective action, 155
   Course corrections, 135
   Criticality, 23
   Deviations from plans, 155
   Leader, 173
   Management, 31, 67
   Manager, 71
   Performance. *See* budget, cycle-time, productivity, quality, schedule
Phases,
   Acceptance, 134
   Delivery, 115
   Development, 86
   Initial analysis, 85
   Integration, 87, 115
   Testing, 87
Progress, tracking and reporting, 154
   Roles, 173
   Team
      Colocation, 22
      Distributed, 22
      Satisfaction, 221
      Self-organizing, 62
      Size, 21
   Time-boxed development, 114

Q
Quality
   Affordable, 172
   Assurance, 133
   Developers' role, 174

R
Reacting to change, 12
Requirements
   Baseline, 149
   Establishing, 16, 132
   Managing changes, 16, 29, 133
Retrospectives, 108, 183
   Capitalize on, 186
   When to hold, 185
Reward system, 41
Rolling out a new method, 215

S
Safety requirements, 24
Scope-creep, 123
Scrum, 8, 205, 257

Daily scrum meetings, 76, 205, 259
Product backlog, 131, 205, 258
Scrum master, 38, 70, 172, 205, 257
Scrum teams, 66, 205, 258
Sprint, 113, 205, 259
Sprint planning meeting, 153, 205, 259
Sprint review, 113, 205, 260
Security requirements, 24
Self-organizing teams, 62
Smoke tests, 91
Software inspections, 108, 166
Staff,
   Considerations about, 37
   Motivated individuals, 61, 68
   Superstars, 37
Statements of work, 15
Stubs, 91
Subcontractors, 26
Synchronization, 90

T
Task switching, source of waste, 179
Team. *See* Project, team
Technical experts, 173
Test automation, 91, 97
Testers, 133, 174
Time-boxed development, 114
Tools,
   Balance with people and processes, 53
   Project success factor, 57
Training, 213

V
Value proposition, 206
Verification and validation, 167

W
Waiting, source of waste, 179
Waterfall lifecycle, 115
Workbook, evaluating agile methods, 45, 191
   Downloading, 45
   Notes, 48
   Ratings, 48
   Summaries, 48
      Practice summary, 48
      Principle summary, 48
      Summary worksheet, 49
      Value summary, 48
   Using, 46

X
XP. *See* Extreme Programming

Recent Titles in the Artech House Computing Library

Achieving Software Quality through Teamwork, Isabel Evans

Action Focused Assessment for Software Process Improvement, Tim Kasse

Advanced ANSI SQL Data Modeling and Structure Processing, Michael M. David

Advanced Database Technology and Design, Mario Piattini and Oscar Díaz, editors

Agent-Based Software Development, Michael Luck, Ronald Ashri, and Mark d'Inverno

Agile Software Development: Evaluating the Methods for Your Organization, Alan S. Koch

Building Reliable Component-Based Software Systems, Ivica Crnkovic and Magnus Larsson, editors

Business Process Implementation for IT Professionals and Managers, Robert B. Walford

Data Modeling and Design for Today's Architectures, Angelo Bobak

Developing Secure Distributed Systems with CORBA, Ulrich Lang and Rudolf Schreiner

Discovering Real Business Requirements for Software Project Success, Robin F. Goldsmith

Future Codes: Essays in Advanced Computer Technology and the Law, Curtis E. A. Karnow

Global Distributed Applications with Windows® DNA, Enrique Madrona

A Guide to Software Configuration Management, Alexis Leon

Guide to Standards and Specifications for Designing Web Software, Stan Magee and Leonard L. Tripp

Implementing and Integrating Product Data Management and Software Configuration, Ivica Crnkovic, Ulf Asklund, and Annita Persson Dahlqvist

Internet Commerce Development, Craig Standing

Knowledge Management Strategy and Technology, Richard F. Bellaver and John M. Lusa, editors

Managing Computer Networks: A Case-Based Reasoning Approach, Lundy Lewis

Metadata Management for Information Control and Business Success, Guy Tozer

Multimedia Database Management Systems, Guojun Lu

Practical Guide to Software Quality Management, Second Edition, John W. Horch

Practical Insight into CMMI®, Tim Kasse

A Practitioner's Guide to Software Test Design, Lee Copeland

The Requirements Engineering Handbook, Ralph R. Young

Risk-Based E-Business Testing, Paul Gerrard and Neil Thompson

Secure Messaging with PGP and S/MIME, Rolf Oppliger

Software Fault Tolerance Techniques and Implementation, Laura L. Pullum

Strategic Software Production with Domain-Oriented Reuse, Paolo Predonzani, Giancarlo Succi, and Tullio Vernazza

Successful Evolution of Software Systems, Hongji Yang and Martin Ward

Systematic Process Improvement Using ISO 9001:2000 and CMMI®, Boris Mutafelija and Harvey Stromberg

Systematic Software Testing, Rick D. Craig and Stefan P. Jaskiel

Testing and Quality Assurance for Component-Based Software, Jerry Zeyu Gao, H. -S. Jacob Tsao, and Ye Wu

Workflow Modeling: Tools for Process Improvement and Application Development, Alec Sharp and Patrick McDermott

For further information on these and other Artech House titles, including previously considered out-of-print books now available through our In-Print-Forever® (IPF®) program, contact:

Artech House	Artech House
685 Canton Street	46 Gillingham Street
Norwood, MA 02062	London SW1V 1AH UK
Phone: 781-769-9750	Phone: +44 (0)20 7596-8750
Fax: 781-769-6334	Fax: +44 (0)20 7630-0166
e-mail: artech@artechhouse.com	e-mail: artech-uk@artechhouse.com

Find us on the World Wide Web at: www.artechhouse.com